MY EXPECTATIONS NEARLY KILLED MY DREAM

The Expectation-Reality Gap

CULTURE | VALUES | CAPABILITY | LEADERSHIP

ANDRIES J. JACOBS

Printed in the United States of America.

Library of Congress Control Number: 2020913700

ISBN	Paperback	978-1-68536-574-5
	eBook	978-1-68536-575-2

Rev date: 4-30-2022

Westwood Books Publishing LLC
Atlanta Financial Center
3343 Peachtree Rd NE Ste 145-725
Atlanta, GA 30326

www.westwoodbookspublishing.com

Also by Andries J. Jacobs

Information System Implementations: Using a Leadership Quality Matrix for Success

First Published: 01/12/2012

CONTENTS

PREFACE

The future belongs to those who believe in the beauty of their dreams.
—Eleanor Roosevelt

WELCOME TO *MY Expectations Nearly Killed My Dream*. This book is ideal for the visual and practical learner, packed with graphics, pictures, and tables to demonstrate and bring across essential concepts. Take a couple of hours, sit back, relax, and gain intellectual capital based on twenty-six years of global business and line management; ten years of portfolio, program and project management; and twelve years of analysis, assessment, and research experience and accomplishments (from a consulting and operations perspective) for your knowledge workers geared toward providing significant momentum to your consulting business or business start-up.

I want to emphasize this book and its insights are based on my personal experiences and viewpoints—mine only. Furthermore, this book is not intended to be an exhaustive list of facts or new inventions; rather, it includes a series of themes that should be viewed together and deserve our attention. The abstracts and stories used in this book are examples of actual occurrences, and to protect the privacy of the persons and organizations, examples and templates are not necessarily complete. I have replaced names, identities, and other specifics of individuals to protect their privacy and integrity and especially protect their right to tell their story if they choose to do so. The facts are representative and accurate, but the lists are not always exhaustive and complete. I recognize some people might not agree with what I have written, and some of my colleagues or ex-colleagues might feel I am too critical or adverse; I am allowing for this. I expect some people might have trouble with some of the concepts and how I apply and present them; I allow for this too.

I am of the same mind as Walt Whitman, who once said, "The words of my book are nothing, the drift of it everything," and Alain Robbe-Grillet, who along the same lines said, "The true writer has nothing to say. What counts is the way he says it." The book contains theological references and might be a source of difficulty for some readers. The theological references represent my experience of divinity. Please feel free to insert your own theological terminology.

In *My Expectations Nearly Killed My Dream*, I created an easy-to-follow framework and a what-is-required approach to make start-up and consulting businesses aware of a couple of pitfalls that might prevent them from achieving their goals and dreams.

Though I do not have to convince you, the reader, let me provide you a synopsis of my experience and qualifications, allowing me to share and make a valuable contribution to the small business world. Directing and orchestrating the start-ups of three companies (project-delivery consulting, internet-based web conferencing, and small event center) bring an understanding of working with all stakeholders gaining control over corporate revenues, profit margins, gross profit, return on equity, debt to equity, project cost, schedule, change, and risk. Twenty-six years of global business and line management; ten years of portfolio, program and project management; and twelve years of analysis, assessment, and research experience equip me to add value and reduce business risk for corporate executives, operations, projects, and stakeholders.

Organizations and their clients directly benefit from my international consulting assignments in agriculture, chemical, energy, health care, information technology, iron and steel, mining and mineral processing, oil refining, and ports and marine sectors in Canada, Brazil, Kazakhstan, Russia, South Africa, and the United States. Insights, knowledge, and experience allow me to champion complex initiatives, be an influencer, and lead multidisciplinary teams.

My knowledge and experience are strengthened by my formal education:

- PhD in corporate governance received from the North-West University, South Africa, in May 2000, with an unpublished thesis titled "Price Decision Support System for the Fertilizer Industry."
- MCom in business economics received from the University of South Africa, South Africa, in 1993, with an unpublished thesis titled "Financial Information for the Management Process."
- BEcon (honors) in business economics from the University of the Free State, South Africa, in 1987
- BAgric in agricultural economics from the University of the Free State, South Africa, in 1983

You may ask, "Why is he writing this book?" A simple answer in a complex and exciting business and project consulting environment. During my time building the consulting business and being a consultant, notable incidents or inspirations eventually provided the spark for this book: consultants with twenty and thirty years of project and business experience unable to engage with clients and find consulting work for themselves and others; employing consultants through referral recruitment not working out; my misperception that all consultants can work independently, are self-driven, and have the willingness to treat the start-up from the owner's perspective; and the impact of my nonconfrontational, controlling, and detail-oriented leadership style. I cannot ignore my desire to build on the insights I have gained in writing my first book: *Information System Implementations: Using a Leadership Quality Matrix for Success.*

In today's world and in general, individuals will very seldom do actions or tasks from which they are not expecting a specific result or outcome. Well, what am I to gain from penciling down the words in this book? Besides others, it satisfies me knowing I am going on record as a business leader who thinks about why I am doing what I do and the way I am doing or have done work and business. Capturing what

I have done in a written piece allows me to give voice and direction to business occurrences that otherwise might rattle around as perceptions of performance success or failure. Critically thinking through what I have done over the past six or seven years, though not always satisfied with the outcome, gives me a sense of achievement.

In November 2010, while leading the project contracts and controls group for a leading EPCM (engineering, procurement, and construction management) organization in Vancouver, British Columbia, Canada, I regularly was challenged by the commercial manager, an advocate for equality between all levels of management. This, together with all the hurdles the project contracts and controls group faced on major capital projects, guided me to prepare an idea map as an outline to start a project contracts and controls consulting organization. Figure Preface.1 demonstrates the idea map that eventually gave birth to the organization PDO Solutions Ltd., with Andries Jacobs as owner and CEO and Elaine Jang as cofounder.

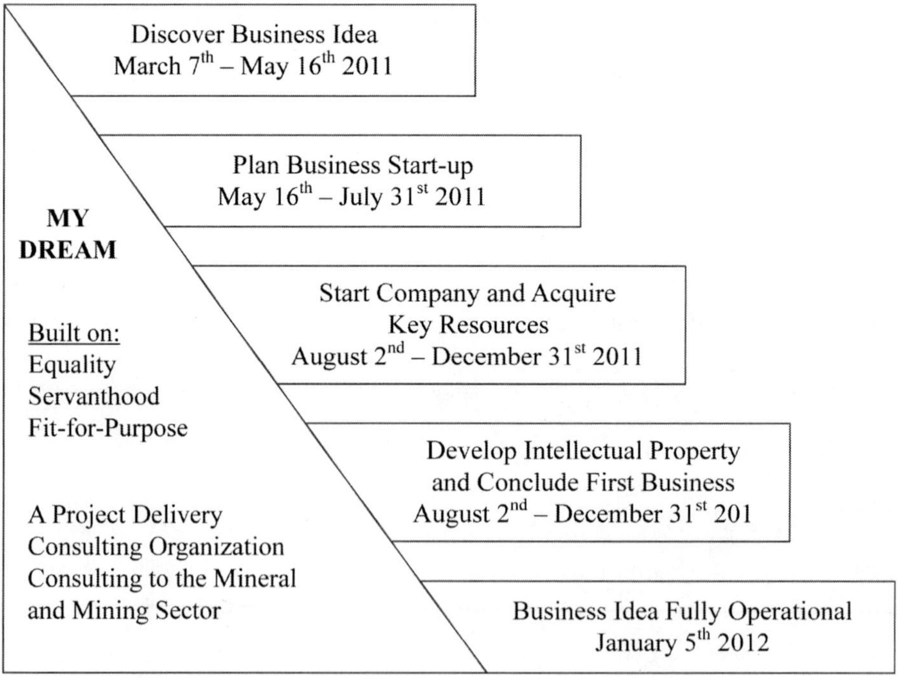

Figure Preface.1: Organization's original idea map.

I am of the belief whether you are having an idea, are ready to initiate, or are building your project consulting organization, you will benefit from the content of this book by not having to work through scenarios the way I had to, and it will help you narrow the expectation-reality gap (ERG). Once your leadership and consultants grasp the themes, they will respond with urgency to become key players and gain significant momentum for your start-up, management consulting, or project contracts and controls consulting business.

As you, the reader, are working through this book, here's a reminder: independent of unsuccessful, ineffective, uninspiring client, project, or business performances, we as business owners have the right to expect more and different from individuals, peers, consultants, and business.

INTRODUCTION

Success is never final and failure never fatal. It's courage that counts.
—George F. Tilton

DO NOT BE misled by the words in the title of this book, *My Expectations Nearly Killed My Dream*. Let me reemphasize the intent is not to focus on a comprehensive list of leadership, business management, communication, client and people engagement concepts, and business processes that guide business ideas; rather, it is to focus on the impact certain misunderstandings, misperceptions, and mistakes regarding these themes have or might have on the operations of a start-up and project consulting organization.

Furthermore, working through the stories and themes described in this book, I several times asked myself, do the misunderstandings, misperceptions, and mistakes reflect poor management or leadership? I cannot help to conclude no. Rather than poor management or leadership, I am of the belief that while every fiber in the leadership team's bodies told them business activities should be done differently, the team took their eyes off the ball by working simultaneously in and on the business. Moreover, the leadership team might not always have asked the right questions or enough questions. Focus and time constraints prevented leadership, making it a practice after seizing on a conclusion to critically reevaluate the actual experience and outcome to see whether it was the correct solution.

A demonstrable gap exists between what is expected of team members and how they perform.

Well, as leader of the group, I fully accept accountability, and though difficult at times, I have the obligation to lead. From there, it is my desire to analyze the various expectation-reality gaps (ERGs) and the business stories in which the ERGs have a visible impact. Analyzing allows me, as a transformational leader, to understand what it takes to show resilience and resolve in the mining market downturn between 2016 and 2020 or to make inroads into other industry sectors. Working in this innovative and multitasking environment allows me to notice the expectation-reality gap, realize red flags, and know something must be done.

The idea of building an organization where the only constant is "being different" is what drove me to give up a lucrative big organization to build a consulting organization. This desire makes sense while operating in an industry where project consulting, including contracts and controls, is fast paced and where innovation has become the holy grail. A thorough understanding of the ERGs allows for building a nontraditional business, having a strong culture, and building future talents in an environment characterized by market and competitive pressure.

These realizations are big motivators for penciling down the words and thoughts in this book. Furthermore, the strong desire to leave a legacy goes beyond myself and drove me to give voice on the topic "expectations nearly killed my dream." The time to scribble down the words and ideas is now while living the ERG and the price the organization paid for the pressure and occurrences of the ERG are fresh in mind.

Although hundreds of books and publications have seen the light on the topics described in this book, I choose to, from experience, highlight ten themes deserving attention. These topics act as enablers in leading and managing project consulting organizations. The ten themes are (1) consulting does not spell adviser, (2) referrals do not spell like-minded, (3) a business plan does not spell action, (4) managing the right KPIs does not spell success, (5) experienced consultants do not spell client engagement, (6) doing the right things right do not spell client wants, (7) talking and selling do not spell consulting, (8) a young company does not spell acting quickly, (9) leadership does not spell immune system, and (10) inspire does not spell leadership.

Let me explain the reasoning behind the phrase "does not spell." For example, with "inspire does not spell leadership." I choose to not use the words "does not mean" because it is well understood and obvious that the meanings of the concepts "inspire" and "leadership" are not the same. The phrase "does not spell" is the method I choose to express my expectations and what the business counts on, strengthen the contrast, and indicate the ERGs.

Realizing the themes exist and understanding the context can be a powerful guideline to consultant engagement leaders during the identification and selection of team members, to client-engagement leaders when engaging consultants, to project leaders in assigning and mentoring team members, and to executive management in starting, leading, and managing project consulting organizations.

Demonstrating and analyzing the ERG, I am using the traditional systems business process analysis technique of addressing input, business process, and outcome as outlined in figure Introduction.1, also known as the input-process-output (IPO) model or pattern. Though the concept might seem complicated and confusing, it will become clear when applied. In the end, neither input nor outcome concepts mean anything unless understood together with the attributes of extent, time, method, and conditions.

From chapter 2 onward, each chapter based on figure Introduction.1 introduces:

- a specific theme of relevance,
- business stories impacted by the various ERGs,
- business input characteristic as a powerful fuel for business and project consulting,
- the result expected from the business input characteristic,
- the expectation-reality gap impacting the specific business stories, and
- an assessment and checklists.

A bird's-eye view diagram at the start of each chapter outlines what to expect. Business input characteristics (business input) represent the knowledge leadership shared and introduced to the team, group, and organization to achieve and satisfy specific business consulting expectations.

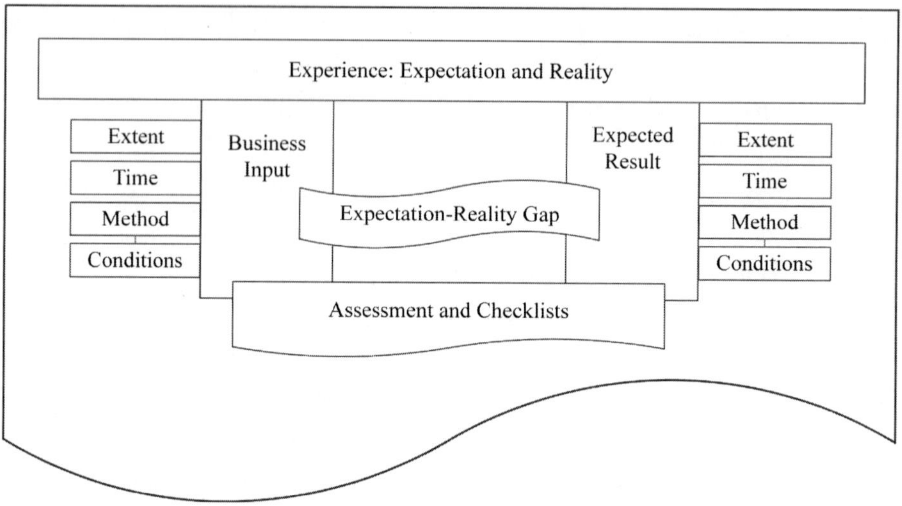

Figure Introduction.1: Chapter bird's-eye view.

Business input refers to an internal or external characteristic of the business process that, together with other business relevant characteristics, is transformed by the business process to produce an expected result. In project-delivery consulting, most of the time, the characteristics are locked up in intellectual capital such as communication, negotiation, discreet and ethical behavior, conflict management, change management, problem-solving, organizational skills, and multitasking. Focusing on business-input elements provides an indication of "how" consulting, management, and leadership are done and the tools leadership places in the hands of consultants to deliver expected result. Moreover, business input exposes a specific delivery method or issues that occurred, or difficulties experienced in terms of the attributes: extent, time, method, and conditions. I will explain shortly.

Expected result refers to the outcome of an input characteristic transformed by the business process to produce an expected output based on anticipation, wants, or promises expected or counted on. Focusing on expected results provides an indication of "how" consulting, management, and leadership are expected to be done or approached, exposing the consulting requirement in terms of the attributes: extent, time, method, and conditions.

Extent describes the degree whereto the input characteristic on its own, or together with one or more characteristics, empowers the business process to produce an expected output. Expected result refers to terms of degree of reach, size, scale, complexity level, scope, or magnitude of impact.

Time describes the period in which an input characteristic, on its own or together with one or more characteristics, empowers the business process to produce an expected result.

Method describes the action by which an input characteristic on its own or together with one or more characteristics in terms of a way, manner, measure, technique, instrument, process, or procedure empowers the business process to produce an expected result. Furthermore, combined with the extent whereto the expected result has been achieved in terms of development, effectiveness, efficiency, practicality, reliability, and usefulness.

Condition describes the premise on which an input characteristic on its own or together with one or more characteristics in terms of prerequisite, restrictions, qualification factor, degree of excellence, fit for purpose, best for use, and ability to satisfy implied needs empowers the business process to produce an expected result

The *expectation-reality gap* (ERG) is described in terms of culture, capability, and leadership. With the expectation-reality gap, the focus is on answering the following two questions: why does the expectation-reality gap occur, and what gaps or inadequacies might exist in terms of culture, capability, and leadership?

The description of business input characteristics is based on thoughts and viewpoints of well-respected and published leaders as outlined in the reference section of this book. The description of the expected results and the expectation-reality gap represents the author's views and direction based on more than thirty years of experience and accomplishments.

Chapters 2–11 each end with a brief assessment checklist. The intent is to put an instrument in the hands of organization leadership and individual consultants to be used to ascertain whether the organization employs practices to avoid or narrow the expectation-reality gap.

Chapters 2–11 also end with two pages for you, the reader, to make notes and jot down reference page numbers. The intent is to facilitate deeper processing of the concepts, and highlight items applicable to your business, and aspects you want to revisit.

Chapter 1 gives a description of the author's dream, a synopsis of seven prominent business stories impacted by the ERGs, and the expectation concepts and themes relevant to each of the mentioned stories.

CHAPTER 1

My Dream and My Expectations

For things to change you need to change. For things to get better you need to get better. The good news is you can change, you can get better and you can start right where you are at and you can go as far as you want to go.
—Jim Rohn

LIVING IN CANADA, the dream of thousands of young boys and girls is to one day play in the National Hockey League. Do you know the origin of ice hockey? It started with the Irish field game, hurling, played in 1788 at King's College in Windsor, Nova Scotia. Around the 1800s, it developed into what is known today as ice hockey. As a bloke from the Southern Hemisphere, where rugby and cricket are king, ice hockey was out of reach. Since I had to find common ground, baseball it was. The early form of baseball was called rounders and originated in England. With Canada being part of the Commonwealth, I do not feel too terrible to not be a total ice hockey fanatic. Since Canada only has the Blue Jays in Major League Baseball, the decision leading up to me supporting the Blue Jays was straightforward.

Why am I telling you this? Looking at the Blue Jays' track record over the past two years, I found comparable characteristics and performances to what I have been experiencing in my own organization since 2011. In 2015, the Blue Jays had an exceptional year, and on September 24, 2016, they were playing a very intense game in Toronto against the New York Yankees with the main goal of staying ahead of the wild card chasers. What a good time to reflect and prepare a final draft of this introductory chapter.

In this chapter, I am sharing my dream of starting, leading, and operating a project consulting organization—an organization built on a strong, well-defined culture, where consultants work and operate in a unique manner. It was not my hope but rather my expectation for consultants to operate in a certain manner within a unique business framework. Besides a detailed description of my dream, this chapter provides insights into the business culture, ten ERG themes, and seven business stories impacted by the ERGs.

Let me reach out. After browsing this book, feel free to share it with friends and business colleagues. The expectation is you will take a couple of minutes to let me know whether the experience and knowledge shared, and insights gained impacted your business for the better.

My Business Dream

As I embark on sharing large amounts of detail, I want to make it clear that I did not go into starting the project consulting business blind. Numerous people—including my brother, an astute business developer and human resources adviser—cautioned me on my business idea, and it was clear my expectations were ambitious and would take significant effort to sustain. At the same time, my inner voice told me to proceed.

In the months leading to the start-up, as insecurity crept in, I found the generally gentle, quiet, and supportive voice increasing in frequency and intensity for me to stay the course. Besides my inner voice, I found a great deal of support for my idea in *Peer-to-Peer Leadership* by Mila Baker (2013). For the record, my idea map was generated in August 2011, while Mila wrote her book in 2013.

It took a long time to get to this moment—well, here we go. My dream in 2010 and 2011 was to start and operate a project consulting organization with a business model where there is equality between consultants; values exist based on the six pillars of trust, pride, camaraderie, transparency, urgency, and commitment; there is a remuneration model where all permanent employees are shareholders; consultants exhibit core competencies to perform their work; principles of servanthood leadership are evident; there is ownership thinking by consultants on projects and in performing business activities; and project activities are based on the fit-for-purpose principle.

As I worked through the vision outlined in the idea map, I asked myself numerous times if it was too different, ambitious, and quick. The vision and original idea were to build a project consulting organization based on only having high-level guiding principles instead of heavy procedures forming the basis of the organization. Very early on, I started to realize, as the size of the consulting team grew and the number of learning profile types increased, that further definition of the guiding principles was required. Not only did we realize the need but also consultants started to ask for a higher degree of written clarity. This higher degree of written clarity to make all consultants feel comfortable had a negative impact on the organization's spirit. Adhering to this request of the consultants at the time was a true sign of an inexperienced leader.

Equality

The workplace resembles equality at all levels, from the individual consultants to leadership. It is an environment where structure is limited and where consultants can participate, fulfill their potential, and be valued, motivated, and treated fairly. It is where the character of consultants and their personal information is protected, work hours respect consultants, and consultants have fun. It is a workplace that has a team of consultants who are committed to equality through recognition of diversity and productivity incentives are equally shared between participating team members. It is a workplace where social identity—gender, race, disability, age, social class, sexuality, and religion—is a nonissue, and each consultant is treated as individual. And there is a knowledge and understanding of all consultants in and outside the work environment; furthermore, respecting individual consultants independent of salary level and, similarly, accepting the salary levels of peers in the organization. When the individual's social identity does not impact others, consultants take one another seriously, and there is an absence of inappropriate and disrespectful language, stereotyping, humiliation, and disrespect.

Ownership Thinking

Ownership thinking is molded through an understanding of the fundamentals of the organization, how the company makes money, and a complete understanding how each consultant adds or takes away value. Leadership uses business *key performance indicators* (KPIs) as an instrument to emulate and mold ownership thinking. All consultants have access to the organization's KPIs and the knowledge of how to exceed KPI targets. KPIs are highly visible, and accountability is well-defined. KPI-driven and self-funded incentive plans are developed to align the consultant's behavior to business objectives.

Fit-for-Purpose

Fit-for-purpose consulting is molded by the method and approach consultants and teams use to engage with clients, develop their projects, and achieve their strategic objectives. Furthermore, it is demonstrated through the quality and comprehensiveness of the as-agreed deliverables and the way in which the organization measures progress and value added.

Delivery Approach

Step 1: Consultants can assess client assignments without bias.

This step allows consultants to get to the heart of the project in a timely and focused manner. The primary focus of this step is for a consultant to review the objectives and structure; define the intended outcomes and outputs of the review; finalize the review work plan, including the scope of work, resource plan, cost estimate, and schedule; and review relevant background material such as project descriptions, execution plans, contract agreements, estimates, and schedules.

Step 2: Consultants can develop with the client an agreed-upon course of action.

The organization's business models, and diagnostic insights should result in the best fit-for-purpose response to the project's needs. During this step, the consultants interview project team members to gain access to insights and opinions about the assignment; synthesize information obtained in the document review and interviews to establish a list of key issues regarding the assignment; review key issues and insights to generate proposed explanations into what activities, decisions, or actions have led to specific outcomes; and review project cost, schedule, progress, and performance data to determine the validity of proposed explanations to generate new insights on the success of the assignment.

Step 3: Consultants can provide tangible, measurable results.

The organization protects the integrity of client projects in a cost-effective manner. The consultant respects the principle of value for money. The primary focus is for the consultant to generate a final report and presentation to the client based on the data, facts, and analysis of the previous steps. There is a clear distinction between fit-for-purpose from a deliverable and measurement perspectives.

Deliverable Perspective

Fit-for-purpose deliverables mean the final deliverables do what they intend to achieve, are good enough to do the work they are designed to do and are of a good enough standard for the clients. Deliverables answer the client's requirements and wants and nothing more. Final deliverables are efficient for the stated purpose. Deliverables represent the right tool to do the work consultants have performed and fulfill the required specifications and stated outcomes. Consultants undertake efficient effort to reach the client's intended goals, including team formation, team integration, stakeholder management, scope-of-work description, time-phasing work activities, and cost of work.

Measurement Perspective

Fit-for-purpose refers to value for money, value added, and transformation. *Value for money* means how deliverables, as inputs, are efficiently used by the client's project-management processes. *Value added* refers to how and to what extent the results derived with deliverables bring the expected change to the client's project-management outcomes. *Transformation* means how and to what extent deliverables empower clients with specific knowledge, information, and insights to make decisions and achieve project management outcomes.

Remuneration Model

A remuneration model is molded by a recognition program focused on creating a work environment where consultants are committed to one another, business activities, clients, business growth, business sustainability, innovation, and management/leadership processes.

Commitment to One Another

Set one another up for success, build up consultants' self-esteem and work status, and promote interaction and sharing of opportunities. Provide mentorship and coaching, increase responsibilities with required authority, and foster team cohesion. Rebuke aggressive, threatening, and hostile behavior: yelling, shouting, and screaming, gossip and monopoly of people, unreasonable criticism, or inappropriate comments. A workplace where consultants respect leadership and guidance.

Commitment to Business-Related Activities.

Consultants partake in business events, attend organization events regularly, and partake in client-engagement events. They accept disciplinary actions for inappropriate behavior, attend business meetings, respond promptly to business administration requests, and perform business administration tasks promptly and timely.

Commitment to client-related activities. Consultants deliver client work promptly and at above-average quality, treat all clients and client personnel with utmost respect, and communicate with clients in a proper fashion.

Commitment to business growth. Consultants partake actively in growing company management through the identification and development of areas proved to be challenging. They contribute by referring consultants to join the organization. They engage with current and potential clients and partners, seeking project work for themselves and other team members.

Commitment to company sustainability. Consultants partake in the identification, evaluation, research, development, and execution of company growth strategies.

Commitment to innovation. Consultants partake in the identification, development, and execution of unique consulting areas and in the development and management of company operations. They partake in the development and execution of client-engagement activities and the identification, development, and execution of competitive edge areas.

Commitment to business management. Consultants partake in the identification and implementation of the business management processes. They carry out and continuously evaluate the agreed-upon business processes.

Values

Consultants are committed to living the organization's values molded in the six pillars of trust, pride, camaraderie, transparency, urgency, and commitment.

Trust

Demonstrated through behavior, reputation, goodwill, experience, and self-reference. Consultants, while working away on construction sites or in client offices, display a behavior of keeping in touch with the organization and other consultants. They are open in dealing with opportunities and challenges in an honest way and do everything applicable in the interest of the organization and other consultants. Consultants are focused on building a reputation of honesty and are fair with fellow consultants, leadership, and clients in doing consulting and business administration work. They display a behavior of goodwill and trustworthiness and do not take advantage of fellow consultants, leadership, or clients. They display experience in dealing with fellow consultants and clients. Consultants understand their self-reference in knowing their own potential, goals, knowledge, strengths, and areas for improvement.

Pride

Demonstrated through defined expectation, regular reviews, appreciation, positivity, focus, and relevant contribution. In both consulting and business administration, there are defined expectations to maximize success through the understanding of duties, tasks, and responsibilities. Regular reviews are requested and scheduled to reinforce the expectations of outcomes and deliverables. Appreciation is visible through the expressed honesty and sincerity consultants display to fellow team members. All consultants, including leadership, focus on keeping consultants engaged and encourage accountability. The team is not focusing on what has gone wrong rather on finding and presenting solutions. The organization, in its totality, focuses on keeping it positive, which means avoiding nagging and blame or negative comments with fellow consultants or clients. All actions are geared toward contribution by allowing all consultants the opportunity and a strong sense of understanding of how to contribute.

Camaraderie

Demonstrated through a sense of belonging where consultants work, accept consultants for what they are, and have a clear message stating and demonstrating all are welcome. Whether working in or on the business, there is a sense of inclusion. The organization makes each consultant an insider and, where possible, accommodates their diverse interests. There are fun, regularly scheduled events with an understanding that some may choose to not participate.

Transparency

Demonstrated through operating in an easy way for outsiders to see what actions are performed based on openness, communication, and accountability. Openness refers to the team's open expression by discussing true feelings and clarifying statements, emotions, and anticipations while speaking from the heart and with integrity and professionalism. Communication refers to the organization's (consultants and business) ability to give, receive, and exchange ideas, information, or messages through the appropriate media while being concise. Furthermore, it applies the skills of reading body language, speaking, writing, and listening. We acknowledge the importance of the skill of listening by demonstrating that we are hearing what is being said. Accountability refers to the obligation of the team and organization to account for its activities and actions while accepting the responsibility for them, as well as disclosing the results in a transparent manner.

Sense of Urgency

Demonstrated by the organization's and consultants' attitudes and process of treating business or personal matters as if one's life depended on them. Consultants are determined to stay focused on results and deadlines until the task or project is completed. Have a consulting team who understands the significance of a sense of urgency. Consultants, leaders, and key decision makers practice a sense of urgency with important projects by focusing on getting things done more quickly. A consulting team realizes the benefit of a sense of urgency and understands all business and personal goals require hard work and commitment. Consultants understand and recognize what is needed and accomplish more than others. Furthermore, they realize that demonstrating a sense of urgency is the best way to meet deadlines. Have a team of high achievers and leaders demonstrating a higher level of a sense of urgency than the competition. Generally accepted leaders who excel at motivating employees have a greater chance of instilling a sense of urgency in a consulting team. The organization's leadership team treating every matter with a sense of urgency on its own merit prevents team burnout.

Commitment

Demonstrated through a consultant team that pledges themselves and their time to the organization and delivers successful projects aligned with the business, culture, remuneration, and leadership model, consistently and persistently pursuing the business's purpose and conduct. Consultants showing commitment to peers leads to trust and camaraderie, and commitment to themselves leads to pride and empowerment.

Leadership

Though the various types of leadership have equal importance, *servanthood leadership* has a soft spot in my transformational leadership style. At the same time, it is the leader's leadership style questioned the most by team members.

Servanthood leadership is molded in serving and meeting needs of fellow consultants and clients. Consultants and leadership continuously focus on developing a team of project consultants to bring out the best in them and encourage self-expression. The organization provides an environment that facilitates the personal growth of consultants and where both leadership and owners are listening well to consultants to build a sense of community and joint ownership. There is an understanding and acceptance of the norm to recruit people who are more knowledgeable and experienced than the business leaders.

Moreover, the organization requires all its consultants, independent of experience level, to demonstrate cooperation, problem-solving, knowledge, get-up-and-go, and example leadership.

Cooperative Leadership

Consultants working both in and on the business are seeking cooperation from fellow consultants whom they, from an organization or project structure perspective, have no control over.

Problem-Solving Leadership

Consultants are addressing issues that might frustrate fellow consultants, even if the actions might make them unpopular.

Leadership by Example

Consultants are taking extreme measures on themselves, doing to fellow consultants as they want to be done to themselves, demonstrating the saying "Walk the walk and talk the talk."

Knowledge Leadership

Consultants demonstrate they have complete knowledge of the business strategies and tactics required. Furthermore, they work with fellow consultants, realizing their experience and potential and, through mentorship, leading them to the highest-possible performance.

Get-Up-and-Go Leadership

Consultants, whether working in or on business activities, demonstrate a "get-up and do what is required of you" attitude, committed to a get-up-and-go business.

Self-Orientation

In the words of the author of *The Trusted Advisor*, the organization strives to have extremely low levels of self-orientation or emotional expense by denouncing whining, gossiping, nonstop talking, grumbling, and bullying.

Whiner

A consultant constantly having the worst day of their life and, most of the time, focuses on themselves.

Gossip

A consultant frequently tells stories about who did what and talks behind the backs of fellow consultants.

Nonstop Talker

A consultant constantly discusses every bit of detail about their personal life, ignoring the open-office environment and not respecting fellow consultants who might prefer a quiet workspace to perform to their potential.

Grumbler

A consultant continuously makes silly jokes or sarcastic comments and regularly requires a reminder of inappropriate remarks.

Bully

A consultant always bosses around fellow consultants and clients and tells them what to do instead of seeking cooperation and requires reminding it is against the company values.

Core Competencies

A highly educated and experienced consultant possesses and demonstrates core consultancy competencies:

Leadership

Consultants are managing change; influencing outcomes; setting strategies; providing clear direction; generating commitment and enthusiasm toward business decisions; acting as a leader, role model, and ambassador for the organization; and motivating and encouraging themselves and fellow team members to work optimally.

Communication

Consultants effectively communicate both verbally and in writing to interact with clients and colleagues, listen attentively and respond in a clear and concise manner, and are aware of their own nonverbal communications.

Teamwork

Consultants establish and maintain positive working relationships and work cooperatively to achieve results, solicit input, value team members' contributions, and place them above personal needs.

Decision-Making

Consultants use analysis, wisdom, sound judgment, experience, and logic to solve problems and make decisions.

Client Focus

Consultants build relationships and meet or exceed the internal and external clients' wants and needs.

Business Acumen

Consultants generate and enhance profit, recognize business opportunities, and anticipate and understand business options to lead to a positive outcome.

Resource Management

Consultants plan, control, and measure resources in a way that balances cost with benefits and enables the organization to meet deliverables. Resources might include money, information, inventory, supplies, people, and time.

People Management

Consultants delegate, set goals, manage performance, motivate, train, develop, hire, and exit employees and contractors in a manner that meets the company's goals. Work quality includes knowledge and skills, ability to meet standards, care and attention to details, ability to follow-through to completion, and frequency of errors.

Quality of Work

Work execution demonstrates speed, efficiency, ability to prioritize and meet deadlines, and ability to organize work.

Accountability

Consultants have responsibility for tasks or assignments and align words with actions.

Adaptability

Consultants demonstrate abilities in mastering new skills and demonstrate flexibility in reacting to changing needs, procedures, and environments. Consultants work well under pressure, handle multiple assignments, and meet deadlines.

Initiative and Innovation

Consultants utilize knowledge and scope to constructively increase productivity and achieve goals, use resourcefulness and creativity in dealing with challenges, and anticipate and react positively to change.

Planning and Organization

Consultants establish an appropriate course of action for themselves and others to accomplish a specific goal, make proper assignments of people and appropriate use of resources, ensure contribution to daily activities, and are timely with the overall short- and long-term business objectives.

My Expectations

My expectations refer to each of the ten themes shaping the core of this book and deserve attention in terms of business models, competencies, leadership style, values, and self-orientation.

Expectation 1

A strong referral-based recruitment process brings a like-minded consultant who accepts the business, capability, remuneration, and leadership models—besides accepting the various models, having the willpower to potentially lose to achieve individual consultant and business success within the start-up and entrepreneurial environments. Table 1.1 outlines leadership's expectation from a consultant defined as like-minded.

Expectation Criteria	Expectations
Models	Accepts organization business and remuneration models
Competencies	Demonstrates teamwork, leadership, adaptability, accountability, planning and organizing, and initiative and innovation
Leadership Styles	Demonstrates cooperative leadership, knowledge leadership, leadership by example, problem-solving leadership, and get-up-and-go leadership
Values	Demonstrates trust, pride, camaraderie, transparency, a sense of urgency, and commitment
Self-Orientation	Avoids gossiping, whining, bullying, and nonstop talking and has low levels of emotional expense

Table 1.1: Like-minded expectation.

Expectation 2

Consultant acts as business adviser to the organization's client base, with an emphasis on business-associated personal relationships and client trust. Table 1.2 outlines what leadership expects from the consultant as adviser.

Expectation Criteria	Expectations
Models	
Competencies	Demonstrates client focus, communication, accountability, adaptability, innovation, and initiative
Leadership Styles	Demonstrates cooperative leadership, knowledge leadership, and get-up-and-go leadership
Values	Demonstrates trust, transparency, and a sense of urgency
Self-Orientation	Avoids gossiping, whining, and nonstop talking and has low levels of emotional expense

Table 1.2: Adviser expectation.

Expectation 3

A detailed business plan communicated through an open-communication leadership model encourages consultant discipline, making the business plan content its own, and drives the organization's business accordingly. As a shareholder, the consultant understands and knows what is required to grow the business from one business life cycle stage to the next. Table 1.3 points out what leadership expects from the take-action-orientated consultant.

Expectation Criteria	Expectations
Models	
Competencies	Demonstrates leadership, decision-making, resource management, planning and organizing, accountability, adaptability, innovation, and initiative
Leadership Styles	Demonstrates cooperative leadership, problem-solving leadership, and get-up-and-go leadership
Cultural Values	Demonstrates camaraderie, commitment, transparency, and a sense of urgency
Self-Orientation	Avoids gossiping, whining, and nonstop talking and has low levels of emotional expense

Table 1.3: Taking-action expectation.

Expectation 4

Well-defined, consulting-based KPIs communicated through an open communication leadership model encourage the consultant to have the discipline to make the real meaning of the KPIs its own and to create and navigate the business accordingly to deliver business results. As a shareholder, the consultant is fully aware of which areas of the business they should be concentrating on to grow the bottom line, resulting in a higher return on invested funds. Table 1.4 points out what leadership expects from a business-success-motivated consultant.

Expectation Criteria	Expectations
Models	Accepts organization, business, and remuneration models
Competencies	Demonstrates leadership, decision-making, resource management, planning and organizing, accountability, adaptability, innovation, and initiative
Leadership Styles	Demonstrates cooperative leadership, problem-solving leadership, and get-up-and-go leadership
Values	Demonstrates commitment, transparency, and a sense of urgency
Self-Orientation	Avoids gossiping, whining, and nonstop talking and has low levels of emotional expense

Table 1.4: Business success expectation.

Expectation 5

A like-minded, seasoned consultant introduced on referral into the organization combined with acceptance of the various organization business, culture, remuneration, and leadership models is a recipe allowing a seasoned consultant to find work for themself and for the more junior consultants. Moreover, this, combined with an environment where the business plan and KPIs are readily visible and demonstrated, provides the consultant an understanding of how the business operates, equipping them to develop business strategies engaging and doing business with clients. Table 1.5 outlines leadership's expectation from a client-engagement-focused consultant.

Expectation Criteria	Expectations
Models	
Competencies	Demonstrates leadership, communication, client focus, business acumen, accountability, planning and organizing, innovation, and initiative
Leadership Styles	Demonstrates cooperative leadership, knowledge leadership, leadership by example, and get-up-and-go leadership
Values	Demonstrates commitment, transparency, and a sense of urgency
Self-Orientation	Avoids gossiping, whining, and nonstop talking and has low levels of emotional expense

Table 1.5: Client engagement expectation.

Expectation 6

Providing industry best-practice readiness, control, and resolution satisfies client requirements and needs. Clients accept the experience base of the organization's consultant and the consulting he or she cannot be without in executing projects. Clients are paying for the consulting and offset the cost against their personal preferences (wants). Table 1.6 points out the leadership expectation from a consultant focused on client wants.

Expectation Criteria	Expectations
Models	
Competencies	Demonstrates leadership, communication, teamwork, client focus, decision-making, resource management, people management, quality of work, accountability, planning and organizing, innovation, and initiative
Leadership Styles	Demonstrates cooperative leadership, knowledge leadership, leadership by example, and get-up-and-go leadership
Values	Demonstrates trust, commitment, transparency, and a sense of urgency
Self-Orientation	Avoids gossiping, whining, and nonstop talking and has low levels of emotional expense

Table 1.6: Client wants expectation.

Expectation 7

It is every consultant's role while consulting to be on the lookout for new engagement opportunities. With the business plan and KPI requirements developed, implemented, and regularly communicated, the consultant understands the importance of each consulting project to the success of the organization. Furthermore, the consultant understands what is required: hard work, commitment, and as a start-up, a bigger effort than the more established competition. Consultants, as shareholders, have the emotional endurance to commit, with their inner resolve, driving them to succeed no matter the circumstances. Table 1.7 points out what leadership expects from the consultant as a consultant.

Expectation Criteria	Expectations
Models	
Competencies	Demonstrates communication, teamwork, decision-making, client focus, people management, quality of work, accountability, planning and organizing, innovation, and initiative
Leadership Styles	Demonstrates cooperative leadership, knowledge leadership, problem-solving leadership, leadership by example, and get-up-and-go leadership
Values	Demonstrates trust, pride, camaraderie, commitment, transparency, and a sense of urgency
Self-Orientation	Avoids gossiping, whining, bullying, and nonstop talking and has low levels of emotional expense

Table 1.7: Consultant expectation.

Expectation 8

Like-minded, seasoned consultants engaged on referral into a young start-up organization still establishing itself in the project-delivery environment realize the importance of practicing a sense of urgency to get work done in a short time and in a fit-for-purpose manner. The consultant understands it is the organization and individual consultants who must kick up their performance to realize beneficial achievements. Furthermore, the consultant understands he or she must work smarter, do more research without charging the client, and deliver quality and acceptable performance. Table 1.8 outlines the leadership expectation from a consultant characterized as quick acting.

Expectation Criteria	Expectations
Models	
Competencies	Demonstrates leadership, communication, teamwork, decision-making, resource management, quality of work, accountability, planning and organizing, innovation and initiative, and a sense of urgency
Leadership Styles	Demonstrates cooperative leadership, problem-solving leadership, knowledge leadership, leadership by example, and get-up-and-go leadership
Values	Demonstrates camaraderie, commitment, transparency, and a sense of urgency
Self-Orientation	Avoids gossiping, whining, and nonstop talking and has low levels of emotional expense

Table 1.8: Act-quick expectation.

Expectation 9

An experienced consultant and member of the organization's leadership team contributes by keeping the president and CEO of the organization on the straight and narrow in decision-making, managing consultants, focusing on consultants' quality of work, and keeping all consultants equally accountable. Furthermore, the consultants, besides being a member of the formal leadership structure, develop informal leadership structures to facilitate and address ordinary business concerns and improve work conditions. Table 1.9 points out the leadership's expectation from a consultant who acts as an immune system for the CEO.

Expectation Criteria	Expectations
Models	Accepts organization, business, and remuneration models
Competencies	Demonstrates leadership, communication, decision-making, resource management, quality of work, accountability, planning and organizing, innovation, and initiative
Leadership Styles	Demonstrates cooperative leadership, knowledge leadership, leadership by example, and get-up-and-go leadership
Values	Demonstrates trust, commitment, transparency, and a sense of urgency
Self-Orientation	Avoids gossiping, whining, and nonstop talking and has low levels of emotional expense

Table 1.9: Immune system expectation.

Expectation 10

Creating an environment for the consultant to become the person and consultant he or she wants to become, assisting with advice and direction in professional development, and generating consultant-specific business or project opportunities with the expectation the consultant will realize the effort, returning the favor by sticking together in the organization, and not just leave when the team dynamics get complicated, executive decisions do not work for them individually, or the business climate obscures the future of the organization. Table 1.10 points out what leadership expects from a leader.

Expectation Criteria	Expectations
Models	Accepts organization, business, and remuneration models
Leadership qualities	Demonstrates positive attitude, judgment, courage, responsibility, vision, passion, self-discipline, character, commitment, charisma, and initiative
Competencies	Demonstrates leadership, communication, decision-making, business acumen, adaptability, people management, planning and organization, and accountability
Leadership Styles	Demonstrates cooperative leadership, problem-solving leadership, knowledge leadership, leadership by example, and get-up-and-go leadership
Values	Demonstrates trust, camaraderie, transparency, and commitment
Self-Orientation	Avoids gossiping, whining, and nonstop talking and has low levels of emotional expense

Table 1.10: Leadership expectation.

Synopsis of Prominent Business Stories

During my thirty years in business, there have been various mainstream thoughts on the best manner to communicate with consultants or teams we are leading. The past eight years are no different. After reading the thoughts and ideas published by Denning (2012), I must admit for the first time, I fully understand the role, place, and importance of storytelling to communicate a specific message.

It is well known and understood in the day-to-day business environment that leaders use different types of stories to achieve or demonstrate their expected business objectives and goals. In the work done by Denning (2012), he demonstrates how leaders could use the same series of occurrences to write a story that could be used in sparking action, communicating who you are, branding, transmitting values, fostering collaborations, taming the grapevine, sharing knowledge, and leading people into the future. In this book, my focus and intent are to share knowledge.

Insight gained through Denning's work allowed me to realize how well knowledge-sharing stories align with my intentions for the book, where the consulting work focuses on a series of occurrences going contrary to expectations. I totally understand that knowledge-sharing stories do not follow the traditional pattern of a wonderful fiction story, and as I refrain from implicating or naming individual consultants, it might not be inherently interesting to you. I instead state the role, seniority, and project experience level of the person operating in the role. Moreover, I refrain from using client names or any project-specific quantitative data. To provide an indication of the relative size of each project or how the various stories compare with each other, I am using Fibonacci story points.

With this in mind, each of the seven stories I compiled is plain, simple, and direct; highlights minor problems, near misses, or weak signals; presents the series of occurrences as it occurred with facts transparent and clear; and presents the experience as it occurred. Slightly different from the traditional knowledge-sharing story, I am not focusing on how the minor problems, near misses, weak signals, or difficulties have been solved but rather on the business input communicated to prevent the resulting in the ERGs. You must read the stories with the context provided and an open mind, which prevents the stories from taking a negative tone.

I want to be clear. I am not classifying the outcomes of the minor problems, near misses, weak signals, or difficulties as mistakes. Furthermore, to detach people from the story, I use roles. Moreover, as an author, I will prevent stories from taking the shape of a scapegoat ("it is all your fault"), victim ("it is all my fault"), or helplessness ("there is nothing we can do").

As the stories happened in the past, I had to dig deep to collect the relevant information and insights to write the stories. I collected information from client-engagement proposals, consulting agreements, consulting task orders, letters between the organization and client, project reports, learnings from retrospectives, and reflection work sessions.

This section outlines seven prominent business stories that contributed to the realization of the various expectation-reality gaps.

Moreover, it addresses the various expectations prominent and visible in each story. The stories primarily stem from 2011 until 2015, a time when capital project activity in the resource sector was at an all-time high—and so was the demand for project-delivery consultants.

Story 1

On June 22, 2011, yet another project-consulting organization registered with the British Columbia province and Canada federal governments. Shortly afterward, a frantic exercise started to identify seasoned consultants to form an integral part of the project-consulting start-up organization. On August 2, 2011, the organization started to reach out to prospective clients for assignments. On board was a group of seasoned project consultants with extensive experience in capital planning, cost management, risk management, and project management. Seasoned consultants with experience to execute the organization's vision by helping clients implement successful projects, decrease project execution risk, and ultimately increase project value. Achieving this by providing consulting in the core areas of cost and schedule management, estimation, procurement, contracts and logistics management, project execution and planning, change, and project risk management. Furthermore, the consultants on board are experienced and skilled to represent the organization, support owners developing capital projects through all project-development life cycle stages, from scoping studies to project execution and in various capacities they required—as full-time members of their project team, as part-time consultants, or as project advisers.

After about twelve months, leadership realized although consultants are experienced in providing consulting work to major capital projects, they found it difficult to simultaneously work in (business administrative tasks) and on (project-specific tasks) business activities. It became apparent that moving from well-established corporate engineering, procurement, and construction management (EPCM) organizations to a small entrepreneurial organization is not for all. It was important that all of this was happening while the organization was operating in the norming and storming group development phases.

In the months to follow, the CEO became impatient and split the in- and on-business roles for some of the experienced consultants. In twenty-twenty hindsight, more patience could have been exercised to gain a better understanding of how to deal with the situation. As a result, the organization lost several experienced consultants.

Referrals do not spell like-minded.

Though initial seasoned consultants were committed to getting the business off the ground and could be described as experts in their field of consulting, several could not totally adjust to accept the business, values, remuneration, and leadership models. Experienced consultants especially expressed concern with the values and remuneration models. Consultants in leadership positions were not comfortable with receiving equal bonuses with junior people even though the chargeability—earning per hour or per month—was different. They were supposedly stuck on the model of receiving bonuses based on chargeability or even the seniority argument, lacking the understanding building the business was complex, the challenges and opportunities were never ending, and sometimes consultants had to step in and do the work of a struggling or underperforming colleague. The toughest of them all was the worry of consultants that all efforts and resulting outcome (success or no success) were a measure of their self-worth, and several friends and family did not approve of the journey.

Business plan availability does not spell action.

Consultants in a matrix format were assigned to one or more than one business leadership stream and a business function. Through these channels, consultants could participate in the development of the business plan, gain access to a breakdown of the business in an organized manner and gain a clear picture of what was required to grow the organization. Consultants seemingly did not have confidence in their own abilities and capabilities to use the information and insights to grow the business accordingly.

Managing the right KPIs does not spell success.

Consultants, though they were engaged and contributed on a yearly basis to determine and set the KPI targets, had access to all the financial and nonfinancial KPIs and KPIs on a biweekly basis during the Friday afternoon parleys evaluated and explained, did not show confidence to focus on related activities delivering positive outcomes or KPI results and making the organization successful.

Experienced consultants do not spell client engagement.

Experienced consultants primarily outside the leadership team, to a limited extent, succeeded in using their contracts and controls functional knowledge and experience to attract clients. On a frequent basis, experienced consultants were unable to convey to clients how and to what extent contracts and controls deliverables (as input) efficiently could be used by client project-management processes (value for money); results derived with project deliverables bring the expected change to client project management outcomes (value added); and project deliverables empower clients with specific knowledge, information, and insights to make decisions and achieve project management outcomes (transformation).

A young company does not spell act quick.

Consultants used to work from templates, slow to custom-build documentation, project processes and procedures to fulfill client expectations, ultimately became the client's reason for contracting the newly started organization. Furthermore, consultants failed to proactively develop unique and nonstandard documentation, including models, templates and procedures, and new ways of performing the project function that would allow quick response to client needs.

Leadership does not spell immune system.

Experienced consultants, with a perceived lack in like-mindedness, were unable to or not feeling accountable to exercise participation and persuasive control to influence or direct the CEO to sound decision-making. Despite a request for and the opportunity to provide a higher level of participation during the weekly Monday afternoon leadership meetings, participating in leading and mentoring of junior consultants, focusing on individual consultant's quality of work, and keeping all consultants equally accountable, experienced consultants chose to leave the organization. Furthermore, the perception was experienced consultants did not fully succeed in completely taking ownership and creating informal leadership structures (communities), facilitating and addressing common business concerns, and improving work conditions.

Inspire does not spell leadership.

Consultants for whom the CEO created an environment to become the person and consultant they wanted to become assisted with advice and direction in professional development and made ideas happen for them in terms of business or project opportunities, not showing resilience by sticking together. Rather, when the team dynamics became complicated, executive decisions did not work for them on an individual basis, or the business climate complicated the future of the company, they chose to leave the organization.

Story 2

Story 2 has a work effort and size equivalent to three Fibonacci story points. In September 2012, one of the largest diversified resources company in Canada awarded the organization an assignment to assist the project development group with capital-procurement activities and the development of procurement procedures. An agreement was reached with the client to provide an intermediate contacts consultant to work under the direct leadership and direction of the senior project procurement consultant. With the organization not having on-site project leadership to support the intermediate contracts consultant, approval from the senior project procurement consultant was required before the consultant could issue documents and critical project communications internally or externally (unless agreed upon).

As the consultant worked primarily in a support capacity, it was expected of the intermediate consultant to attend weekly action-planning sessions and record and issue the work in progress. In situations where the consultant was approached by the small project groups for procurement support, these requests were agreed to by the senior project-procurement specialist before making any commitments, allowing the senior project-procurement specialist to prioritize and allocate resources accordingly.

Procurement activities were primarily directed toward the organization's small capital projects. The intermediate consultant was required to provide input to the procurement plan development, preferred bidders' list, and preparation of bid commercial documents; assemble and issue procurement inquiry packages; receive and respond to bidders' queries; coordinate pre-bid meetings; issue addendums; prepare and coordinate the evaluation of proposals; prepare and issue award documentation; and prepare procurement-related closeout documentation.

Besides the day-to-day procurement activities, the senior project procurement specialist—on an as-needed-basis—received support from two intermediate consultants to develop procedures and templates. This included gathering the current state processes and procedures information, analyzing business processes and procedures, writing a synopsis of practices, developing business process and procedure forms and templates, and performing business process and procedure technical reviews. The consultants also coordinated business process and procedure approvals and authorizations.

Consulting does not spell adviser.

The consultants did not have confidence in the client senior project-procurement specialist they were supporting. The client senior project-procurement specialist frustrated our consultants. Consultants were unable to understand the senior project procurement specialist's qualities and ways of working, which could be respected. The mountain became too high, and they were unable to build on the good qualities that could bring them together as a team. Our consultants were unable to put their own credibility at stake on behalf of the senior project-procurement specialist despite the shortcomings. Furthermore, consultants were unable to use their personal strengths to improve the client both personally and professionally.

Talking and selling do not spell consulting.

Our intermediate consultant offended the senior project-procurement specialist by talking too much and listening too little, telling too much and asking too few clarification questions, talking in a disrespectful manner to the client, and assuming the consultant knew better than the senior project procurement specialist. The senior project-procurement specialist spread the word that the organization was incompetent and difficult to deal with. This resulted in making the environment more difficult for other consultants working in different functional areas to get their work done and the client not providing follow-up work in the specific department and broader organization.

Experienced consultants do not spell client engagement.

As the client is important to the stability and growth of the organization, the organization engages several well-seasoned consultants. The consultants, well aware of the presence and profile of the client in the resource industry sector, did not engage in discussion to get the work arrangements extended. The perception was consultants fear failure, embarrassment, appearing to be ignorant or incompetent, and loss of reputation or security. Despite this fear resulting in great timely delivery of cost engineering work through several stages of the project life cycle, the organization was unable to hold on to the client and eventually partially lost it to the competition.

Story 3

Story 3 has a work effort and size equivalent to five Fibonacci story points. With capital projects in the resources sector on a high and the supply curve for consultants 100 percent elastic, the organization in August 2012 submitted a proposal to provide project consulting for a junior Canadian precious metal company with flagship projects in Nunavut, Canada. The organization's project setup team lead clearly described our understanding of the project requirements, outlined the approach the consultant would follow to satisfy these requirements, and identified the resources, timelines, and estimated costs required to successfully complete the project scope. To be different, with a specific focus on attracting new assignment opportunities and putting forward an attractive offer, the organization's proposal provided proposed contracts and controls in a modularized format, allowing the client to select consulting as and when needed. This proposal primarily concentrated on supporting the pre-feasibility study and identified future recommended consulting.

With the proposal, the client took advantage of the modularized format and agreed for the organization to, in the short term, provide a project coordinator to the vice president and project development to assist in managing the execution of the pre-feasibility study, with the potential to—over the medium and long term—provide ongoing project coordination support, project controls and accounting consulting, and owner's team representation.

The project coordination task included day-to-day coordination and management of project-development activities such as writing scopes of work for consulting contracts, preparing request for proposal documents, evaluating and awarding requests for proposals, handling project cost control and invoice administration, preparing project documentation, and other duties as assigned by the client. Shortly after, the client requested planning and scheduling support. This included developing, monitoring, and maintaining the execution schedule for the pre-feasibility study. The schedule was developed in Microsoft Project during the early stages of the pre-feasibility study and was to be updated weekly or biweekly throughout the study phase.

In about November 2012, the client requested contracts support primarily for an exploration program. A seasoned contracts-formation consultant was assigned to support the client's construction management team. The scope of work included preparing a list of necessary contracts, forming the contract terms and conditions, issuing tenders and requests for proposals to proponents, adjudicating bids and reviewing proposals, and issuing recommendations to the client's responsible person.

After about six months' involvement with the client, in January 2013, the organization secured an agreement with the objective of developing a temporary solution for improving project cost management and reporting for the project. The assignment included the development of project management tools, procedures, a contracts and controls workflow, and reporting criteria. Furthermore, it included a critical review of the communication and responsibilities around cost reporting and forecasting. Cost transparency and realistic cost forecasts to ensure accurate and adequate information were available to support project decision-making considering the long-term plan of the client to implement an enterprise resource planning (ERP) system. Based on the outcomes, the organization developed an issues/solutions memorandum to describe the key areas of improvement and recommended solutions to implement.

Referrals do not spell like-minded.

The organization assigned a member of its leadership team to the client with the purpose of leading the organization's client-engagement activities and acting as the organization's project sponsor. The consultant managed to build an exceptional relationship with the client. The experienced consultant was not successful in leading the cost control and contracts formation activities. The organization realized the consultant concentrated on developing opportunities for himself or herself and, sadly, left the organization with the client's business relationship.

Talking and selling do not spell consulting.

The assigned cost-control consultant was too inexperienced to realize the client project director was a busy person and did not want to be interrupted with unimportant questions or barraged with requests for information or lengthy reports on matters considered to be an unwarranted intrusion of their time.

Experienced consultants do not spell client engagement.

A member of the leadership assisted the client with the selection of an ERP application. From an organization perspective, it enhanced the organization's profile and gained acceptance. The experienced system transformation consultant came across too strongly and made the client feel as if they have not been heard. The consultant failed to properly understand the client's requirements, objectives, and timelines.

A young company does not spell act quick.

On short notice, the client made a request, and the organization assigned an experienced contracts-formation consultant. The consultant was very experienced, had previously worked for major organizations on major execution life cycle phase projects, and was used to working with large, complex template contracts. The organization failed to deliver fit-for-purpose contracts based on the specific type of contracting services and aligned with the specific life cycle stage.

Story 4

Story 4 has a work effort and size equivalent to three Fibonacci story points. In early January 2013, the organization engaged with a rapid-growing global mining company with operating mines in North and South America, providing project consulting for the early-stage activities of the execution phase.

Early-stage activities refer to those project activities scheduled to take place before receiving environmental assessment approval and before the start of the post-environmental assessment detail engineering phase, with the target date of first quarter of 2014. Three full-time-equivalent consultants were assigned to the project management team to cover the early-stage cost management, procurement and planning, and scheduling requirements. Providing the relevant project support required for the early-stage project activities, the organization—within the framework of the three full-time-equivalent staff—made available a larger number of people with the required skills and experience. Besides ensuring the availability of consultants familiar with the project work, this approach would ensure the availability of a well-organized and project-experienced team by the time detailed engineering was scheduled to start in the first quarter of 2014.

Making use of the now typical modularized consulting offer, the client expressed a need for scheduling assistance, producing a level 2 schedule with the immediate focus on environmental and community affairs, biweekly updating of the level 2 schedule, and biweekly and monthly time progress reporting. To ensure a successful outcome and deliverables adhering to the fit-for-purpose principle, the consultant agreed to a collaborative and iterative process with all the project stakeholders in compiling the schedule in compliance with the organization's scheduling, project management, and project execution standards. To facilitate the collaborative and iterative process, the consultant agreed to spend at least 50 percent of the allotted time in the client's office and to produce the level 2 schedule in Primavera P6.

Producing the level 2 Primavera schedule included—besides the schedule as a core deliverable—progress monitoring and reporting, schedule analysis, schedule statusing, trend analysis and forecasting, and option evaluation. The consultant applied schedule change control and baseline changes and version control.

In May 2013, with scheduling support well under way, the client requested cost management and procurement support. The client asked for simplicity in producing cost management reporting. The organization developed an Excel-based tool to report biweekly and cumulative current dollars and hours budgeted, spent, forecast, and earned. The cost management report included monthly and overall cost and schedule performance indicators and monthly and cumulative schedule and cost variances. The Excel-based model was sound and allowed for overall project cost management after the capital cost estimate work breakdown structure and allowed for integration of all changes with the cost management system.

Contract arrangement sensitivities on the project made information gathering difficult, leading to the implementation of a request for an information system between the client and the organization. To further speed up information gathering and eliminate any uncertainty, the cost management consultant developed an earned value progress reporting work instruction and—in preparation for the progress curves—a template for the gathering of historical information from the consultants regarding budgets, deliverables, forecasts, and change control.

In parallel with the cost management, the organization—upon request of the client—started providing procurement support. A series of request for proposal and contract templates were developed and used on two different contracts. To keep the client informed, the contracts-formation consultant developed and implemented an Excel-based purchasing and contracts schedule status report.

Experienced consultants do not spell client engagement.

Engaging a senior leader to lead the organization's client-engagement activities—thoroughly understanding and recognizing meeting recurring needs of the client—would be the organization's bread and butter. Unsuccessful in keeping the client engaged, primarily the inability to understand the client's needs made up only 50 percent of their "wants." Adhering to their wants was more important than their desire for the organization to take a personal interest in managing the outcome of their project.

Doing the right things right does not spell client wants.

The cost-control consultant was very experienced with strong verbal and writing skills and concentrated on delivering best-practice control and reporting. The consultant was not asking adequate qualifying questions and confirming with the client the organization's interpretation of the needs was in line with the client's wants. That would confirm the client wanted a more simplified solution based on the project life cycle stage.

Talking and selling do not spell consulting.

The client-engagement team spent significant time driving five hundred kilometers to engage with the client, and two days later, the team presented our skills and capabilities to the client. A week later, they signed an agreement with the client. Concentrating on supplying capabilities and getting chargeable work, our consultants could not manage to put themselves in the client's shoes, breaking down requirements into smaller individual pieces to determine the root cause for not being successful in delivering satisfactory consulting.

A young company does not spell act quick.

The contracts-formation consultant was very experienced, had previously worked for major organizations, on major execution life cycle phase projects, and with large, complex template contracts. The organization failed to accommodate and be receptive of unusual needs from the client based on the specific type of contracting services and specific life cycle stage.

Story 5

Story 5 has a work effort and size equivalent to five Fibonacci story points. In February 2014, the organization provided project planning and scheduling for an intermediate gold mining company with four producing assets and three significant development projects. It created realistic work plans based on project estimates, drawings, and construction execution strategies with resource loading, organizing and coding, and reviewing logic sequence.

The consultant was experienced in providing expert skills in Primavera P6, efficient and effective in the use of project time, and a master in schedule management. With eight years of experience, including several years at construction sites and doing the needed scope of work, the consultant had the capabilities to assist the client in the successful implementation of the project, decrease the project execution risk, and ultimately increase project value.

The consultant continued with the development of the existing level 3 Primavera P6 schedule for both owners and EPCM-managed scope of work. Schedule development included resource loading, organizing and coding, and reviewing of the logic sequence. The consultant, based on experience, managed to achieve an acceptable standard building schedule based on layout, P&ID (piping and instrumentation diagram), general arrangements and issue for construction drawings, construction sequencing, and EPC (engineering, procurement, and construction) work package management. Furthermore, the schedule reflected the project execution strategy, EPCM resource loading, and cost, procurement, and schedule integration, including a complete schedule analysis. Value added included the consultant's ability to understand and improve existing schedules and balance the requirements of the project manager and construction manager.

Referrals do not spell like-minded.

The organization, after spending extensive time engaging with the client, assigned a consultant to provide project scheduling. The organization had high expectations since the consultant was referred to the organization by a member of the organization's leadership. The consultant provided quality work and managed to build an exceptional relationship with the client. In the end, the consultant decided to leave the organization and joined the client—with the organization losing the revenue from client engagement.

Experienced consultants do not spell client engagement.

One of the organization's experienced consultants who worked on two previous projects with client, on request, engaged with a client by providing EPCM commercial management work. Though the consultant had an exceptional relationship with the client and had delivered quality work in the past, resulting in a return on investment for the client, the consultant was unable to generate more business opportunities.

Story 6

Story 6 has a work effort and size equivalent to one Fibonacci story point. In September 2013, the organization received a work order from the fastest-growing, lowest-cost senior gold producer to assist with the requirement definition, development, and testing of their project management application. Furthermore, the assignment included project controls standard development, implementation, and other project controls support as required. The final task of the assignment was a request to develop a project schedule and cost range analysis workshop for a feasibility project.

The organization assigned a senior consultant with a wide range of experience to support the project development group in developing project controls guidelines and procedures for use on all stages of the client's projects. The scope of work included drafting purpose and objectives for project controls guidelines, drafting guidelines documents, preparing and publishing the guidelines, and implementing the projects. The guidelines included work breakdown structures, cost management, planning and scheduling, change management, progress and performance, cash flow forecasting, project accounting, and project systems. The expectation was all deliverables would follow the AACE International project controls best practices.

The organization assigned a seasoned consultant to perform risk assessment with the main objective of determining a more realistic project completion cost using the Monte Carlo analysis as a risk-based probabilistic model. The Monte Carlo cost and schedule risk analysis was conducted on the overall project, including the owner's and EPCM scope of work. It determined the probable project completion cost and validated the cost contingency necessary to complete the project with a ±50 percent confidence level.

Consulting does not spell adviser.

The organization's experienced cost management consultant did not value the client's project controls manager's knowledge and experience. The client's project controls manager's methods of engagement and collaboration frustrated the consultant. The organization's experienced consultant was unable to realize the project controls manager's qualities and ways of working, which could be appreciated. The mountain became too high, and the consultant was unable to build on the good qualities that could bring them together as a team. The consultant was unable to put their own credibility at stake and support the project controls manager despite the inadequacies. Furthermore, the consultant was unable to use their personal strengths to improve client relations on a personal and work activity level.

Experienced consultants do not spell client engagement.

The organization engaged a newly recruited consultant on assignment to assist client with their project management office's project controls practice development and centralized project controls—reporting from an organization perspective to enhance organization's profile, gaining acceptance, and developing new business for organization. The experienced project controls management consultant came across too strongly, making the client feel as if they had not been heard. The experienced consultant failed to properly understand the client's requirements, objectives, and timelines.

Talking and selling do not spell consulting.

The project controls consultant, although a seasoned consultant who had worked in various corporate and project environments, failed to realize the client was expecting an independent, innovative, and creative contribution with minimum interruption of the client's leadership group—without a barrage of requests for information on matters the client considered an unwarranted intrusion of their time.

Story 7

Story 7 has a work effort and size equivalent to twenty-one Fibonacci story points. In November 2013, with a request for proposal, the organization was contracted to provide the world's largest iron ore producer with purchase and contract formation consulting. Pre-award duties included preparation and approval of bidders' lists, review of technical specifications for request for proposal, commercial assembly, including discussions with quality assurance, expediting, project management, cost control, and accounting. It included arranging clarification meetings, preparation of any agendas, commercial analysis, and formulating the overall evaluation with a combination of technical and commercial components. Furthermore, it required leading negotiations with selected tenderers before award, managing all technical and commercial clarifications, recommendations for contract award, and closure of contracts and procurement packages.

Consulting does not spell adviser.

The organization assigned an intermediate consultant performing groundbreaking client-engagement work for organization. The consultant, after a period, decided to end verbal dialogue and communication with the organization and grew close to the client's leadership. Though the client appreciated the contracts administrator, they were not using the consultant to their full potential. Though the client confirmed a long-term assignment with the organization for the consultant, the client regularly raised issues about consultant's behavior.

Experienced consultants do not spell client engagement.

The organization engaged with the client on a continuous basis for more than two years in delivering work at pre-agreement levels. Though the client continued to provide assignments to the organization, the client showed signs of tension through poor communication and refusal to having regular project sponsor meetings.

Doing the right things right does not spell client wants.

Though the organization engaged with the client on an ongoing basis for the past two years, the consultants were unable to get fully engaged. The consultants were unable to produce packages of work from start to end in satisfying wants of the client's procurement leadership. The organization, with the best intentions, was unable to assign consultants who could produce and interact per the client's requirements, resulting in a high turnover of consultants.

Chapter 2 will shed light on the theme that "referral does not spell like-minded," focusing on the referral/like-minded expectation-reality gap.

This page is for you, the reader, to make notes and jot down reference page numbers.

Use this table to make notes and jot down system-related reference page numbers.

Note	Page Number		
	People	Process	Application

Use this table to make notes and jot down IPO-related reference page numbers.

Note	Page Number		
	Input	Process	Output

Use this table to make notes and jot down theme-related reference page numbers.

Note	Page Number				
	Business Models	Competencies	Leadership	Values	Self-Orientation

This page is for you, the reader, to make notes and jot down ERG-related reference page numbers.

Note	Page Number
Referral Does Not Spell Like-Minded	
Consulting Does Not Spell Adviser	
Business Plan Availability Does Not Spell Business Action	
Managing Right KPIs Does Not Spell Business Success	
Experienced Consultant Does Not Spell Client Engagement	
Doing the Right Things Right Does Not Spell Client Wants	
Talking and Selling Do Not Spell Consulting	
A Young Company Does Not Spell Act Quick	
Leadership Does Not Spell Immune System	
Inspire Does Not Spell Leadership	

CHAPTER 2

Referral Does Not Spell Like-Minded

True regret is knowing you missed your only opportunity to be simply a good friend to someone that was exactly like you.
—Shannon L. Alder

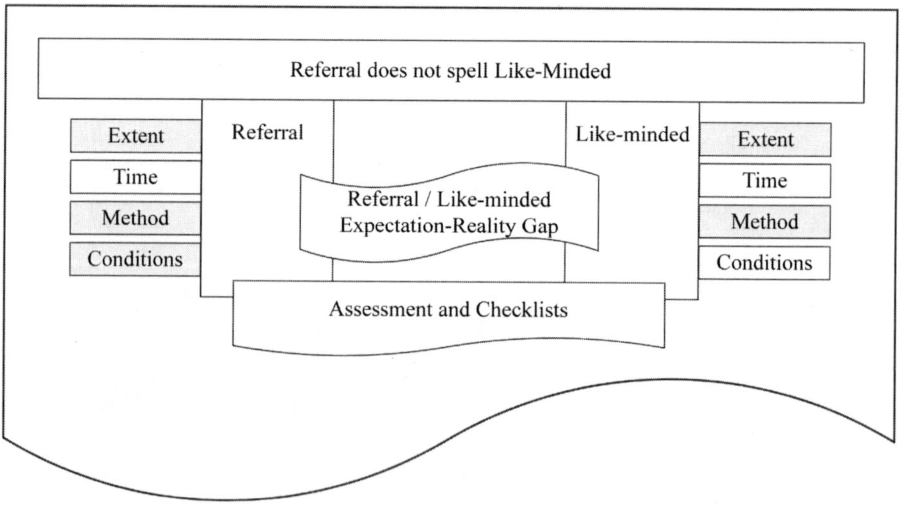

Introduction

THE FIRST THEME requiring our attention is "referral does not spell like-minded."

It is the summer of 2016, and I avoided working on this chapter for the longest of time. As I am entering the last decade of my business career, my focus is on leaving a legacy. Starting the organization, I counted on engaging a group of consultants who could assist me in doing so and, at the same time, build a legacy for themselves.

With the focus on being unique and different, several people told me starting a business on my predefined guiding principles was a pure experiment, questioning my true intentions. The emphasis on the like-minded concept was a must from as early as the idea mapping. In fact, I realize to build the organization I want with the various models outlined in chapter 1 of this book, I will need consultants who are compatible, in harmony, and capable of providing an unanimous front, which is easier said than done.

As it was second nature, before I started with my writing, I browsed the internet, read the news, and listened to music. Going over several music tracks, I stumbled over a music piece by Val Matthew Emmich—an American actor, musician, and writer—titled "Like Minded." The lyrics of this piece of music made me realize I was not the only one in search of like-mindedness. Though in a different context, I cannot help but quote the following, which says it all:

> It's so hard when you arrive where you've been the whole time, in your struggle to find the like-minded … I get lonely as can be searching for somebody like me, understands without having to speak, the like-minded … I think … I'm mad. I think … I'm mad already. The like-minded, can't find them.

The focus of this chapter is to provide an understanding of the leadership's expectation from a referral-based recruitment process as input characteristic; an understanding of the actions taken by the organization to support the referral input characteristic; the circumstances bringing about the realization a referral/like-minded expectation-reality gap exists; and an analysis of the organization's culture, capabilities, and values identifying potential inadequacies that might cause the referral/like-minded expectation-reality gap.

Expected Result

Expectation 1

A referral-based recruitment process brings like-minded consultants who accept the business value, remuneration, and leadership models. Besides acceptance of the various business models, consultants have the willpower to lose within the entrepreneurial environment to achieve individual consultant and business success.

Business Input

To deliver the expected result and develop like-minded consultants, the leadership introduced as input "referrals" (a characteristic of the recruitment function within the human resources business process) to the equation. Furthermore, to promote and prepare consultants to be like-minded and strengthen the chance of achieving the expected outcome of like-minded consultants, leadership—through knowledge transfer—introduces to the organization, the team, and individual consultants the following relevant business characteristics: leadership style, team development stage, team performance, and team contribution.

The leadership team is confident a referral program can do wonders for the start-up business by producing like-minded consultants, bringing a high retention rate, and increasing project and business engagement. To generate the referral program, start with creating a work culture that has a positive employer brand and become an organization that consultants will refer. To implement the referral program, it is critical for leadership to:

- report feedback or responses in a short time frame, giving precedence to referrals, have specific and separate deadlines for interviewing these candidates, and allow referred candidates to choose the time and date of their interview or offering online assessments

- allow all team members to refer outside of their own areas of expertise, allow nonemployee referrals, and commit to discourage bad referrers
- request referrals from new consultants right away, continuously promote and send notifications, keep the referred aware of needs and updated on the status of leads, and provide feedback on each referral
- continuously relay the importance of good talent to team members and effectively communicate how that affects them, recognize a good referral through a personalized thank-you note, reward and encourage consultants when they bring in a good candidate—regardless of the outcome—and set and communicate the goals of the leadership for team referrals.

It is well known that an organization's values influence the way people think about the business, and an awareness of cultural feelings toward business helps consultants communicate efficiently and effectively when working with clients from other cultures. The flip side of the coin in recent years draws a fair amount of attention: seeking clarification whether the language the consultants speak influences the way they think and execute their work. The organization leadership, as input for creating a strong business culture and advance the like-minded thinking, introduces the use of similar terminology and the elimination of specific words from day-to-day use.

Leadership chooses the concept of terminology, which is a collection of vocabulary, to strengthen the project consulting offer to clients and to align the consultants. The leadership's emphasis is to create a consistent vocabulary, shared language, common reference book, and a set of words used and understood by the industry and clients through terminology to mean the same ideas they think they mean. From a terminology perspective, the emphasis is on using the word and concept of "consulting" rather than a "service." The following six actions are important to ensure expected results are achieved:

- describing relevant terminology,
- making a simple glossary a mandatory part of the organization's documentations,
- ensuring consultants can ask clarification questions,
- validating the terminology against the business's objectives and goals,
- validating the terminology with all consultants, and
- defining known aliases to bring mind-sets and conversations together.

Leadership, as input to create like-mindedness around the consulting culture, promotes the elimination of the words "like" and "but." Linguists agree the word "like" is a filler word and, though it has been in use since the Middle Ages, it is becoming an epidemic and is used more than ever before. Furthermore, excessive and unnecessary use of the word "like" delays expressing an actual idea. Sara McCord—a well-known publisher on *Forbes*, Mashable, *Newsweek*, Time Inc., and Business Insider and writer/editor for the Daily Muse—suggests a five-step process to eliminate the word "like" from business speak:

- slow down,
- use different descriptive filler words,
- focus on word choice,
- reinforce your good habits by forcing yourself to sidestep "like" 24/7, and
- forgive yourself when you occasionally use the word.

The second is elimination of the word "but" since the leadership is confident the word that comes after "but" doesn't matter because it is stopping the consultant from accomplishing the intent. It is our brain's way of giving us an easy way out and makes giving up acceptable. With a variety of articles, studies, and blogs, the leadership focused on the elimination of the word "but" from business speak to prevent:

- holding consultants back,
- stopping consultants from accepting their own faults and failures,
- making a mess of their self-esteem,
- making consultants apathetic,
- draining the consultants' energy,
- halting their progress,
- allowing consultants to hide who they really are,
- limiting and preventing the consultant from change, and
- blocking personal growth and strengthening.

Leadership, for similar reasons, also discouraged the use of the words "hate," "hope," "things," "it," and "nice."

To strengthen the chances of achieving the organization's objective of recruiting through the referral program and development of like-minded consultants, leadership adopted the concepts and approaches of the group-development process, Belbin team role, and team performance models.

Through sharing and transferring knowledge regarding the Tuckman-Jensen group development diagnostic (figure 2.1), the emphasis is on making sure each consultant understands where the team is in terms of maturity.

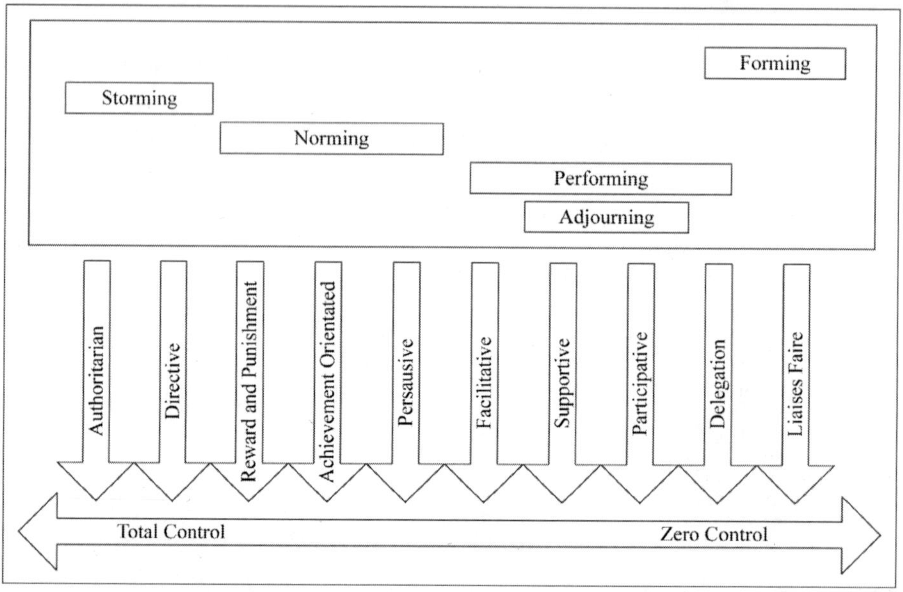

Figure 2.1: Tuckman-Jensen group-development process (Pinto and Millet 1999) combined with leadership continuum (Tannenbaum, R., and Schmidt, Warren H., May to June 1972).

With knowledge from the Tuckman-Jensen group-development process, understanding the reality of interpersonal differences will occur during the development stages of the organization, especially the norming and storming stages, where leadership has collaborated with the team on the Belbin team roles model (figure 2.2). The expectation is consultants will proactively study their own and their peer's tendency to behave, contribute, and interrelate.

A thorough understanding of the Belbin team roles model allows consultants, without babysitting and spoon-feeding from their leaders, to identify strengths, weaknesses, and characteristics of themselves and their peers. Leadership is confident a thorough understanding will bring like-mindedness, speed up the building of a productive working relationship, develop a high-performing team, build mutual trust and understanding, and raise self-awareness and personal effectiveness.

TEAM CONTRIBUTION			
TEAM ROLE	**CONTRIBUTION**	**CHARACTER**	**PERMISSIBLE WEAKNESS**
The plant	Introduces new ideas	Unorthodox thinking	Absent-minded
Resource investigator	Investigate possibilities, develops contacts	Communicative, extrovert	Over-optimistic
Coordinator	Encourages decision-making processes, delegates	Independent, responsible	Appears manipulative
Shaper	Overcomes obstacles	Dynamic, works well under pressure	Impatient, provocation
Monitor	Examine feasibility	Level-headed, strategic, critical	Uninspired
Team worker	Improves communication, get things moving	Cooperative, diplomatic	Indecisive
Implementor	Put ideas into practice	Disciplined, reliable, effective	Inflexible
Completor	Ensure optimal results	Conscientious, prompt	Timid, hardly, delegates
Specialist	Provides specialist knowledge	Self-reliant, committed	Gets lost in details

Figure 2.2: Belbin team roles (Belbin, M., Belbin, N., and Bainbridge, D., published on belbin.com).

Business leadership accepting team development, especially in the early start-up stages of an organization, can be one of the largest and most complicated challenges. Leadership counted on communicating and sharing the Drexler/Sibbet team performance framework (figure 2.3) as a road map to provide the consultants an understanding of balancing commitment, skill sets, communication, and goals, and foster like-mindedness. The leadership's expectation is that referral-based recruitment will bring like-mindedness to the extent where team members literally can read the minds of teammates, anticipating their needs and moves, and become a seamless supportive unit. According to the model, team members want to indefinitely stay in the performance stage, and it is only when the team reaches the "wow" moment the organization from a performance expectation perspective has a like-minded team.

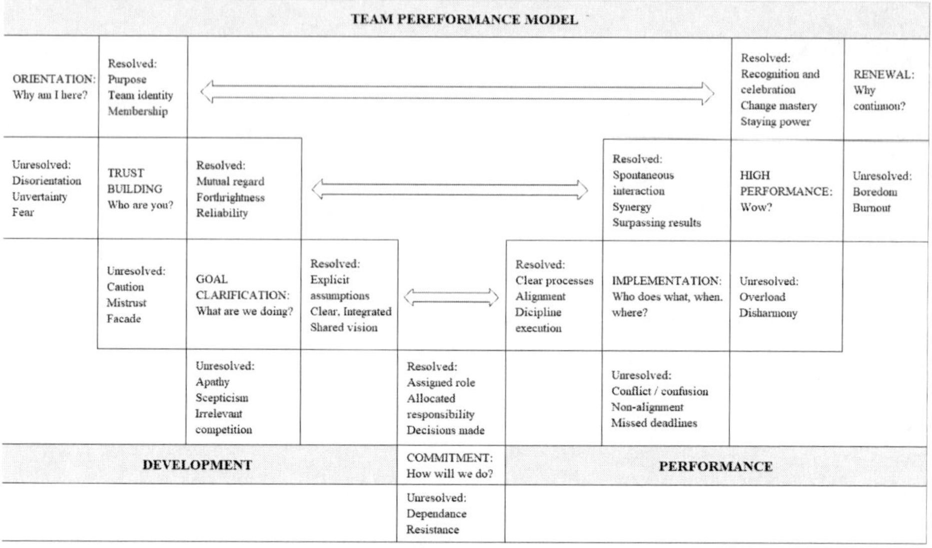

Figure 2.3: Sibbet and Drexler's Team Performance model (Sibbet, D., and Drexler, A., 1993, *Team Performance: Principles, Practices*).

Reality: Referral does not spell like-minded.

Story 1

Though initial consultants are committed to getting the business off the ground and could be described as professionals in their field of consulting, several could not fully adjust to accept the business, values, remuneration, and leadership models. Experienced consultants especially expressed concern with values and remuneration models. The leadership team members were not comfortable receiving equal bonuses with junior people even though the chargeability—earning per hour or per month—was different, assumingly stuck on the model of receiving bonuses based on chargeability or even the seniority argument. They lacked the understanding that building a business is complex, the challenges and opportunities are never ending, and sometimes, an individual must step in and do work of a struggling colleague. The hardest of them all is the worry of consultants that its effort and resulting outcome (success or no success) are a measure of own self-worth, and several friends and family did not approve of the journey.

Table 2.1 shows when it comes to consultants recruited on a referral basis accepting the business, values, remuneration, and leadership models, the organization experienced difficulties in terms of the method and condition of the "referral" input characteristic. The table further indicates when it comes to consultants referred to the organization, leadership counted on high levels of like-mindedness and recognized gaps exist in the extent of like-mindedness in the organization.

Character	Difficulties Experienced or Issues Occurred		Counted On	
	Referrals		Like-Minded	
Extent			◇	Scale of like-mindedness Complexity of a start-up Magnitude of effort required
Time				
Method	◇	Method of reward system Way of interacting with peers Manner of working as a team		
Condition	◇	Prerequisite to accepting equality Fit-for-purpose capability		

Table 2.1: Acceptance of business models: referral input characteristic difficulties and level of like-mindedness.

Story 3

The organization assigned an organization leader to the client with the purpose of leading the organization's client-engagement activities and act as organization project sponsor. The consultant managed to build an exceptional relationship with the client. The experienced consultant was unsuccessful in leading the cost control and contracts formation activities. In the end, the consultant concentrated on developing opportunities for himself or herself, leaving the organization with the client's business relationship.

Table 2.2 shows when it comes to professional consultants successfully leading teams, the organization experienced difficulties in terms of the method and conditions of the "referral" input characteristic. The table further indicates although the organization counted-on professional consultants for high levels of like-mindedness, inadequacies were identified in terms of the extent and method of like-mindedness.

Character		Difficulties Experienced or Issues Occurred		Counted On
		Referrals		Like-Minded
Extent			◇	Scale of like-mindedness Magnitude of effort required
Time				
Method	◇	Method of reward system Way of interacting with peers Manner of working as a team Reliability of leadership	◇	Way of interacting with client Way of interacting with peers Manner of working as a team Process of dealing on behalf of the company
Condition	◇	Prerequisite to accepting equality		

Table 2.2: Professional consultants as leaders: referral input characteristic difficulties and level of like-mindedness.

Story 5

The organization, after spending extensive time engaging with the client, assigned a consultant to provide project scheduling. The organization had high expectations because the consultant was referred to the organization by one of the organization's leaders. The consultant provided quality work and managed to build an exceptional relationship with the client. The consultant left the organization and joined the client, with the organization losing the revenue from the assignment.

Table 2.3 shows when it comes to referred professional consultants sticking with the organization, the organization experienced difficulties in terms of the method of the "referral" input characteristic. The table further indicates when it comes to referred professional consultants, the organization counted on a high level of link-mindedness, while shortcomings were recognized in terms of the extent and method of like-mindedness.

Character	Difficulties Experienced or Issues Occurred		Counted On	
	Referrals		Like-Minded	
Extent			◇	Scale of like-mindedness
Time				
Method	◇	Way of interacting with client Method of leadership interaction Process of dealing on behalf of the company	◇	Lack of reliability Communication with leadership team

Table 2.3: Referred consultants sticking with organization: referral input characteristic difficulties and level of like-mindedness.

Expectation-Reality Gap

To identify the reasoning behind the referral/like-minded expectation-reality gap with referral input characteristic difficulties and level of like-mindedness in mind, an analysis was done on the organization's culture, consultant capabilities, and organization leadership.

Table 2.4 shows the various misalignments in the organization's culture (equality, ownership thinking, fit for purpose, and values) that might exist and could have led to the referral/like-minded expectation-reality gap.

Equality			
Limited organization structures		Consultants enjoying themselves	
Consultant participation	◆	Equal productivity incentives	◆
Fulfill potential		Social identity	
Treated fairly		Knowing our peers	
Character protected		Absence of inappropriate and disrespectful language	
Work hours respected		Absence of stereotyping	
Personal information protected		Taking consultants seriously	
Recognition of diversity			
Ownership thinking			
Understanding the fundamentals of the organization	◆	Forecasting and achieving the business's key performance indicators	
Understanding how the company makes money		Key performance indicators highly visible and accountable	
Understanding how each consultant adds—or takes away—value	◆	Having self-funded incentive plans	◆
Knowing the business's key performance indicators		Incentive plans aligning the consultants' behavior to the business's objectives	◆
Fit for Purpose			
Deliverables do what they intend to achieve		Final deliverables are efficient enough for the stated purpose	
Deliverables are good enough to do the work they are designed to do		Deliverables represent the right tool to do the work consultants have to do	
Deliverables are of a good enough standard for clients		Deliverables fulfill the requirement specifications and stated outcome	
Deliverables answer the client's requirements and wants and nothing more	◆	Consultants are undertaking enough and have efficient effort to reach the client's intended goals	◆
Deliverables are comprehensive to the extent that they answer the client's requirements and wants and nothing more	◆		

Values			
Trust		Transparency	
Pride		Sense of urgency	◆
Camaraderie		Commitment	◆

Table 2.4: Referral/like-minded expectation-reality gap: culture.

Table 2.5 shows the various shortcomings in organization core competencies that might exist and could have led to the referral/like-minded expectation-reality gap.

Core Competencies			
Leadership	◆	Work quality	
Sense of urgency		Quantity of work	
Teamwork	◆	Accountability	◆
Decision-making		Adaptability	◆
Client focus		Initiative	◆
Business acumen		Innovation	◆
Resource management		Planning and organizing	
People management	◆	Communication	

Table 2.5: Referral/like-minded expectation-reality gap: capability.

Table 2.6 shows the various inadequacies in organization leadership styles that might exist and could have led to the referral/like-minded expectation-reality gap.

Styles			
Cooperative leadership		Whiner	
Problem-solving leadership		Gossiper	
Leadership by example	◆	Nonstop talker	◆
Knowledge leadership	◆	Grumbler	
Get-up-and-go leadership	◆	Bully	◆

Table 2.6: Referral/like-minded expectation-reality gap: leadership.

Assessment and Checklists

With the circumstances bringing about the realization a referral/like-minded expectation-reality gap exists and an analysis of the organization's culture, capabilities, and values identifying potential inadequacies, which might cause the referral/like-minded expectation-reality gap, table 2.7 provides a list of questions and phrases used to assess the extent whereto the organization's culture, capabilities, values, and leadership support the referral recruitment process, contractual agreement with consultants, assignment of consultants to work, and mentoring and coaching of consultants.

Item	Description	Score
A	Culture	
	Equality	
2	Consultant participation is evident in preparedness, and consultants stay focused on the main topics, keep control of tasks, discuss the salient issues, and contribute to ideas and information.	
10	The organization has implemented equal productivity incentives to reward consultants and ensure the organization retains top-performing consultants. The consulting incentive plan increases consultant loyalty, increase sales and profit growth, utilize consultants to assist with sales, and strengthen client relationships.	
	Ownership Thinking	
1	Consultants understand the fundamentals of the organization and how the organization runs the business within the following six departments: people, administration, business information management, client engagement, projects, and commercial and day-to-day operations.	
3	The organization and the team members understand how each consultant adds—or takes away—value.	
7	The organization has implemented self-funded incentive plans	
8	The organization has implemented incentive plans that align the consultants' behavior with the business's objectives.	
	Fit for Purpose	
4	Consultants produce deliverables answering the client's requirements and wants and nothing more.	
5	Consultants produce deliverables comprehensive to the extent it answers the client's requirements and wants and nothing more.	
9	Consultants are undertaking enough and have efficient effort to reach the client's intended goals.	

Item	Description	Score
B	Values	
5	Consultants demonstrate a sense of urgency through attitude and the process of treating key business or personal matters as if one's life depended on it. Consultants have the determination to stay focused on results and deadlines until the task or project is completed.	
6	Commitment is demonstrated through a consultant base that pledges themselves to the organization; delivers successful projects aligned with the business, culture, remuneration, and leadership model; and consistently and persistently pursues the business's purpose and conduct.	
C	Capabilities	
1	Consultants have leadership skills, including managing change; influencing outcomes; setting strategies and providing clear direction; generating commitment and enthusiasm toward business decisions; acting as a leader, role model, and ambassador for the organization; and motivating and encouraging themselves and other team members to work optimally.	
3	Consultants have teamwork competencies, including the ability to establish and maintain positive working relationships and to work cooperatively to achieve results. They solicit input, value team members' contributions, and place them above personal needs.	
8	Consultants apply people management to day-to-day work execution, including the ability to delegate, set goals, manage performance, motivate, train, develop, hire, and exit employees and contractors in a fashion that meets the company's goals.	
11	Consultants have accountability competencies, including the ability to take responsibility for tasks or assignments and align words with actions.	
12	Consultants are showing adaptability abilities in mastering new skills and demonstrate flexibility in reacting to changing needs, procedures, and environments. They work well under pressure, handle multiple assignments, and meet deadlines.	
13	Consultants have initiative and innovation, utilizing knowledge and scope to constructively increase productivity and achieve goals. They use resourcefulness and creativity in dealing with challenges and anticipate and react positively to change.	
D	Leadership	
3	Consultants take extreme measures on themselves, doing to other consultants as they would want them to do unto them. They "walk the walk and talk the talk."	

Item	Description	Score
4	Consultants provide knowledge leadership and know the strategies and tactics required, realize experience and potential in consultants, and mentor.	
5	Consultants provide a get-up-and-go leadership, getting up and doing what is required of them, and committing themselves to a get-up-and-go business.	
8	The organization does not have consultants who always discuss every bit of detail about their personal lives and ignore the fact that the team is working in an open-office environment and do not respect other consultants who prefer a quiet working environment.	
10	The organization does not have consultants who always boss other people around and tell them what to do and require reminding it is against the company culture.	
	Average Score	
Rate a score of 1, 3, or 5. Score: 1 = Seldom, 3 = Sometimes true, 5 = Almost always true		
Interpretation of average score: 88 - 99 signs of a referral/like-minded expectation-reality gap, 55 - 83 likely a referral/like-minded expectation-reality gap exists, 1- 54 certainly the referral/like-minded expectation-reality gap exists.		

Table 2.7: Assessment: referral/like-minded expectation-reality gap.

Paying attention to the circumstances bringing about the realization of a referral/like-minded expectation-reality gap, the outcome of the analysis of the organization's culture, capabilities, and values identifying potential shortfalls causing the referral/like-minded expectation-reality gap, could allow the organization to:

- narrow or reduce the referral/like-minded expectation-reality gap,
- recruit and build a team of like-minded consultants,
- adjust the referral program as input characteristic, and
- adjust the actions taken by the organization to support the referral input characteristic.

Chapter 3 will shed light on the theme "consulting does not spell adviser," focusing on the consultant/adviser expectation-reality gap.

This page is for you, the reader, to make notes and jot down reference page numbers.

Use this table to make notes and jot down system-related reference page numbers.

Note	Page Number		
	People	Process	Application

Use this table to make notes and jot down IPO-related reference page numbers.

Note	Page Number		
	Input	Process	Output

Use this table to make notes and jot down theme-related reference page numbers.

Note	Page Number				
	Business Models	Competencies	Leadership	Values	Self-Orientation

This page is for you, the reader, to make notes and jot down ERG-related reference page numbers.

Note	Page Number
Referral Does Not Spell Like-Minded	

CHAPTER 3

Consulting Does Not Spell Adviser

Your customer doesn't care how much you know until they know how much you care.
—Theodore Roosevelt

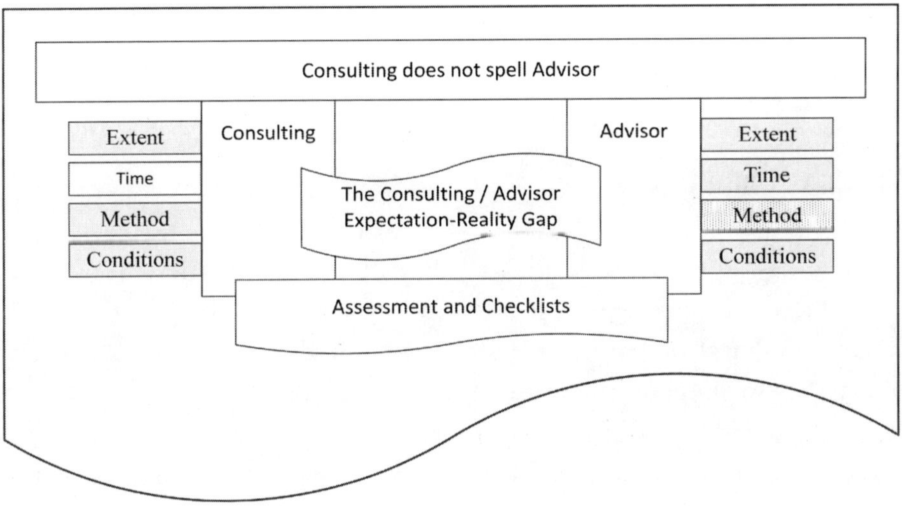

Introduction

IT IS SATURDAY evening, August 29, 2015. As I am lounging on my bed and scribbling away, I am witnessing dusk over the hydroelectrical construction campsite near Gillam in Northern Manitoba, Canada.

Realizing once I have removed the distractions preventing me from writing and focused on influences that inspire me to write, it is easy to take my writing on the road.

The second theme requiring our attention is "consulting does not spell adviser." The focus of this chapter is to provide an understanding of leadership's expectations from project and business consulting as input characteristic; the actions taken by the organization to support the consulting input characteristic; the circumstances bringing about the realization a consulting/adviser expectation-reality gap exists; and an analysis of the organization's culture, capabilities, and values identifying potential shortfalls causing the consulting/adviser expectation-reality gap.

Expected Result

Expectation 2

All consultants act as business or project adviser to the organization's client base with a focus on business-associated personal relationships and client trust.

Business Input

To deliver the expected result and develop trusted advisers, leadership introduced as input the concept of consulting to the equation. Furthermore, to promote and prepare consultants to be advisers and strengthen the chance of achieving the expected outcome of adviser, leadership—through knowledge transfer—introduces to the organization, team, and individual consultants the following business-relevant characteristics: relationship types, trusted adviser, and trust base.

Leadership is confident consultants focused on being professionals and engaging on projects as project and business consultants can benefit the start-up business by assisting in development of advisers and bringing a trust base to the organization's clients.

To promote and prepare consultants to be advisers and strengthen the chance of achieving the expected outcome of consultants being advisers, leadership handed each consultant the book *The Trusted Advisor,* a practical guide outlining the types of client-adviser relationships, types of relationships, and the breadth of business issues and personal relationships.

Introducing the four types of relationships, characteristics of the various types of relationship levels, and the evolution of a client-adviser relationship (figure 3.1).

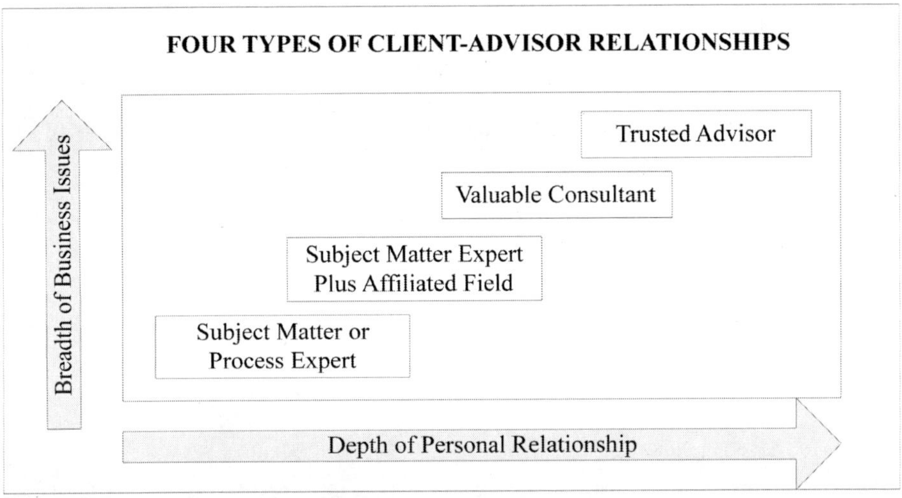

Figure 3.1: Four types of client-adviser relationships (Maister, David H., Green, Charles H., and Galford, Robert M. 2000).

Through sharing of knowledge and collaborating on the evolution of client-adviser relationship with *The Trusted Advisor* as basis, leadership is confident individual consultants, by combining consulting experience, and business and interpersonal skills, have the knowledge required to be trusted advisers to clients (figure 3.1).

Being trusted advisers to our clients will ensure clients communicate and collaborate with consultants and do not just terminate an agreement when concerns arise in terms of crises, change, triumph, or defeat in business or personality issues.

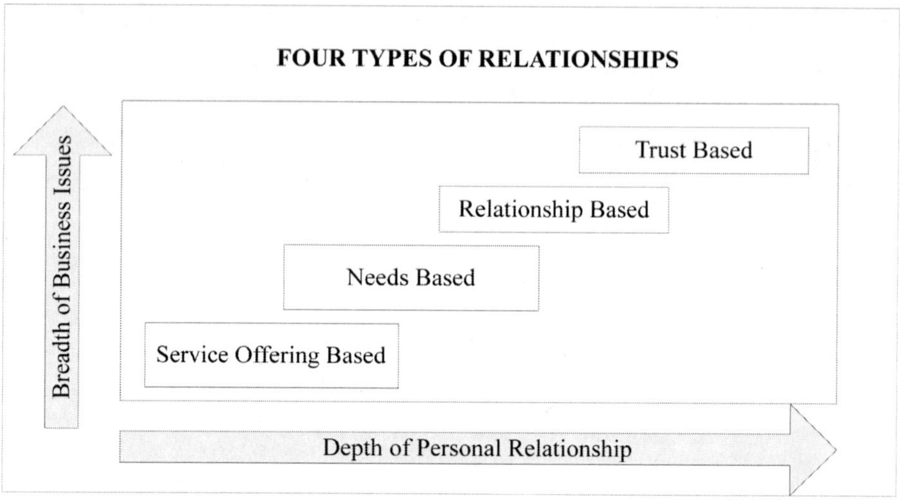

Figure 3.2: Four types of relationships (Maister, David H., Green, Charles H., and Galford, Robert M. 2000).

Having the goal to have consultants as trusted advisers is not enough to ensure success. Leadership furthermore introduced to consultants, with *The Trusted Advisor* as basis, four different types of relationships (figure 3.2). The expectation is with the background knowledge gained, consultants can determine the appropriate relationship to support their clients, realizing in certain situations the client requires service- or needs-based support, while in other situations, the requirement might go beyond support to a relationship or trust base.

FOUR TYPES OF RELATIONSHIPS

	Service Based	Needs Based	Relationship Based	Trust Based
Focus On	Answers, Expertise, input	Business Problems	Client Organization	Client as Individual
Energy Spend on	Explaining	Problem Solving	Providing Insights	Understanding the Client
Client Receives	Information	Solutions	Ideas	Safe Haven for Hard Issues
Indicators of Success	Timely, High Quality	Problem Solved	Repeat Business	Varied: Creative, Pricing, and Other

Breadth of Business Issues

Depth of Personal Relationship

Figure 3.3: Breadth of business issues and depth of personal relationships (Maister, David H., Green, Charles H., and Galford, Robert M. 2000).

Leadership, furthermore, equips consultants with knowledge to understand what each relationship type requires in terms of focus, time and energy spent, client deliverables, and indicators of success (figure 3.3). With an understanding, consultants will equip themselves with the skills required in each client interaction to realize what the focus should be, the amount of time and energy required, the appropriate deliverables, and the indicators demonstrating success.

Reality: Consulting does not spell adviser.

Story 2

The mountain becomes too high, and consultants are unable to identify and build on the good qualities of the client to bring them together as a team. The reality is that consultants are unable to put their own credibility at stake and use their personal strengths to support the client both personally and professionally.

Table 3.1 shows when it comes to experienced consultants providing consulting, the organization experienced difficulties in terms of the extent, method, and condition of the "consulting" input characteristic. The table further indicates although leadership counted on high levels of advisory, gaps were identified in the method of delivering advice.

Character	Difficulties Experienced or Issues Occurred	Counted On
	Consulting	Adviser
Extent	Degree of difficult clients Degree of inexperienced clients Level of technical skills	
Time		
Method	Practice to proactively deal with difficulties Practice of working without supervision Sense of urgency while on project to realize the opportunity and generate work	Practice of being patient Focus on supporting the client Focus on educating client Building client relationship
Condition	Asking questions Nontechnical skills	

Table 3.1: Providing consulting: consulting input characteristic difficulties and level of advisory.

Story 4

It is thoroughly understood and recognized that meeting the recurring needs of the client is the organization's bread and butter. The reality is that consultants are unsuccessful in keeping the client engaged. Not fully comprehending client's needs makes up only 50 percent of their "wants." In general, client wants are more important than their desire for the consulting organization to take a personal interest in managing the outcome of their project.

Table 3.2 shows when it comes to experienced consultants being able to meet recurring needs, the organization experienced difficulties in terms of the extent, method, and condition of the "consulting" input characteristic. The table 3.2 further indicates although the organization counted on senior team members for high levels of advisory, gaps were identified in the extent, time, and method of delivering advice.

Character		Difficulties Experienced or Issues Occurred		Counted On
		Consulting		Adviser
Extent	◇	Level of early-stage project experience Degree of project IP to sell to client as a package Degree of focus on technical	◇	Degree of client support and mentoring of organization
Time			◇	Juncture of developing assignment through different life cycle stages
Method	◇	Technique to build a client relationship Practice of growing past a single business connection Modus operandi in pricing consulting Modus operandi to calculate project cost	◇	Technique to develop a personal and advisory capacity relationship Sense that consulting is more than only a commodity
Condition	◇	Listening to the client wants		

Table 3.2: Meeting recurring needs: consulting input characteristic difficulties and level of advisory.

Story 4

It is well understood that experienced consultants should always work with clients following work methods, which can be appreciated, and allowing the individuals to achieve agreed business and project qualities. The reality is the consultant is unable to put its own credibility at stake and use its personal strengths to support the client personally and professionally.

Table 3.3 shows when it comes to consultants following work methods allowing to achieve agreed qualities, the organization experienced difficulties in terms of the extent, method, and condition of the "consulting" input characteristic. Furthermore, the table indicates while the organization counted on consultants for high levels of advisory, a gap was identified in the extent, and method of delivering advice.

Character	Difficulties Experienced or Issues Occurred	Counted On
	Consulting	Adviser
Extent	Level of consultant experience Scale of selling and delivering	Degree of consultants taking over account management
Time		
Method	Technique of client communication Practice of proactive and independent work Modus operandi in escalating client competencies Modus operandi in getting direct client replaced	Practice of being patient Consultant to focus on supporting the client Building client relationship Practice of generating more work while on project
Condition	Listening skills Nontechnical skills	

Table 3.3: Consultant credibility: consulting input characteristic difficulties and level of advisory.

Story 7

The importance of continuous communication between the consultant and the organization is emphasized to ensure long-term client engagement and consultant time utilization. Consultant discipline and behavior requirements on this matter are well documented and are built into the contractor agreements. Overshadowing the fact that groundbreaking client-engagement work for the organization is done, a break in verbal dialogue and communication with the organization allows the client to take over management of the consultant, opening the door for the client to not use the consultant to their full potential and regularly raise issues regarding the consultant's behavior.

Table 3.4 shows when it comes to consultants keeping a continuous line of communication between consultant and the organization, the organization experienced difficulties in terms of the extent and method of the "consulting" input characteristic. Though the organization counted on high levels of advisory, shortcomings existed in terms of the extent, method, and condition of delivering advice.

Character		Difficulties Experienced or Issues Occurred		Counted On
		Consulting		Adviser
Extent	◇	Magnitude of personal issues Degree where to contractual agreement impacts personal interaction Degree of contractor business acceptance	◇	Scale of longer-term contract
Time				
Method	◇	Sense of worrying about future work Sense of worrying about career Design of subcontract agreement versus employment	◇	Building client relationships Modus operandi in viewing contractors and employees as equals
Condition			◇	Setting of contractor work on behalf of the organization Setting which contractor keeps working within the spirit of a start-up company

Table 3.4: Break in communication: consulting input characteristic difficulties and level of advisory.

Expectation-Reality Gap

To identify the reasoning behind consulting/adviser expectation-reality gap with the advisory input characteristic difficulties and level of advisory in mind, an analysis has been done on the organization's culture, consultant capabilities, and organization leadership.

Table 3.5 indicates the various misalignments in organization culture (equality, ownership thinking, fit for purpose, and values) that might exist and could have led to the consulting/adviser expectation-reality gap.

Equality			
Limited organization structures		Consultants can enjoy themselves	
Consultant participation	◇	Equal productivity incentives	
Fulfill potential		Social identity	
Treated fairly		Knowing our peers	
Character protected		Absence of inappropriate and disrespectful language	
Work hours respected		Absence of stereotyping	
Personal information protected		Taking consultants seriously	
Recognition of diversity			
Ownership Thinking			
Understanding the fundamentals of the organization	◇	Forecasting and achieving the business's key performance indicators	
Understanding how the company makes money		Key performance indicators are highly visible and accountable	
Understanding how each consultant adds—or takes away—value	◇	Having self-funding incentive plans	
Knowing the business's key performance indicators	◇	Incentive plans aligning the consultants' behavior to the business's objectives	◇
Fit for Purpose			
Deliverables do what they intend to achieve		Final deliverables are efficient enough for the stated purpose	
Deliverables are good enough to do the work they are designed to do		Deliverables represent the right tool to do the work consultants have to do	
Deliverables are of a good enough standard for clients		Deliverables fulfill the requirement specifications and stated outcome	
Deliverables answer the client's requirement and wants and nothing more	◇	Consultants are undertaking enough and have efficient effort to reach the client's intended goals	
Deliverables are comprehensive to the extent that they answer the client's requirement and wants and nothing more			
Values			
Trust	◇	Transparency	
Pride		Sense of urgency	
Camaraderie	◇	Commitment	◇

Table 3.5: Consulting/adviser expectation-reality gap: culture.

Table 3.6 indicates the various gaps in organization core competencies that potentially exist and could have led to the consulting/adviser expectation-reality gap.

Core Competencies			
Leadership		Work quality	
Sense of urgency		Quantity of work	
Teamwork	◆	Accountability	◆
Decision-making		Adaptability	◆
Client focused	◆	Initiative	
Business acumen	◆	Innovation	
Resource management		Planning and organizing	
People management	◆	Communication	◆

Table 3.6: Consulting/adviser expectation-reality gap: capability.

Table 3.7 shows the various inadequacies in organization leadership styles that might exist and could have led to the consulting/adviser expectation-reality gap.

Styles			
Cooperative leadership	◆	Whiner	
Problem-solving leadership		Gossiper	
Leadership by example		Nonstop talker	◆
Knowledge leadership	◆	Grumbler	
Get-up-and-go leadership	◆	Bully	

Table 3.7: Experienced consulting/adviser expectation-reality gap: leadership.

Assessment and Checklists

With the circumstances bringing about the realization of a consulting/adviser expectation-reality gap and an analysis of the organization's culture, capabilities, and values identifying potential inadequacies causing the consulting/adviser expectation-reality gap, table 3.8 provides a list of questions and phrases to be used to assess the extent whereto the organization's culture, capabilities, values, and leadership support the advisory process, contractual agreement with consultants, assignment of consultants to work, and mentoring and coaching of consultants.

Item	Description	Score
A	Culture	
	Equality	
2	Consultant participation is evident in preparedness, staying focused on the main topics, keeping control of tasks, discussing the salient issues, and contributing to ideas and information.	
	Ownership Thinking	
1	Consultants understand the fundamentals of the organization and how the organization runs the business within the following six departments: people, administration, business information management, client engagement, projects, and commercial and day-to-day operations.	
3	The organization and the individual team members understand how each consultant adds—or takes away—value.	
4	Individual team members are aware of the business's key performance indicators.	
8	The organization has implemented incentive plans that align the consultants' behavior to the business's objectives.	
	Fit for Purpose	
5	Consultants produce deliverables that are comprehensive to the extent that they answer the client's requirement and wants and nothing more.	
B	Values	
1	Consultants have people-management competencies, including the ability to delegate, set goals, manage performance, motivate, train, develop, hire, and exit employees and contractors in a fashion that meets the company's goals.	

Item	Description	Score
3	Camaraderie is demonstrated through a sense of belonging where consultants work, acceptance for who consultants are, a sense of inclusion where the organization makes everyone an insider, occasional fun events that are planned to meet diverse interests, clear messages stating that all are welcome, and understanding for those who don't choose to participate.	
6	Commitment is demonstrated through a consultant base that pledges themselves to the organization and delivers successful projects aligned with the business, culture, remuneration, and leadership model, consistently and persistently pursuing the business's purpose and conduct	
C	Capabilities	
3	Consultants have teamwork competencies including the ability to establish and maintain positive working relationships and to work cooperatively to achieve results, solicit input, value team members' contributions, and place them above personal needs.	
5	Consultants, from a business perspective, can generate and enhance profit; recognize business opportunities; and anticipate, understand, and act on business options to lead to a positive outcome.	
6	Consultants demonstrate business acumen, including the ability to generate and enhance profit; recognize business opportunities; and anticipate, understand, and act on business options to lead to a positive outcome.	
8	Consultants apply people management day-to-day work execution including the ability to delegate, set goals, manage performance, motivate, train, develop, hire, and exit employees and contractors in a fashion that meets the company's goals.	
11	Consultants have accountability competencies, including the ability to take responsibility for tasks or assignments and align words with actions.	
12	Consultants have adaptability, showing abilities in mastering new skills and demonstrating flexibility in reacting to changing needs, procedures, and environments; work well under pressure; handle multiple assignments; and meet deadlines.	
16	Consultants have people-management competencies, including the ability to delegate, set goals, manage performance, motivate, train, develop, hire, and exit employees and contractors in a fashion that meets the company's goals.	
D	Leadership	
1	Have consultants and team members who are seeking cooperation from all consultants, seeking cooperation from consultants whom they have no control over.	

Item	Description	Score
4	Have consultants providing knowledge leadership, who know the strategies and tactics required, realizing experience and potential in the consultants, and mentoring.	
5	Have consultants providing get-up-and-go leadership, getting up and doing what is required of them, and committing themselves to get-up-and-go business.	
8	The organization does not have consultants who are always discussing every bit of detail about their personal lives and ignoring the fact that the team is working in an open-office environment and not respecting other consultants who prefer a quiet working environment.	
	Average Score	
Rate a score of 1, 3 or 5. Score: 1 = Seldom, 3 = Sometimes true, and 5 = Almost always true		
Interpretation of average score: 75 - 90 signs of a consulting/adviser expectation-reality gap, 50 - 74 likely a consulting/adviser expectation-reality gap exists, 1 - 49 certainly the consulting/adviser expectation-reality gap exists.		

Table 3.8: Assessment: consulting/adviser expectation-reality gap.

Paying attention to the circumstances bringing about the awareness a consulting/adviser expectation-reality gap exists, the outcome of the analysis of the organization's culture, capabilities, and values identifying potential shortfalls causing the consulting/adviser expectation-reality gap and the assessment will allow the organization to:

- narrow or reduce the consulting/adviser expectation-reality gap,
- recruit and build a team of advisers,
- adjust the referral program as input characteristic, and
- adjust the actions taken by the organization to support the consultant input characteristic.

Chapter 4 will shed light on the theme "business plan availability does not spell business action," focusing on the business plan/business action expectation-reality gap.

This page is for you, the reader, to make notes and jot down reference page numbers.

Use this table to make notes and jot down system-related reference page numbers.

Note	Page Number		
	People	Process	Application

Use this table to make notes and jot down IPO-related reference page numbers.

Note	Page Number		
	Input	Process	Output

Use this table to make notes and jot down theme-related reference page numbers.

Note	Page Number				
	Business Models	Competencies	Leadership	Values	Self-Orientation

This page is for you, the reader, to make notes and jot down ERG-related reference page numbers.

Note	Page Number
Consulting Does Not Spell Adviser	

CHAPTER 4

Business Plan Availability Does Not Spell Business Action

Vision is not enough; it must be combined with venture. It is not enough to stare up the steps, we must step up the stairs.
—Vaclav Havel

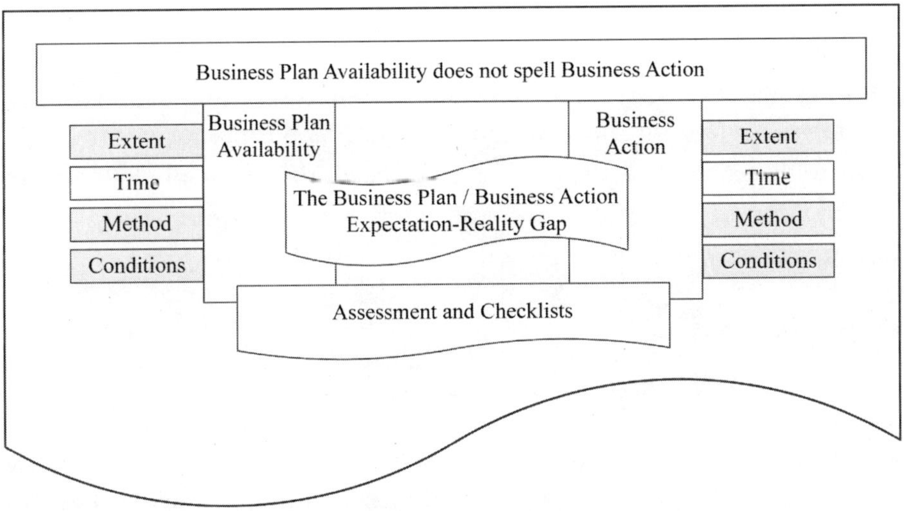

Introduction

WITH AN AUDIO headset on, keeping my mind off the busy and noisy project surroundings, listening to Mozart's "Piano Concerto No.

21, in C Major: Andante," the music in my ears prompted my urge to write. I pull closer my computer, inspired and ready to start scribbling down the words for chapter 4.

The third theme requiring our attention is "business plan availability does not spell business action." The focus of this chapter is to provide an understanding of actions taken by leadership to make clear their expectation of consultants playing their part in building the business, including a business plan as input characteristic; an understanding of actions taken by the organization to support the business plan input characteristic; circumstances bringing about the awareness a business plan/business action expectation-reality gap exists; and an analysis of the organization's culture, capabilities, and values identifying potential inadequacies causing the business plan/business action expectation-reality gap.

Expected Result

Expectation 3

A detailed business plan and a leadership model based on open communication encourage consultants to have the discipline making the business plan content their own and conducting business accordingly. As shareholders—or with the possibility of becoming a shareholder within a year—consultants understand and know what is required to grow the business from one business growth life-cycle stage to the next.

Business Input

The primary business input is for leadership to equip consultants with the insight to generate business, strengthen current project work, take the business forward, and move the company from one business cycle to another. Leadership uses the organization's business plan (table 4.1) to communicate how each business plan activity is in support of a specific equity risk lever and business excellence criteria.

NUMBER	PLAN	IN SUPPORT OF BUSSINESS SCORECARD	BUSINESS AREA IMPACTED	IN SUPPORT OF RISK LEVERS	IN SUPPORT OF BUSINESS EXCELLENCE
P.1.0	Well defined PDO Solutions roles and responsibilities	Capability	People	Intellectual capital	Mgmt Processes
P.1.2	Building relationships and experience that will allow people to act empowered and forster a project culture	Culture	People	Consultant loyalty	Sustainability
COM.1.0	Develop and implement our proposal and RFP risk review process	Longterm Sustanability	Commercial	Quality of fee income	Mgmt Processes
COM.1.1	Protect on a corporate level and project basis revenue targets and margins	Longterm Sustanability	Commercial	Management quality	Sustainability
CE.1.0	Increase Lead Generating activities; Target 50 per month, company wide	Sales Growth	Client Engagement	Sales and profit growth	Business Growth
CE.1.1	Engage with existing clients to increase scope or explore new opportunities on current projects	Work Availability	Client Engagement	Sales and profit growth	Business Growth
A.1.0	Optimal use of office infrastructure to support flexible work culture	Longterm Sustanability	Administration	Management quality	Sustainability
A.1.1	Increase efforts to pro-actively manage company debt – procedures and reporting	Longterm Sustanability	Administration	Management quality	Sustainability
BI.1.1	Procedures Development	Corporate Valuation	Business Info Management	Intellectual capital	Innovation
BI.1.2	PM Application Implementation	Corporate Valuation	Business Info Management	Intellectual capital	Business Growth
BI.1.3	New Practice Areas	Corporate Valuation	Business Info Management	Market positioning	Business Growth
P.1.0	Implement and monitor on-project peer reviews	Client Satisfaction	Projects	Quality of fee income	Mgmt Processes
P.1.3	Implement project sponsorship	Retention	Projects	Client relationships	Mgmt Processes
P.1.5	Further develop and implement our fit-for-purpose framework	Deliver-as-agreed	Projects	Quality of fee income	Mgmt Processes

Figure 4.1: Abstract from organization business plan.

With consultants having insight into the various activities and a thorough understanding of the business plan, leadership in a proactive manner aligned consultants based on functional knowledge, experience, and preferences to plan business activities; on a continuous basis, tracking the outcome of the various business activities, implementing corrective plan of action, and collaborating with consultants.

Leadership, through the business plan, strives to communicate the focus areas of the organization's strategy, being clear on what is included or excluded. Emphasis is placed on how each line item in the business plan can support individual consultants to define and manage specific measurable objectives; provide a single point to track dates and deadlines; prioritize actions to align with business growth, management, and financial health; and delegate responsibility; furthermore, putting action steps in writing aligns expectations and course of actions.

To achieve its objectives with the organization's business plan, leadership builds the business plan on the following three methodologies: the Equity Growth Wheel, the European model for business excellence, and the balanced scorecard.

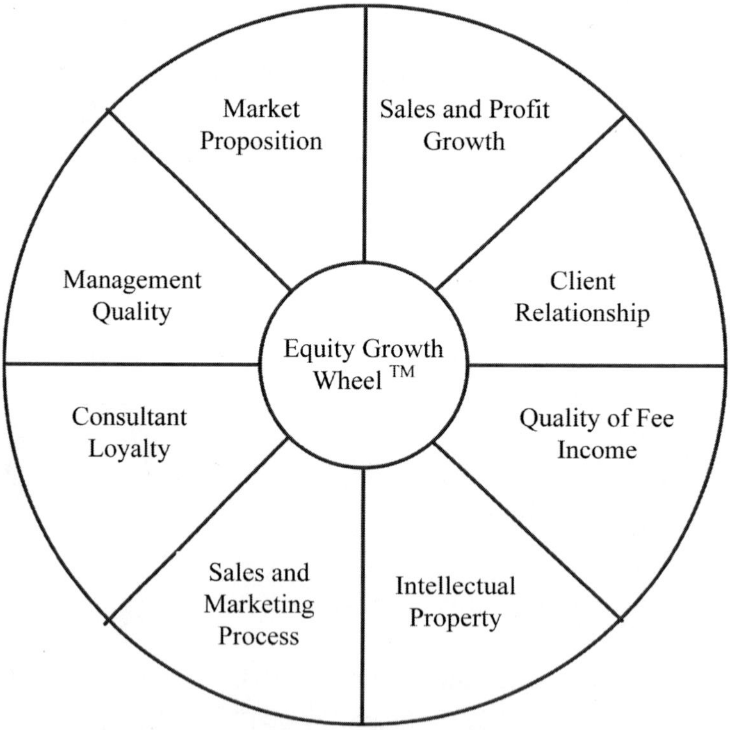

Figure 4.2: The Equity Growth Wheel (source: http://www.equiteq.com/equiteq-edge/grow-your-business/the-8-levers-of-equity-value.aspx).

Consultants, as shareholders invested in the organization leadership, made all efforts to ensure individual consultants and the group understand and know what is required to grow the business and increase the organization's valuation. The organization's founders, at a time when they were at a very bleak position, were stumbling across a consultant from the organization Equiteq, who became a highly regarded friend, mentor, and coach. The founders made a strategic decision to use the Equity Growth Wheel risk levers (figure 4.2) to assist in determining the organization's value and guide the organization's growth. Each business plan action item is assigned to a specific risk lever, allowing leadership to utilize organization's business plan as an instrument to guide the growth and valuation journey. Business plan action items are assigned to one of the following risk levers: sales and profit growth, sales and marketing process, market proposition, management quality, client relationships, quality of fee income, intellectual property, or consultant loyalty (figure 4.2).

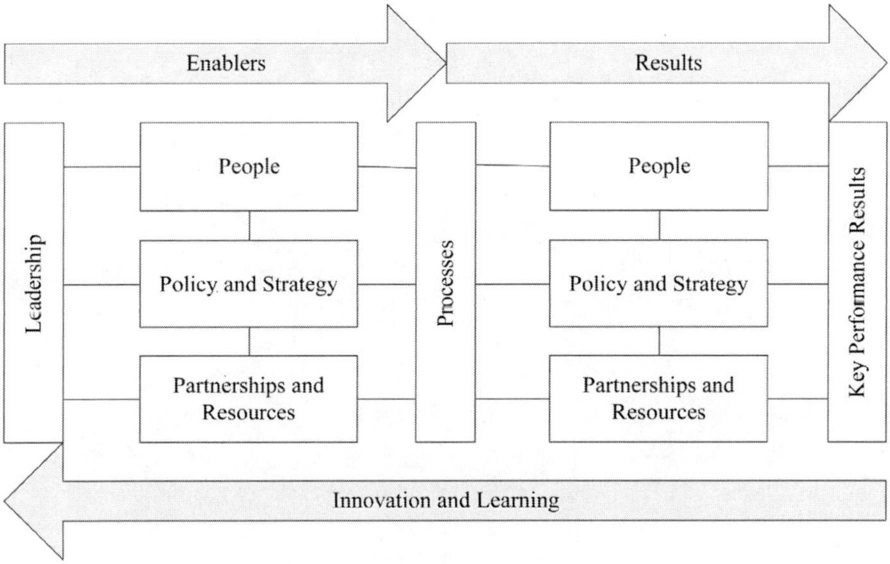

Figure 4.3: European model for business excellence (source: http://www.trimo.eu/company/business-excellence/European-model-of-business-excellence-efqm-8412).

As the pursuit for success and excellence is a long, winding journey and never ends, leadership adopted the European model for business excellence and assigned selected business plan action items to a specific business excellence initiative. To prevent exhaustion and avoid becoming overwhelmed, the organization embarked on only four business excellence initiatives: business growth, innovation, sustainability, and management processes. Considering all the consultants joining this newly formed organization came from different backgrounds, leadership focused on introducing the excellence initiatives to rally the individual consultants and bring them together on the business excellence journey. Furthermore, the organization used the business plan as an instrument to connect day-to-day activities individual consultants are involved in and assigned to guide the organization in a structured manner, create the change required to make all consultants proud of the organization, and build the organization into a world-class entity.

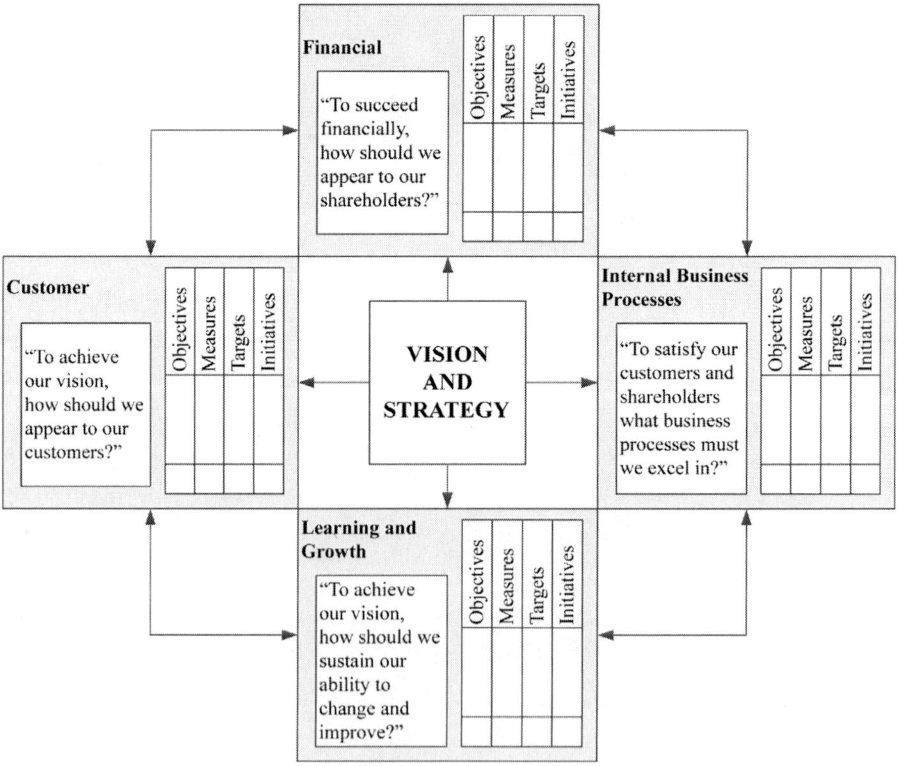

Figure 4.4: The balanced scorecard: translating strategy into action (David P. Norton and Robert S. Kaplan. 1996).

The final component making up the backbone of the organization's business strategy as relayed through the business plan is the Norton and Kaplan balanced scorecard (figure 4.3). Integrating the balanced scorecard with the organization's business plan allowed the organization to leverage the business plan as a mechanism to translate the strategic vision into concrete goals and actions. Every line item in the organization's business plan is also aligned with a specific balanced scorecard item, allowing the business to have a clear guideline on how business plan items assist in reaching the organization's short-term and longer-term goals. To mention a couple, the balanced scorecard included corporate valuation, deliver as agreed, person fit for purpose, culture, capability, work availability, sales growth, consultant loyalty, client satisfaction, retention, and predictability of performance.

Leadership is confident that introducing consultants to the balanced scorecard principles allows them to gain a thorough understanding of how best practices methodologies cascade through the entire organization, and through this awareness, team members are focused on supporting one another to succeed. The balanced scorecard methodology helps the cross-department and functional team to have a more open channel of communication, enabling understanding of business goals and strategies at all levels of an organization.

Based on this experience, the balanced scorecard is an ideal methodology to transform strategy into action and create desired behaviors because the concept provides strategic feedback and learning, and initiatives are continually measured and evaluated against industry standards.

Reality: Business plan availability does not spell business action.

Story 1

To allow consultants to participate in the development of the organization's business plan, in a matrix format, consultants, based on experience, strengths, and passion, are assigned to one or more business leadership streams and a business function. Through these channels, consultants can participate in the development of the business plan and have access to a breakdown of the business and a clear map of what is required to grow the specific functional area in the organization. The reality is consultants seemingly do not have faith in their own abilities and capabilities to use the information and insights to grow the business accordingly.

Table 4.1 indicates when it comes to embracing the organization's business plan and growing the business accordingly, difficulties were experienced in terms of the extent, method, and condition of the business plan input characteristic. The table further indicates although leadership counted on high levels of business action and participation, gaps exist in the extent, method, and condition of business action.

Character	Difficulties Experienced or Issues Occurred		Counted On	
	Business Plan		Business Action	
Extent	◇	Corporate business plan not translating into personal plans Not understanding the principles of the business plan	◇	Shareholders will show interest in business management Business plan not only managerial and proactive leadership drive
Time				
Method	◇	Not asking questions Not showing ownership	◇	Shareholders focus on the business plan enhancing the organization and generating more profit
Condition	◇	Ability to handle project and business work together Working beyond eight hours a day	◇	Business plan not only sitting on the shelf exercise

Table 4.1: Embrace business plan: business plan input characteristic difficulties and level of business action.

Expectation-Reality Gap

To identify the reasoning behind the business plan/business action expectation-reality gap with the referral input characteristic difficulties and level of business participation in mind, an analysis has been done on the organization's culture, consultant capabilities, and organization leadership.

Table 4.2 indicates the various misalignments in organization culture (equality, ownership thinking, fit for purpose, and values) that might exist and could have led to the business plan/business action expectation-reality gap.

Equality			
Limited organization structures	◇	Consultants can enjoy themselves	
Consultant participation	◇	Equal productivity incentives	
Fulfill potential		Social identity	
Treated fairly		Knowing our peers	
Character protected		Absence of inappropriate and disrespectful language	
Work hours respected	◇	Absence of stereotyping	
Personal information protected		Taking consultants seriously	
Recognition of diversity			
Ownership Thinking			
Understanding the fundamentals of the organization	◇	Forecasting and achieving the business's key performance indicators	◇
Understanding how the company makes money	◇	Key performance indicators are highly visible and accountable	◇
Understanding how each consultant adds—or takes away—value	◇	Having self-funding incentive plans	
Knowing the business's key performance indicators	◇	Incentive plans aligning the consultants' behavior to the business's objectives	

Fit for Purpose			
Deliverables do what they intend to achieve		Final deliverables are efficient enough for the stated purpose	
Deliverables are good enough to do the work they are designed to do		Deliverables represent the right tool to do the work consultants have to do	
Deliverables are of a good enough standard for clients		Deliverables fulfill the requirement specifications and stated outcome	
Deliverables answer the client's requirement and wants and nothing more		Consultants are undertaking enough and have efficient effort to reach the client's intended goals	◆
Deliverables are comprehensive to the extent that they answer the client's requirement and wants and nothing more			

Values			
Trust		Transparency	
Pride		Sense of urgency	◆
Camaraderie		Commitment	◆

Table 4.2: Business plan/business action expectation-reality gap: culture.

Table 4.3 shows the various shortcomings in organization core competencies that might exist and could have led to the business plan/ business action expectation-reality gap.

Core Competencies			
Leadership		Work quality	
Sense of urgency	◆	Quantity of work	
Teamwork		Accountability	◆
Decision-making	◆	Adaptability	
Client focused		Initiative	◆
Business acumen	◆	Innovation	
Resource management		Planning and organizing	
People management		Communication	

Table 4.4: Business plan/business action expectation-reality gap: capability.

Table 4.5 indicates the various inadequacies in organization leadership styles that might exist and could have led to the business plan/business action expectation-reality gap.

Styles			
Cooperative leadership		Whiner	
Problem-solving leadership	◇	Gossiper	
Leadership by example		Nonstop talker	
Knowledge leadership	◇	Grumbler	
Get-up-and-go leadership	◇	Bully	

Table 4.5: Business plan/business action expectation-reality gap: leadership.

Quotient and Checklists

With the circumstances bringing about the realization of an experienced business plan/business action expectation-reality gap and an analysis of the organization's culture, capabilities, and values identifying potential inadequacies causing the experienced consulting/adviser expectation-reality gap, table 4.6 provides a list of questions and phrases to be used to assess the extent whereto the organization's culture, capabilities, values, and leadership support the referral recruitment process, contractual agreement with consultants, assignment of consultants to work, and mentoring and coaching of consultants.

Item	Description	Score
A	Culture	
	Equality	
1	The organization encourages all employees to become more active and productive by giving them more roles in the decision-making process.	
2	Consultant participation is evident in preparedness, staying focused on the main topics, keeping control of tasks, discussing the salient issues, and contributing to ideas and information.	
6	Organization and consultants respect work hours and operate under the principle to get work done in the most effective way, honoring work-life balance, and high level of trust to overcome the concerns of "out of sight can mean out of mind" and "when you're in the flow, time has no meaning."	
	Ownership Thinking	
1	Consultants understand the fundamentals of the organization and how the organization runs the business within the following six departments: people, administration, business information management, client engagement, projects, and commercial and day-to-day operations.	
2	Consultants understand how the business makes money through project work in terms of commercial agreements, delivering quality work, pricing work, reporting, and analysis.	
3	The organization and the individual team members understand how each consultant adds—or takes away—value.	
4	Individual team members are aware of the business's key performance indicators.	
5	The organization, on agreed intervals, forecasts and monitors and controls business key performance indicators.	
6	Organization leadership is clear on key performance indicators, makes it visible to all team members, and keeps responsible people accountable.	
	Fit for Purpose	
9	Consultants are undertaking enough and have efficient effort to reach the client's intended goals.	
B	Values	
5	Consultants demonstrate a sense of urgency through attitude and the process of treating key business or personal matters as if one's life depended on it. Consultants have the determination to stay focused on results and deadlines until the task or project is completed	
6	Commitment is demonstrated through a consultant base that pledges themselves to the organization and delivers successful projects aligned with the business, culture, remuneration, and leadership model, consistently and persistently pursuing the business's purpose and conduct.	

Item	Description	Score
C	Capabilities	
2	Have a consulting base that understands the significance of a sense of urgency. Demonstrated through the organization's and consultants' attitude and the process of treating key business or personal matters as if one's life depended on it. Consultants demonstrate the ability and determination to stay focused on results and deadlines until the task or project is completed.	
4	Using analysis, wisdom, sound judgment, experience, and logic to solve problems and make decisions.	
6	Consultants demonstrate business acumen, including the ability to generate and enhance profit; recognize business opportunities; and anticipate, understand, and act on business options to lead to a positive outcome.	
11	Consultants have accountability competencies, including the ability to take responsibility for tasks or assignments and align words with actions.	
13	Consultants have initiative and innovation utilizing knowledge and scope to constructively increase productivity and achieve goals, use resourcefulness and creativity in dealing with challenges, and anticipate and react positively to change.	
D	Leadership	
2	Have problem solvers who are addressing the issues that frustrate individual consultants, addressing the issues—even if they make them unpopular.	
4	Have consultants providing knowledge leadership, who know the strategies and tactics required, realizing experience and potential in the consultants, and mentoring.	
5	Have consultants providing get-up-and-go leadership, getting up and doing what is required of them, and committing themselves to get-up-and-go business.	
	Average Score	
Rate a score of 1, 3, or 5. Score: 1 = Seldom, 3 = Sometimes true, 5 = Almost always true		
Interpretation of average score: 75 - 90 signs of a business plan/business action expectation-reality gap, 50 - 74 likely business plan/business action expectation-reality gap exists, 1 - 49 certainly a business plan/business action expectation-reality gap exists.		

Table 4.6: Assessment: business plan/business action expectation-reality gap.

Paying attention to the circumstances bringing about the realization a business plan/business action expectation-reality gap exists, the outcome of the analysis of the organization's culture, capabilities, and values, and identifying potential shortfalls causing the business plan/business action expectation-reality gap could allow the organization to:

- narrow or reduce the business plan/business action expectation-reality gap,
- recruit and build a team of business-orientated consultants,
- adjust the business plan as input characteristic, and
- adjust the actions taken by the organization to support the business plan input characteristic.

Chapter 5 will shed light on the theme "KPIs do not spell business success," focusing on the KPI/business success expectation-reality gap.

This page is for you, the reader, to make notes and jot down reference page numbers.

Use this table to make notes and jot down system-related reference page numbers.

Note	Page Number		
	People	Process	Application

Use this table to make notes and jot down IPO-related reference page numbers.

Note	Page Number		
	Input	Process	Output

Use this table to make notes and jot down theme-related reference page numbers.

Note	Page Number				
	Business Models	Competencies	Leadership	Values	Self-Orientation

This page is for you, the reader, to make notes and jot down ERG-related reference page numbers.

Note	Page Number
Business Plan Availability Does Not Spell Business Action	

CHAPTER 5

Managing Right KPIs Does Not Spell Business Success

Coming together is a beginning, keeping together
is progress, and working together is success.
—Henry Ford

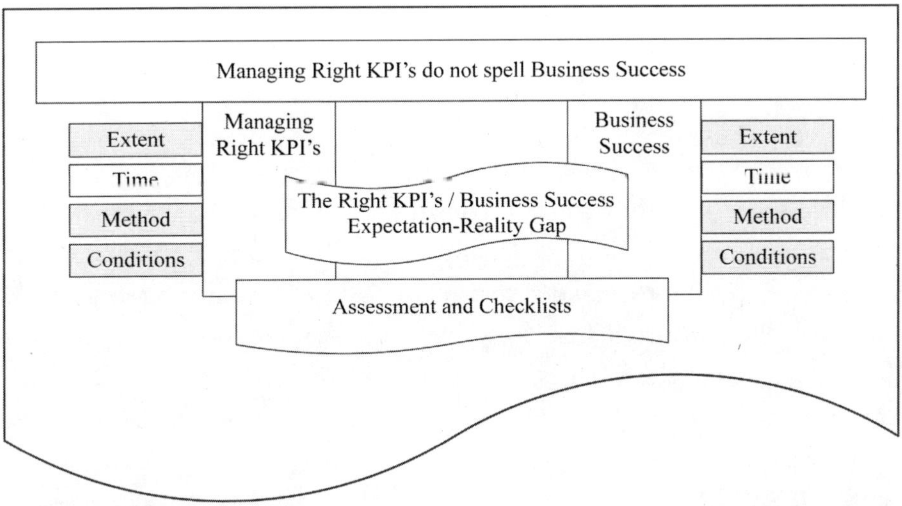

Introduction

AS A PERSON, I imitate the leadership style of Ingvar Kamprad, founder, and CEO of Ikea. This leadership style is very closely influenced by the company culture, structure, and business model. The transformational leadership style is characterized by intellectual stimulation, inspirational motivation, individualized consideration, and idealized influence, including a strong democratic component asking for input from team members and at the same time the autocrat making the ultimate decisions and ensuring continuation of the entrepreneurial vision. From there, my happiness was to pen down thoughts on KPIs as it resembles the transformational leader, allowing for asking input and at same time providing a control mechanism.

The fourth theme requiring our attention is "KPIs do not spell business success." The focus of this chapter is to provide an understanding of leadership's expectations from managing the right KPIs as input characteristics; an understanding of the actions taken by the organization to support the KPIs' input characteristics; the circumstances bringing about the realization a KPI/business success expectation-reality gap exists; and an analysis of the organization's culture, capabilities, and values identifying potential inadequacies and causing the KPI/business success expectation-reality gap.

Expected Result

Expectation 4

Well-defined and thought-out consulting based KPIs, together with an open communication leadership model, encourage consultants to have the discipline to make it their own and deliver business results. As shareholders, consultants are fully aware of what areas of the business to focus on to grow the business's bottom line, resulting in a higher return on their invested funds.

Business Input

As an understudy of Peter Drucker, Tom Peters, and Edwards Deming, here are a couple of their quotations that have stayed with me throughout the years: "what gets measured gets managed" and "no decision has been made unless carrying it out in specific steps has become someone's work assignment and responsibility." These quotations brought the realization that the organization's business plan is the most relevant instrument to reside and make them tangible to the organization and individual consultants, especially considering the way the organization's business plan is structured. Each line in the business plan is aligned with an organization's long-term and short-term goals.

As most of the long- and short-term goals are quantified, it allows for easy measuring of success and/or failure, comparing the results of the organization and the individual consultants with the business goals. *Quantified* refers to the fact that each business plan line item is time bound with specified frames for evaluation and outlining the method of how it will be measured and what will be measured.

To develop, support, and achieve the organization's objective with KPIs, leadership builds the business plan on the following two methodologies: Six Sigma process improvement and goal-setting theory. To facilitate rollout and implementation of KPIs, leadership took direction from the KPI definition process, KPI metrics flow, and KPI metrics-reporting process.

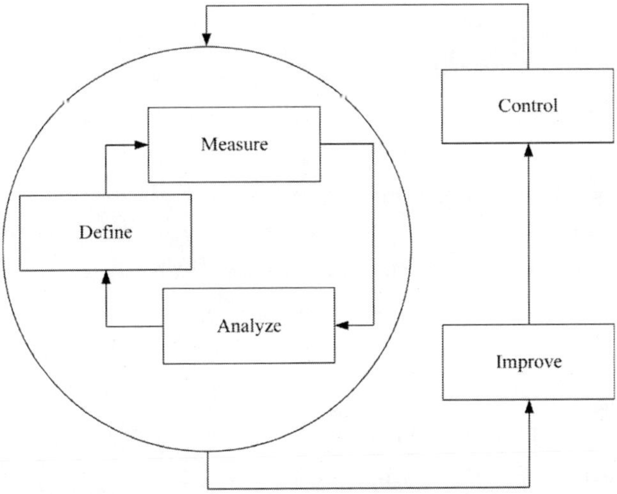

Figure 5.1: Six Sigma: process improvement (source: https://ianjseath.wordpress.com/2014/01/23/dont-let-anyone-tell-you-which-dmaic-is-a-linear-process/).

Leadership, though Six Sigma is not formally implemented, follows the data-driven discipline of the Six Sigma approach and methodology to identify areas for improvement in the consulting business process (figure 5.1). Following the principles of the Six Sigma approach, leadership uses the business plan to set the scene for what needs to be measured in the organization's consulting business process.

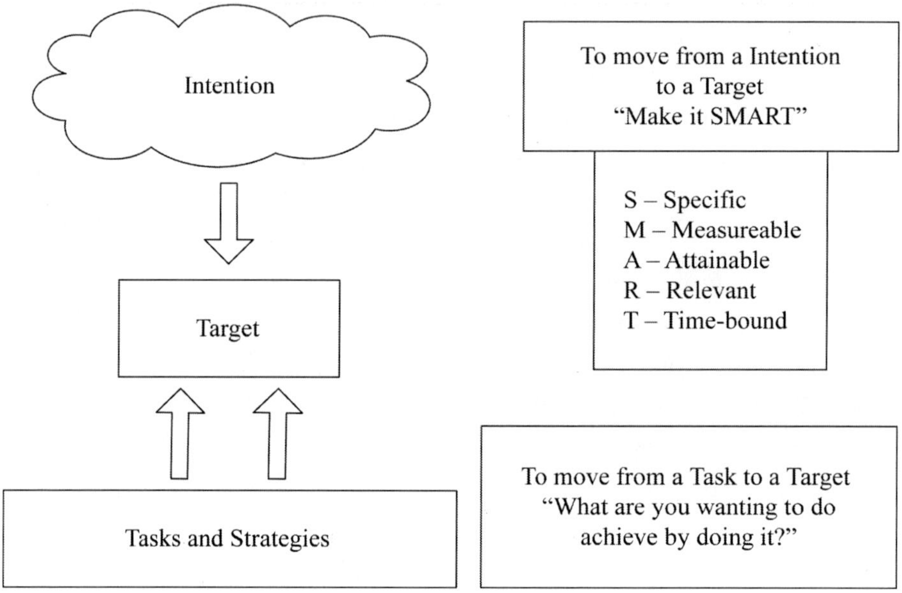

Figure 5.2: Goal-setting theory (source: https://ianjseath.wordpress.com/2014/01/23/dont-let-anyone-tell-you-which-dmaic-is-a-linear-process/).

Totally accepting the fact that leadership cannot motivate the individual consultants, they embrace the work and theories of Locke and Latham in the 1960s and later in the 1990s and implemented the goal-setting theory principles (figure 5.2), expressing the outcomes of the various business plan line items in "SMART" terms: specific, measurable, attainable, relevant, and time bound. Leadership implements the SMART theory to ensure an environment, and targets exist wherein the organization and individual consultants can be motivated through achieving the targets, growing the organization, and increasing their own shareholder value.

Number	In Support of Risk Levers	In Support of Short Term Goals	Review Period	Deliverable	Description	Start Date	Due Date	Hours	Cost
P.1.0	Intellectual capital								
P.1.1	Consultant loyalty								
P.1.2	Consultant loyalty								
COM.1.0	Quality of fee income								
COM.1.1	Quality of fee income								
COM.1.2	Quality of fee income								
CE.1.0	Sales and profit growth								
CE.1.1	Sales and profit growth								
CE.1.2	Sales and profit growth								
CE.1.3	Market positioning								
A.1.0	Management quality								
A.1.1	Management quality								
A.1.2	Management quality								
A.1.3	Management quality								
BI.1.1	Intellectual capital								
BI.1.2	Intellectual capital								
BI.1.3	Market positioning								
BI.1.4	Intellectual capital								
P.1.0	Quality of fee income								
P.1.1	Client relationships								
P.1.2	Quality of fee income								
P.1.3	Quality of fee income								

Figure 5.3: Abstract from organization business plan (SMART targets)

Collaborating on and applying the SMART principles, leadership expects the organization and individual consultants to recognize the importance of setting targets to achieve business and personal success. Furthermore, individual consultants will accept the targets and adapt their behaviors and ways of working to achieve them.

Leadership, in conjunction with the organization and individual consultants to be successful in achieving the targets, strives to use clear and challenging targets, allowing time for consultants to commit themselves to achieving the targets (figure 5.3). Supporting continuous knowledge transfer and providing a feedback loop mechanism, selected business plan line items—and targets available in report format—are collaborated on during weekly business meetings.

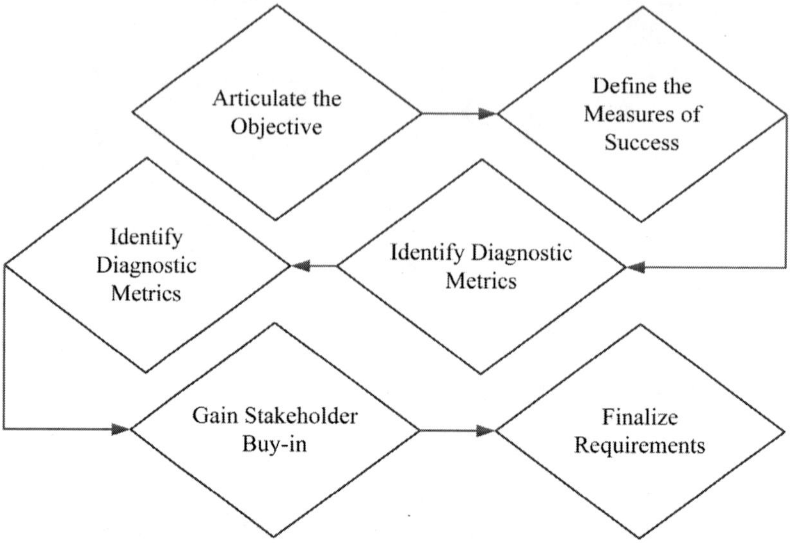

Figure 5.4: KPI definition process (source: http://www.dianliwenmi.com/postimg_743052.html).

The organization leadership followed the KPI definition process to appeal for involvement of consultants and eventual buy-in (figure 5.4). The KPI definition process guides the organization to ensure defined KPIs are metrics clearly indicating how the organization is performing against specific business objectives. Moreover, individual consultants can identify KPIs and provide actionable recommendations that impact the business's bottom line.

Utilizing the KPI definition process, keeping in mind the organization is young and in a start-up phase, leadership and individual consultants identified both KPIs to measure and optimize internal business performance (internal KPIs) and build strategic road maps for the organization (external KPIs).

Overall Business Strategy
"What is it the business wants to achieve?"

Goals and Objectives
"What are the long and short term objectives to achieve the business strategy?"

Key Business Drivers
"What are the core business execution steps to achieve the goals and objectives?"

Key Performance Indicators
"What measure of success are tied to the business drivers?"

Supporting Metrics
"What are the detailed metrics to augment and support the key performance indicators?"

Figure 5.5: KPI metrics flow (source: http://kpi.davidparmenter.com/finding-measure-public-sector/).

The organization followed a step-by-step approach as presented in figure 5.5 to ensure appropriate KPIs are selected to support the overall business strategy. In the run-up to selecting the organization's KPI, the organization considers the specific consulting-based business process of relevance, clear objectives for selected business processes, an active approach to finding and remedying identified business process variances, and predefined quantitative and qualitative measurements.

Using both the KPI definition process and the KPI metrics flow leadership guides and involves consultants from all business areas, including administration, commercial, client engagement, business information management, projects, and people (figure 5.6).

The focus is on working with the organization and consultants to define single and not compounding KPIs. Allowing for KPIs to be calculated independently and regularly and capable of facilitating timely and directed decision-making. Making provision for high level of understanding and consensus KPIs are expressed in either numeric or ratio format with specific constraint criteria (figure 5.6). Easily recognizable KPIs make it possible to include all key areas in the business and allow for consultant involvement and role and responsibility assignment and for a consistent reinforcement of the terminology.

KPI #	MANAGEMENT AREA	DELIVERABLE			
		Specific	Constraint	Units	Measurable
A.1.0	Administration	Year-after-year EAIT growth	MIN	%	
A.1.1	Administration	Annual EAIT	MIN	%	
A.1.2	Administration	EAIT	MIN	$	
A.1.3	Administration	EAIT Y-on-Y	MIN	$	
A.1.4	Administration	Total revenue	MIN	$	
BI.1.1	Business Info Mgmt	Monthly BIM spend as % of total revenue	MAX	%	
BI.1.2	Business Info Mgmt	Monthly BIM spend/person	MAX	$	
BI.1.3	Business Info Mgmt	BIM spend/chargeable hour	MAX	$	
BI.1.4	Business Info Mgmt	Opportunity cost/cost effectiveness of internal hours	MAX	$/Hr	
CE.1.0	Client Engagement	COCA - cost of client acquisition	MAX	$ / Hr	
CE.1.1	Client Engagement	Fees from new projects	MIN	% of fees	
CE.1.2	Client Engagement	Fees from new clients	MIN	% of fees	
CE.1.3	Client Engagement	Fees generated from owners team projects	MIN	% of fees	
CE.1.4	Client Engagement	Have clients in multiple industries	MIN	% of fees	
COM.1.0	Commercial	Average rate per hour	MIN	$	
COM.1.1	Commercial	Permanent employee rate per hour	MIN	$	
COM.1.2	Commercial	Contractors rate per hour	MAX	$	
COM.1.3	Commercial	Empolyee cost as % of rate	MAX	%	
COM.1.4	Commercial	Contractor cost as % of rate	MAX	%	
PE.1.0	People	Have a capable workforce	MIN	Industries	
PE.1.1	People	Cost of recruitment as % of salaries	MIN	%	
PE.1.2	People	Have a stable workplace - Resignations	MAX	%	
PE.1.3	People	Employee engagement as % of fees	MAX	%	
P.1.0	Projects	Average chargeability	MIN	%	
P.1.1	Projects	Permanent employees chargeability	MIN	%	
P.1.2	Projects	Contractors chargeability	MIN	%	
P.1.3	Projects	Permanent Employee : Contractor Hours	MIN	%	
P.1.4	Projects	Quality of consulting surveys	MIN	# / Quarter	
P.1.5	Projects	Project Sponsors connect with client team	MIN	# / 6 months	
P.1.6	Projects	Have a structured session to get feedback	MIN	# / Quarter	

Figure 5.6: Abstract from organization business plan (KPIs).

With the identification and definition of KPIs completed, leadership puts in place applicable reporting and ongoing monitoring of the KPIs. As an integral part of the knowledge-transfer process, leadership engages consultants from the beginning of business planning and metric identification to metric reporting (figure 5.7). Following a structured metric-reporting process to support individual consultants and leadership ownership, allow for time commitments, agreement of calculations and the data source, and a thorough understanding of report formats and context. Weekly business meetings ensured knowledge transfer and a central location for responsible consultants to get access to data, information, and insights.

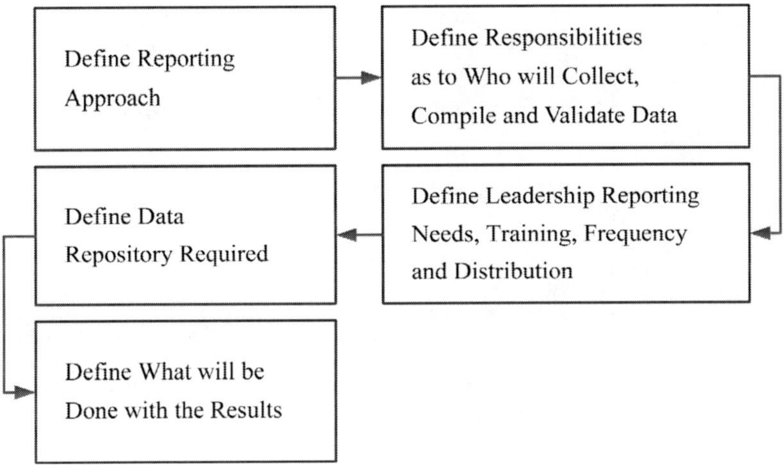

Figure 5.7: KPI metrics reporting process (source: http://www.slideshare.net/anandsubramaniam/project-metrics-measures).

Reality: Managing the right KPIs does not spell business success.

Story 1

Consultants, though they contribute on a yearly basis to determine and set the KPI targets, have access to all the financial and nonfinancial KPIs—KPIs are evaluated and explained on a biweekly basis during the Friday afternoon parleys—do not show confidence to focus on related activities delivering positive outcomes or KPI results and contribute to the organization's business bottom line.

Table 5.1 shows when it came to experienced consultants participating in setting, accepting, and living the organization KPIs, difficulties were experienced in terms of the extent, method, and condition of the KPI input characteristic. The table further indicates although leadership counted on high levels of business success, inadequacies were identified in the extent, method, and condition of business success.

Character	Difficulties Experienced or Issues Occurred	Hoped for or Counted On
	Managing Right KPIs	Business Success
Extent	◇ The understanding of the principles of KPIs Taking and showing ownership	◇ As shareholders show interest in business management Business KPIs not only a managerial and proactive leadership drive
Time		
Method	◇ Translating business KPIs into personal KPIs Asking questions and executing	◇ As shareholders, consultants focus on the business's KPIs, enhancing the organization and generating more profit
Condition	◇ Ability to handle project and business work together. Entrepreneurial spirit to work beyond eight hours per day	◇ Business KPIs not only sitting on the shelf exercise

Table 5.1: Senior team members: right KPIs input characteristic difficulties and level of business success.

Expectation-Reality Gap

To identify the reasoning behind the right KPIs/business success expectation-reality gap with the right KPIs input characteristic difficulties and level of business success in mind, an analysis has been done on the organization's culture, consultant capabilities, and organization leadership.

Table 5.2 indicates the various misalignments in organization culture (equality, ownership thinking, fit for purpose, and values) that might exist and could have led to the right KPIs/business success expectation-reality gap.

Equality			
Limited organization structures		Consultants can enjoy themselves	
Consultant participation	◇	Equal productivity incentives	
Fulfill potential		Social identity	
Treated fairly		Knowing our peers	
Character protected		Absence of inappropriate and disrespectful language	
Work hours respected	◇	Absence of stereotyping	
Personal information protected		Taking consultants seriously	
Recognition of Diversity			
Ownership Thinking			
Understanding the fundamentals of the organization	◇	Forecasting and achieving the business's key performance indicators	◇
Understanding how the company makes money		Key performance indicators are highly visible and accountable	◇
Understanding how each consultant adds—or takes away—value		Having self-funding incentive plans	
Knowing the business's key performance indicators	◇	Incentive plans aligning the consultants' behavior to the business's objectives	

Fit for Purpose			
Deliverables do what they intend to achieve		Final deliverables are efficient enough for the stated purpose	
Deliverables are good enough to do the work they are designed to do		Deliverables represent the right tool to do the work consultants have to do	
Deliverables are of a good enough standard for clients		Deliverables fulfill the requirement specifications and stated outcome	
Deliverables answer the client's requirement and wants and nothing more		Consultants are undertaking enough and have efficient effort to reach the client's intended goals	
Deliverables are comprehensive to the extent that they answer the client's requirement and wants and nothing more			

Values			
Trust		Transparency	◇
Pride		Sense of urgency	◇
Camaraderie		Commitment	◇

Table 5.2: Right KPIs/business success expectation-reality gap: culture.

Table 5.3 indicates the various shortcomings in organization core competencies that might exist and could have led to the right KPIs/ business success expectation-reality gap.

Core Competencies			
Leadership	◇	Work quality	
Sense of urgency	◇	Quantity of work	
Teamwork		Accountability	◇
Decision-making		Adaptability	◇
Client focused		Initiative	◇
Business acumen	◇	Innovation	◇
Resource management		Planning and organizing	
People management		Communication	

Table 5.3: Right KPIs/business success expectation-reality gap: capability.

Table 5.4 indicates the various inadequacies in organization leadership styles that might exist and could have led to the right KPIs/business success expectation-reality gap.

Styles		
Cooperative leadership	Whiner	
Problem-solving leadership	Gossiper	
Leadership by example	Nonstop talker	
Knowledge leadership	Grumbler	
Get-up-and-go leadership	Bully	

Table 5.4: Right KPIs/business success expectation-reality gap: leadership.

Assessment and Checklists

With the circumstances bringing about the realization of a KPIs/business success expectation-reality gap, and an analysis of the organization's culture, capabilities, and values identifying potential inadequacies causing the KPIs/business success expectation-reality gap, table 5.5 provides a list of questions and phrases to be used to assess the extent whereto the organization's culture, capabilities, values, and leadership support the referral recruitment process, contractual agreement with consultants, assignment of consultants to work, and mentoring and coaching of consultants.

Item	Description	Score
A	Culture	
	Equality	
2	Consultant participation is evident in preparedness, staying focused on the main topics, keeping control of tasks, discussing the salient issues, and contributing to ideas and information.	
6	Organization and consultants respect work hours and operate under the principle to get work done in the most effective way, honoring work-life balance, and high level of trust to overcome the concerns of "out of sight can mean out of mind" and "when you're in the flow, time has no meaning."	
	Ownership Thinking	

Item	Description	Score
1	Consultants understand the fundamentals of the organization and how the organization runs the business within the following six departments: people, administration, business information management, client engagement, projects, and commercial and day-to-day operations.	
4	Individual team members are aware of the business's key performance indicators.	
5	The organization, on agreed intervals, forecasts and monitors and controls business key performance indicators.	
6	Organization leadership is clear on key performance indicators, makes it visible to all team members, and keeps responsible people accountable.	
	Fit for Purpose	
B	Values	
4	Organization and consultants demonstrate through operating in such a way that it is easy for outsiders to see what actions are being performed based on openness, communication, and accountability.	
5	Consultants demonstrate a sense of urgency through attitude and the process of treating key business or personal matters as if one's life depended on it. Consultants have the determination to stay focused on results and deadlines until the task or project is completed.	
6	Commitment is demonstrated through a consultant base that pledges themselves to the organization and delivers successful projects aligned with the business, culture, remuneration, and leadership model, consistently and persistently pursuing the business's purpose and conduct.	
C	Capabilities	
1	Consultants have leadership skills, including managing change; influencing outcomes; setting strategy and providing clear direction; generating commitment and enthusiasm toward business decisions; acting as a leader, role model, and ambassador for the organization; and motivating and encouraging self and other team members to work optimally.	
2	Have a consulting base that understands the significance of a sense of urgency, demonstrated through the organization's and consultants' attitude and the process of treating key business or personal matters as if one's life depended on it. Consultants demonstrate the ability and determination to stay focused on results and deadlines until the task or project is completed.	

Item	Description	Score
6	Consultants demonstrate business acumen, including the ability to generate and enhance profit; recognize business opportunities; and anticipate, understand, and act on business options to lead to a positive outcome.	
11	Consultants have accountability competencies, including the ability to take responsibility for tasks or assignments and align words with actions.	
12	Consultants have adaptability, showing abilities in mastering new skills and demonstrating flexibility in reacting to changing needs, procedures, and environments; work well under pressure; handle multiple assignments; and meet deadlines.	
13	Consultants have initiative and innovation utilizing knowledge and scope to constructively increase productivity and achieve goals, use resourcefulness and creativity in dealing with challenges, and anticipate and react positively to change.	
14	Intentionally blank	
D	Leadership	
1	Have consultants and team members who are seeking cooperation from all consultants, seeking cooperation from consultants whom they have no control over.	
2	Have problem solvers who are addressing the issues that frustrate individual consultants, addressing the issues—even if they make them unpopular.	
3	Have consultants who are taking extreme measures on themselves, doing to other consultants as we would want them to do unto us: "walk the walk" and "talk the talk."	
4	Have consultants providing knowledge leadership, who know the strategies and tactics required, realizing experience and potential in the consultants, and mentoring.	
5	Have consultants providing get-up-and-go leadership, getting up and doing what is required of them, and committing themselves to get-up-and-go business.	
	Average Score	
Rate a score of 1, 3, or 5. Score: 1 = Seldom, 3 = Sometimes true, 5 = Almost always true		
Interpretation of average score: 75 - 90 signs of a KPI/business success expectation-reality gap, 50 - 74 likely a KPI/business success expectation-reality gap exists, 1 - 49 certainly a KPI/business success expectation-reality gap exists.		

Table 5.5: Assessment: KPI/business success expectation-reality gap.

Paying attention to the circumstances bringing about the realization a KPI/business success expectation-reality gap exists, the outcome of the analysis of the organization's culture, capabilities, and values identifying potential shortfalls causing the KPI/business success expectation-reality gap and the assessment, could allow the organization to:

- narrow or reduce the KPI/business success expectation-reality gap,
- recruit and build a team of business-orientated consultants,
- adjust the KPI as input characteristic, and
- adjust the actions taken by the organization to support the KPI input characteristic.

Chapter 6 will shed light on the theme "experienced consultants do not spell client engagement," focusing on the experienced consultant-client-engagement expectation-reality gap.

This page is for you, the reader, to make notes and jot down reference page numbers.

Use this table to make notes and jot down system-related reference page numbers.

Note	Page Number		
	People	Process	Application

Use this table to make notes and jot down IPO-related reference page numbers.

Note	Page Number		
	Input	Process	Output

Use this table to make notes and jot down theme-related reference page numbers.

Note	Page Number				
	Business Models	Competencies	Leadership	Values	Self-Orientation

This page is for you, the reader, to make notes and jot down ERG-related reference page numbers.

Note	Page Number
Managing Right KPIs Does Not Spell Business Success	

CHAPTER 6

Experienced Consultant Does Not Spell Client Engagement

I had to make my own living and my own opportunity! But I made it! Don't sit down and wait for the opportunities to come. Get up and make them.
—C. J. Walker

Get closer than ever to your customers. So close which you tell them what they need well before they realize it themselves.
—Steve Jobs

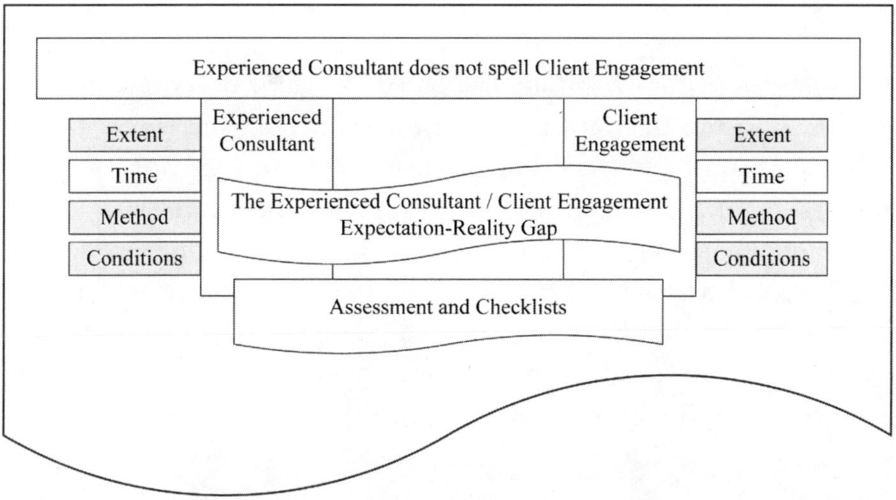

Introduction

IT IS SATURDAY afternoon, September 5, 2015, and I am still at the hydroelectrical construction campsite near Gillam in Northern Manitoba, Canada. Desperately in need of inspiration, I started to focus on what individuals with a strong abstract conceptualization and active experimentation learning style do best: focusing on a specific theme, treating the theme as a unique case, digging into the theory, and performing a systematic analysis. What better way to do this than through writing another chapter in this book?

The fifth theme requiring our attention is "experienced consultant does not spell client engagement." The focus of this chapter is to provide an understanding of leadership's expectation from experienced consultant as input characteristic, an understanding of the actions taken by the organization to support or strengthen the experienced consultant's input characteristic, the circumstances bringing about the realization an experienced consultant/client-engagement-expectation-reality gap exists, and an analysis of the organization's culture, capabilities, and values, identifying potential shortcomings causing the experienced consultant-client-engagement expectation-reality gap.

Expected Result

Expectation 5

Like-minded seasoned consultants, based on referral, recruited into the organization and their acceptance of the various organization business, culture, remuneration, and leadership models, are a driving factor for the experienced consultants to find work for themselves and for the more junior consultants. Furthermore, having an environment where the business plan and KPIs are available and communicated on a regular basis should be enough for experienced consultants to understand how business operates and allow them to develop business strategies to be used when working with clients.

Business Input

After years of experience leading business and project management teams and making numerous mistakes by bringing on board consultants who were not willing to align with leadership's vision and goals, I have come to the realization of the importance of having a structured questionnaire during the recruitment process, addressing all the relevant components of business and projects, to select consultants with a high level of fit. It is especially important for the employment-engagement questionnaire to align with the organization's business plan line items and long-term and short-term goals. Leadership's emphasis with the employment-engagement questionnaire is to accurately assess competency, fit, and motivation, prevent value-added candidates from being improperly assessed, and shift the decision to career growth rather than compensation maximization.

As practice, before the employee-engagement questionnaire is distributed to the potential consultant for completion, the consultant returns a ranked questionnaire for review and discussion during the official interview (figure 6.1). Based on how the potential consultants score themselves, the scores are analyzed to provide an indication of overall fit, like-mindedness, client-engagement capabilities, business leadership, business and project management, and consultant advisory capability.

Similarly, the organization has implemented a client-engagement questionnaire to assess client competency and fit areas, including commitment level, culture fit, competence level, business sector experience, client-engagement experience, business leadership experience, project experience, and business sustainability.

Client engagement expectations are clearly spelled out in leadership, director, and shareholder role and responsibility descriptions. Experienced consultants, acting as directors of the organization, have the general responsibility to provide strategic guidance to the organization, ensuring a strategic direction consistent with the opportunities and challenges facing the organization and the needs of its stakeholders. Experienced consultants, doing their best to ensure this strategic direction, are well known in the organization, and decision-making reflects the strategic direction of the organization.

Employee Engagement Questionnaire	
Commitment Level (3 Questions)	
What is you employment preference? (Yes=1, No=leave blank)	
Are you interested in having equity in company?	What is your preferred investment range? (Mark with 1)
Culture Fit Level (10 Questions)	
Ownership Thinking, How many years of experience do you have?	Ownership Thinking, How many years of experience do you have?
Fit-for-Purpose, How many years of experience do you have?	What languages are you able to do business in (Read and write)? (Yes=1, No=leave blank)
Equality - What is your viewpoint on the following actions?	Equality - What is your viewpoint on the following actions?
Competence Level (6 Questions)	
How do you rate you competency against the following soft skills?	How do you rate you competency against the following soft skills?
How do you rate you competency against the following soft skills?	How do you rate you competency against the following soft skills?
Sector and Discipline Experience (10 Questions)	
Business Areas, How many years working experience do you have?	Business Departments, How many years working experience do you have?
How many projects have you done in each Inductry sector?	How many projects have you done in each Inductry sector?
Client Engagement (6 Questions)	
Marketing, How many years of experience do you have?	How many Client relationships do you own at each management level?
What is the max. repeat business from client relationships? (Mark with 1)	Indicate the total fees generated from client relationships owned (Mark with 1)
Project Experience (8 Questions)	
How many projects over $50,000 completed within each Contract Type?	How many projects completed in each of the Project Lifecycle Phases?
How many projects completed in each of the Project Stages?	Readiness Stage, How many projects completed in each of the following areas?
Business Sustainability (6 Questions)	
What was your avg. charge-out rate / hour over past 3 years? (Mark with 1)	What was your avg. remuneration rate/hour over past 3 years? (Mark with 1)
IP Development, How many years experience do you have?	IP Development, How many years experience do you have?
Comments (2 Questions)	
Mention and rate your 4 biggest business and or personal frustrations	Mention and rate your 4 biggest business and or personal enjoyments

Figure 6.1: Abstract from organization—Employee-Engagement Questionnaire.

Furthermore, directors are responsible for providing both strategic and tactical leadership across all the organization's consulting projects while still partaking in the day-to-day project activities with a focus on meeting deliverable requirements, ensuring overall quality of deliverables, and ensuring overall client satisfaction. Experienced consultants working on client projects have the responsibility to build key client relationships to maintain an acceptable position in the marketplace. In conjunction with the director-client engagement, they deliver presentations, collaborate on proposal development, and participate in consulting and business industry professional events. With the director-commercial, they engage in contractual negotiations with clients and prospective clients.

It is expected of experienced consultants to uphold and maintain client-engagement standards and maintain the highest standards of business ethics, professionalism, and accountability.

To strengthen the chances of achieving the organization's objective of recruiting experienced consultants to participate in client-engagement activities, leadership adopted the concepts and guidelines of client-engagement leadership skills, Kolb leadership profile and types, and the client-engagement process.

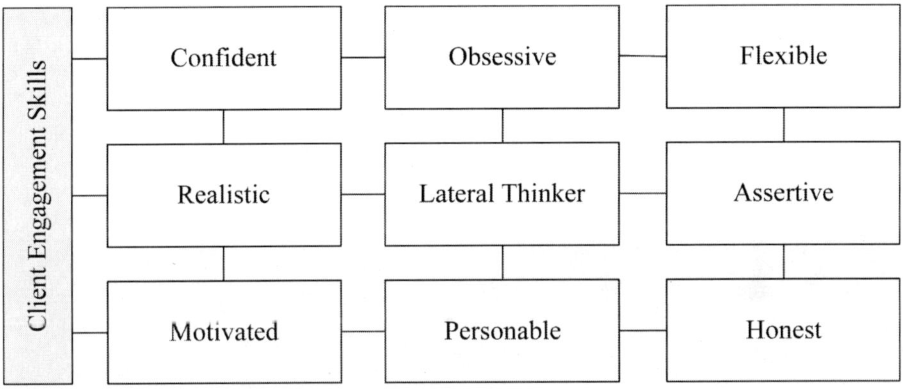

Figure 6.2: Client engagement skills (source: http://www.techrepublic.com/blog/it-consultant/10-personality-traits-of-a-highly-effective-independent-consultant-247228/).

Leadership, throughout day-to-day technical work, knowledge transfer sessions, and business management meetings, focuses on building up the confidence of individual consultants to be self-assured that they have the capabilities to collaborate and engage with their clients to take on consulting work from themselves and the organization.

Besides the people and technical skills, leadership arranged mock sessions to transfer knowledge on how to sell oneself and negotiate terms and conditions, and personal motivation and discipline to perform work on an independent basis at client sites. On a continuous basis, emphasis is placed on capabilities required to engage with clients, such as confidence, motivation, possessiveness, lateral thinking, personable, realistic, flexibility, assertiveness, and honesty (figure 6.2).

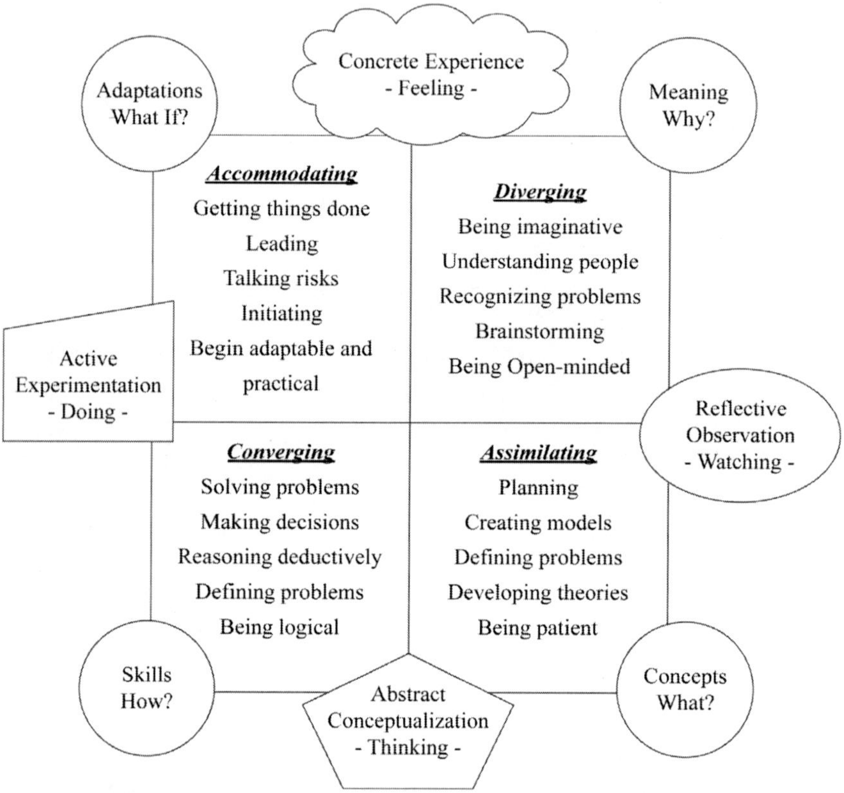

Figure 6.3: Kolb leadership profile and type (David and Kolb 1976).

Supporting the consultants to adapt to and adopt the new role of client engagement, leadership assists the consultants in understanding what their preferred method of learning is. To understanding the learning style, leadership used the Kolb Learning Style questionnaire. The focus of introducing the individual consultants to the KOLB Learning style is to make them understand how the best take in knowledge and best deal with knowledge. Consultants can either take in knowledge by concrete experience or abstract conceptualization and can deal with knowledge either through reflective observation or active experimentation (figure 6.6).

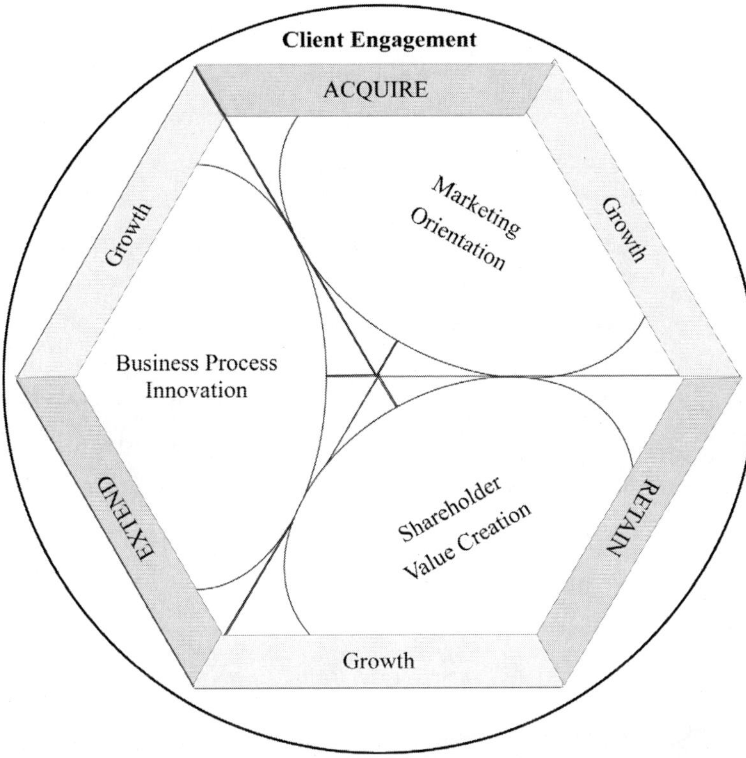

Figure 6.4: Client engagement process (source: http://www.marketingteacher.com/business-strategy-and-crm/).

To introduce experienced consultants to the domain of client engagement, leadership focused on both phases of client engagement: the process of engaging the client and the contextual factors of client relationship, which means what it takes to grow the relationship and business with the client (figure 6.4).

The client-engagement process consists of three core phases—namely, acquisition, retention, and extension. Leadership emphasizes knowledge transfer primarily around what it will take to move client engagement from one phase to the other with the core around market orientation or business offer, value creation within the consulting offer, and, finally, improvement of the consulting offer.

Leadership, to equip consultants with the tools to engage the clients, developed statement of qualifications and key project write-ups. Furthermore, assisting the experienced consultant to gain an understanding of what consulting offer components will be supplementary to the existing offer—or a totally new offer—to support new offer development of the director-client engagement and to assist in developing new or supplementary intellectual property.

With a thorough understanding of their client-engagement roles and responsibilities, soft skills required, an understanding of preferred personal leadership style and the client-engagement process, leadership aligned experienced consultants, through the organization's business plan, to specific client-engagement activities. Leadership, through the business plan, strives to communicate the main points of the company's client-engagement strategy, being clear on what is included or excluded. Emphasis is placed on how the client-engagement line items in the business plan support the individual consultants in their client-engagement efforts.

MANAGEMENT AREA	DELIVERABLE			
	Specific	Constraint	Units	Measurable
Client loyalty	Receive referale from existing clients	Min	% of Clients	
Longterm sustainability	Client provide at a high consistency a high volume of hours - quadrant 1	Min	# of Clients	
Cost of client acquisition	Client engagement cost per chargeable hour	Max	% of Fees	
Cost of client acquisition	Client engagement cost per client	Max	% of Fees	
Lead generation	Early stage - number of opportunities within 3 - 6 months of award	Min	# of Projects	
Lead generation	Late stage - number of opportunities within 1 - 3 months of award	Min	# of Projects	
Longterm sustainability	Fees from new projects as percentage of total fees	Min	%	
Longterm sustainability	Fees from new clients as percentage of total fees	Min	%	
Longterm sustainability	Fees generated from owner's team project participation	Min	%	
Diversified clientele	Have client's in multiple industries	Max	%	

Figure 6.5: Abstract from organization—client-engagement KPIs

The focus is on working with the organization and consultants to define single and not compounding client-engagement KPIs, allowing for client-engagement KPIs to be calculated independently and regularly and capable of facilitating timely and directed decision-making.

Making provision for high level of understanding and consensus, KPIs are expressed in either numeric or ratio format with specific constraint criteria (figure 6.5). Easily recognizable client-engagement KPIs make it possible to ensure key client-engagement areas in the business are covered and all experienced consultants are involved and understand what is required to achieve the business's long- and short-term goals.

Reality: Experienced consultant does not spell client engagement.

Story 1

Experienced consultants primarily outside of the leadership team, only to a limited extent, succeed in using their functional knowledge and experience as an attraction for clients. Furthermore, consultants frequently are unable to succeed in conveying to clients how the organization's consulting (as input) could be used efficiently in client project-management processes (value for money); how and to what extent the results derive from the organization's consulting can bring the expected change to client project management outcomes (value add); and how and to what extent outcomes from the organization's consulting can empower clients with specific knowledge, information, and insights to make decisions and achieve project management outcomes (transformation).

Table 6.1 shows the organization's experienced consultants have difficulties leveraging their technical skills to attract clients in terms of the extent, method, and condition of the experienced consultant's input characteristic. The table further shows the organization counted on using the superior technical skills of consultants to produce high levels of client-engagement activity, and inadequacies were identified in the extent, method, and condition of client-engagement actions.

Character		Difficulties Experienced or Issues Occurred		Hoped for or Counted On
		Experienced Consultants		Client Engagement
Extent	◆	Consultants being stuck in a fixed way of executing work	◆	Experienced consultants able to develop work for themselves Experienced consultants able to develop work for others
Time				
Method	◆	Only focused on doing the work assigned Understanding how to translate technical work into business discussion	◆	Experienced consultants have an established client base Through previous work, built up a relationship that translates into work opportunities
Condition	◆	Understanding how to have a business discussion	◆	Awareness of consultants available to perform project work

Table 6.1: Technical capability: experienced consultants input characteristic difficulties and level of client engagement.

Story 2

As the client is important to the stability and growth of the organization, the organization engages several senior and experienced consultants. The consultants, aware of the presence and profile of the client in the mining and mineral processing industry sector, fear failure, embarrassment, appearing ignorant or incompetent, or loss of reputation or security. Despite this fear resulting in great timely delivery of cost engineering work through several stages of the project life cycle, the organization is unable to hold on to the client and partially lost it to the competition.

Table 6.2 shows the organization's experienced consultants have difficulties leveraging their technical skills as an attraction for clients in terms of the extent, method, and condition of the experienced consulting input characteristic. The table further indicates although the organization counted on its experienced consultants to produce high levels of client engagement, shortcomings were identified in terms of the extent, and method of client engagement.

Character		Difficulties Experienced or Issues Occurred		Hoped for or Counted On
		Experienced Consultants		Client Engagement
Extent	◇	Focused on providing client needs and not wants	◇	Focused on the wants of the client
Time				
Method	◇	Consultants being stuck in a fixed way of executing work Bad-mouthing clients as unknowledgeable and without personal skills	◇	Client relationship that will foster or result in mentorship from the client Engaging with clients instead of only providing technical work Staying connected through person-to-person communication rather than only email communication
Condition	◇	Working off-site away from the clients Inability to travel and work on-site with clients		

Table 6.2: Delivery and communications: experienced consultants input characteristic difficulties and level of client engagement.

Story 3

Engaging a senior leader on the assignment to assist the client with the selection of an ERP application. From an organization perspective, the objective was to enhance the organization's profile and gain acceptance. The seasoned system-transformation consultant came across too strongly and made the client feel as if they had not been heard. The consultant failed to properly understand the client's requirements, objectives, and timelines.

Table 6.3 shows when it comes to the organization's experienced consultants leveraging their technical skills to enhance the organization's profile and gain acceptance, difficulties were experienced in terms of the extent and method of the experienced consultant's input characteristic. The table further indicates when it comes to leveraging the organization's management level consultants, the organization counted on a high level of client engagement, while shortcomings were experienced in the extent and method of client engagement.

Character	Difficulties Experienced or Issues Occurred	Hoped for or Counted On
	Experienced Consultants	Client Engagement
Extent	Focused on providing the needs and not the wants Consultant not educated enough and experienced enough in the groundbreaking work	Focused on the wants of the client
Time		
Method	Consultant not able to make a personal connection with the decision maker Consultant unable to relate the work at hand with the client timelines, project status, and health of the client's business Consultant too strong with individual functional clients	Client relationship that will foster or result in mentorship from the client Consultant will have built a strongenoughrelationshipwith influencers to assist decision makers Consultants will communicate via person-to-person communication rather than only email communication
Condition		

Table 6.3: Management level: experienced consultants input characteristic difficulties and level of client engagement.

Story 4

Engaging one of the organization's leaders to lead the organization's client-engagement activities—who thoroughly understands and recognizes meeting recurring needs of the client—is the organization's bread and butter. Unsuccessful in keeping the client engaged because of the inability to accept the client's needs make up only 50 percent of their "wants," which is more important than their desire to take a personal interest in managing the outcome of their project.

Table 6.4 indicates when it comes to leveraging experienced consultant understanding and recognizing meeting recurring needs, the organization experienced difficulties in terms of the extent, method, and condition of the experienced consultant's input characteristic. The table further indicates the organization counted on the senior consultant's requirement definition skills to engage client, while inadequacies were experienced in the extent and method of client engagement.

Character	Difficulties Experienced or Issues Occurred		Hoped for or Counted On	
	Experienced Consultants		Client Engagement	
Extent	◇	Focused on providing the needs and not the wants Education and expertise in the groundbreaking work	◇	Focus on the wants of the client
Time				
Method	◇	Ability to personally connect with the client decision maker Consultant too strong with individual functional clients	◇	Client relationship that will foster or result in mentorship from the client Consultant will have built a strong enough relationship with influencers to assist decision makers
Condition	◇	Ability to relate the work at hand with the client timelines, project status, and health of the client's business		

Table 6.4: Requirement definition: experienced consultants input characteristic difficulties and level of client engagement.

Story 5

One of the organization's most experienced consultants with two previous project relationships with the client, once more on request of the client, provides commercial management work. Though the consultant has an exceptionally good relationship with the client and in the past delivered quality work resulting in a significant return on investment, the consultant is unable to generate more business opportunities.

Table 6.5 indicates when it comes to experienced consultants leveraging existing relationships with the client and previously delivered quality work, the organization experienced difficulties in terms of the extent and method of the experienced consultant's input characteristic. The table further indicates when it comes to leveraging experienced consultants with a perceived business relationship to result in high levels of client engagement, shortcomings were recognized in terms of the extent and method of client engagement.

Character	Difficulties Experienced or Issues Occurred	Hoped for or Counted On
	Experienced Consultants	Client Engagement
Extent	Understanding how to translate technical work into business discussion Ability to expand visual presentation of value added to client and project Expressing and reporting results and benefits in terms of value added and risk minimization terms	Generating work for consultants not having work Interest and knowledge to sell other disciplines to the client Capacity to make the client believe the organization is more than a recruitment organization
Time		
Method	Organization's ability to train, mentor, and educate on how to perform work and client engagement at the same time Developing a compelling story about the business and business strength	Built a relationship that will foster mentorship from the client Consultant will have built a strong enough relationship with influencers to assist decision makers
Condition		

Table 6.5: Business relationships: experienced consultants input characteristic difficulties and level of client engagement.

Story 6

The organization engages a newly recruited experienced consultant on an assignment to assist the client with their project management office developing the project controls practices and centralized project controls reporting. From an organization perspective, the strategic placement is to enhance the organization's profile, gaining acceptance and developing new business for the organization. The experienced project controls management consultant comes across strongly, making the client feel as if they have not been heard. Furthermore, the consultant fails to properly understand the client's requirements, objectives, and timelines.

Table 6.6 indicates when it comes to leveraging experienced consultant skills to properly understand the client's requirements, objectives, and timelines, the organization experienced difficulties in terms of the extent, method, and condition of the experienced consultant's input characteristic. The table further indicates although the organization counts on experienced consultants' listening skills to generate high levels of client engagement, shortcomings were recognized in terms of the method of client engagement.

Character	Difficulties Experienced or Issues Occurred		Hoped for or Counted On	
	Experienced Consultants		Client Engagement	
Extent	◇	Confidence in dealing with difficult clients Confidence in dealing with inexperienced clients		
Time				
Method	◇	Proactively dealing with client and project difficulties Working on client sites independent of senior supervision Ability to generate work and realize the opportunity	◇	Patience when working on projects and working through project difficulties Abilities and capability to support clients Abilities and capability to educate clients Focus to build a relationship
Condition	◇	Listening skills Unsupervised consultants Nontechnical skills of consultant Experienced consultants with practical technical skills		

Table 6.6: Listening skills: experienced consultants input characteristic difficulties and level of client engagement.

Story 7

The organization is engaged with the client on a continuous basis for a two-year period. Though the client continues to provide assignments to the on-site consultants, the client is showing its questioning of the relationship through poor communication and refusal to have regular project sponsor meetings.

Table 6.7 shows when it comes to the organization's experienced consultants building business relationships, the organization experienced difficulties in terms of the extent and method of the experienced consultant's input characteristic. The table further indicates although the organization counts on leveraging the perceived business relationships for high levels of client engagement, shortcomings were realized in terms of the extent and method of client engagement.

Character	Difficulties Experienced or Issues Occurred	Hoped for or Counted On
	Experienced Consultants	Client Engagement
Extent	Ability and approach to go above the technical task at hand	Focus and ability to develop the client project work into a long-term client Capacity to make the client believe the organization is more than a recruitment organization
Time		
Method	Organization's ability to train, mentor, and educate on how to perform work and client engagement at the same time Developing a compelling story about the business and business strength Experience and personality to reach decision makers and influencers	Built a relationship that will foster mentorship from the client Consultant will have built a strong enough relationship with influencers to assist decision makers
Condition		

Table 6.7: Business relationship: experienced consultants input characteristic difficulties and level of client engagement.

Expectation-Reality Gap

To identify the reasoning behind the experienced consultant-client-engagement expectation-reality gap with the experienced consulting input characteristic difficulties and level of client engagement in mind, an analysis has been done on the organization's culture, consultant capabilities, and organization leadership.

Table 6.8 shows the various misalignments in the organization culture (equality, ownership thinking, fit for purpose, and values) that might exist and could have led to the experienced consultant/client-engagement expectation-reality gap.

Equality			
Limited organization structures	◆	Consultants can enjoy themselves	
Consultant participation	◆	Equal productivity incentives	
Fulfill potential		Social identity	
Treated fairly		Knowing our peers	
Character protected		Absence of inappropriate and disrespectful language	
Work hours respected		Absence of stereotyping	
Personal information protected		Taking consultants seriously	◆
Recognition of diversity			
Ownership Thinking			
Understanding the fundamentals of the organization	◆	Forecasting and achieving the business's key performance indicators	
Understanding how the company makes money	◆	Key performance indicators are highly visible and accountable	
Understanding how each consultant adds—or takes away—value	◆	Having self-funding incentive plans	
Knowing the business's key performance indicators		Incentive plans aligning the consultants' behavior to the business's objectives	
Fit for Purpose			
Deliverables do what they intend to achieve	◆	Final deliverables are efficient enough for the stated purpose	◆
Deliverables are good enough to do the work they are designed to do		Deliverables represent the right tool to do the work consultants have to do	
Deliverables are of a good enough standard for clients	◆	Deliverables fulfill the requirement specifications and stated outcome	
Deliverables answer the client's requirement and wants and nothing more	◆	Consultants are undertaking enough and have efficient effort to reach the client's intended goals	
Deliverables are comprehensive to the extent that they answer the client's requirement and wants and nothing more			

Values			
Trust		Transparency	
Pride	◆	Sense of urgency	◆
Camaraderie		Commitment	◆

Table 6.8: Experienced consultant-client-engagement expectation-reality gap: culture.

Table 6.9 indicates the various shortcomings in the organization's core competencies that might exist and could have led to the experienced consultant-client-engagement expectation-reality gap.

Core Competencies			
Leadership		Work quality	
Sense of urgency		Quantity of work	
Teamwork		Accountability	◆
Decision-making		Adaptability	◆
Client focused	◆	Initiative	◆
Business acumen	◆	Innovation	
Resource management		Planning and organizing	◆
People management		Communication	

Table 6.9: Experienced consultant-client-engagement expectation-reality gap: capability.

Table 6.10 indicates the various inadequacies in organization leadership styles that might exist and could have led to the experienced consultant-client-engagement expectation-reality gap.

Styles			
Cooperative leadership	◇	Whiner	
Problem-solving leadership		Gossiper	
Leadership by example	◇	Nonstop talker	
Knowledge leadership	◇	Grumbler	
Get-up-and-go leadership	◇	Bully	

Table 6.10: Experienced consultant-client-engagement expectation-reality gap: leadership.

Assessment and Checklists

With the circumstances bringing about the realization an experienced consultant-client-engagement expectation-reality gap exists and an analysis of the organization's culture, capabilities, and values identifying potential inadequacies causing the experienced consultant-client-engagement expectation-reality gap, table 6.11 provides a list of questions and phrases to can be used to assess the extent whereto the organization's culture, capabilities, values, and leadership support the referral recruitment process, contractual agreement with consultants, assignment of consultants to work, and mentoring and coaching of consultants.

Item	Description	Score
A	Culture	
	Equality	
1	The organization encourages all employees to become more active and productive by giving them more roles in the decision-making process.	
2	Consultant participation is evident in preparedness, staying focused on the main topics, keeping control of tasks, discussing the salient issues, and contributing to ideas and information.	
15	Consultants are taken seriously as they are confident and know what they are talking about; they are engaged in multiple-level conversation, say what they need to say and get to the point, and stay serious about work most of the time.	

Item	Description	Score
	Ownership Thinking	
1	Consultants understand the fundamentals of the organization and how the organization runs the business within the following six departments: people, administration, business information management, client engagement, projects, and commercial and day-to-day operations.	
4	Individual team members are aware of the business's key performance indicators.	
5	The organization, on agreed intervals, forecasts and monitors and controls business key performance indicators.	
6	Organization leadership is clear on key performance indicators, makes it visible to all team members, and keeps responsible people accountable.	
	Fit for Purpose	
1	Consultants produce deliverables that give what the assignment intends to deliver to achieve the project or business value.	
3	Consultants produce deliverables that are of a good enough standard for clients in terms of quality, risk, and safety.	
4	Consultants produce deliverables that answer the client's requirement and wants and nothing more.	
6	Consultants produce deliverables that are doing the right things according to the stated purpose.	
B	Values	
2	Pride, demonstrated in defined expectations, keeps people engaged; encourages accountability, not focusing on who did what wrong rather on the solution; and reinforces expectations of outcomes, appreciation, keeping it positive, allowing each person the opportunity and strong sense of how they contribute and do the right things for the right reasons.	
C	Capabilities	
5	Consultants, from a business perspective, can generate and enhance profit; recognize business opportunities; and anticipate, understand, and act on business options to lead to a positive outcome.	
6	Consultants demonstrate business acumen, including the ability to generate and enhance profit; recognize business opportunities; and anticipate, understand, and act on business options to lead to a positive outcome.	
11	Consultants have accountability competencies, including the ability to take responsibility for tasks or assignments and align words with actions.	

Item	Description	Score
12	Consultants have adaptability, showing abilities in mastering new skills and demonstrating flexibility in reacting to changing needs, procedures, and environments; work well under pressure; handle multiple assignments; and meet deadlines.	
13	Consultants have initiative and innovation utilizing knowledge and scope to constructively increase productivity and achieve goals, use resourcefulness and creativity in dealing with challenges, and anticipate and react positively to change.	
14	Intentionally blank	
15	Consultants have planning and organization competencies, including establishing an appropriate course of action for themselves and/or others to accomplish a specific goal, making proper assignments of people and appropriate use of resources, and ensuring which daily activities contribute to and are timely with the overall business's short- and long-term objectives.	
D	Leadership	
1	Have consultants and team members who are seeking cooperation from all consultants, seeking cooperation from consultants whom they have no control over.	
3	Have consultants who are taking extreme measures on themselves, doing to other consultants as we would want them to do unto us: "walk the walk" and "talk the talk."	
4	Have consultants providing knowledge leadership, who know the strategies and tactics required, realizing experience and potential in the consultants, and mentoring.	
5	Have consultants providing get-up-and-go leadership, getting up and doing what is required of them, and committing themselves to get-up-and-go business.	
	Average Score	
Rate a score of 1, 3 or 5. Score: 1 = Seldom, 3 = Sometimes true, and 5 = Almost always true		
Interpretation of average score: 83 - 99 signs of an experienced consultant/client-engagement expectation-reality gap, 53 - 82 likely an experienced consultant/client-engagement expectation-reality gap exists, 1 - 52 certainly an experienced consultant/client-engagement expectation-reality gap exists.		

Table 6.11: Assessment: experienced consultant/client-engagement expectation-reality gap.

Paying attention to the circumstances and bringing about the realization of an experienced consultant-client-engagement expectation-reality gap, the outcome of the analysis of the organization's culture, capabilities, and values identifying potential shortfalls causing the experienced consultant-client-engagement expectation-reality gap, could allow the organization to:

- narrow or reduce the experienced consultant-client-engagement expectation-reality gap,
- recruit and build a team of experienced consultants,
- adjust the experienced consultant as input characteristic, and
- adjust the actions taken by the organization to support the experienced consultant's input characteristic.

Chapter 7 will shed light on the theme "doing right things right does not spell client wants," focusing on the doing the right things right/client wants expectation-reality gap.

This page is for you, the reader, to make notes and jot down reference page numbers.

Use this table to make notes and jot down system-related reference page numbers.

Note	Page Number		
	People	Process	Application

Use this table to make notes and jot down IPO-related reference page numbers.

Note	Page Number		
	Input	Process	Output

Use this table to make notes and jot down theme-related reference page numbers.

Note	Page Number				
	Business Models	Competencies	Leadership	Values	Self-Orientation

This page is for you, the reader, to make notes and jot down ERG-related reference page numbers.

Note	Page Number
Experienced Consultant Does Not Spell Client Engagement	

CHAPTER 7

Doing the Right Things Right Does Not Spell Client Wants

Sell people what they want … not what you think they need.
—Michael Blandvold

Initiative is doing the right thing without being told.
—Victor Hugo

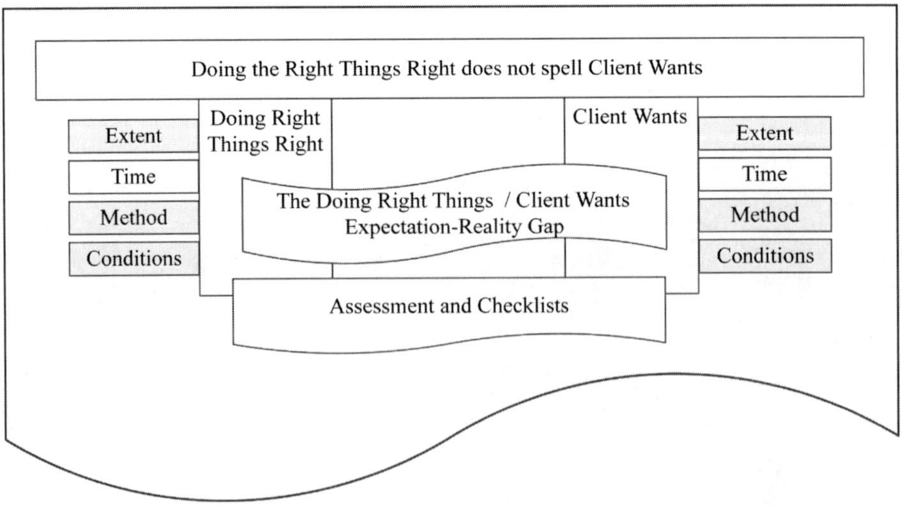

Introduction

FOR SOME REASON, the first week in November for the past seven years, on a personal level, has proved to be challenging for me. I have been tracking the activities that have caused me to experience significant challenges, causing the rare feeling of stress. November 2015 certainly follows the same trend. The year is closing, long-term assignments in the business are coming to an end, and new assignments in the pipeline are taking their course.

By the time I reached Sunday evening, November 15, at the end of the day, I collapsed on the couch, completely drained, coffee in hand, doing a retrospect, reminding myself to take deep breaths and time-outs, doing one thing at a time, focusing on the now, and taking care of what I have control over.

I remind myself of the article I read a while back, which talked about how happiness in stressful times comes from a relationship with ourselves. I realized although the busyness and stress of the week gave me a fresh perspective, it certainly was not enough perspective to make me want to give up my dream of sharing my experiences through this book. Opening my computer, I could not get a better topic to focus me for the week to come than "doing the right things right does not spell client wants."

The sixth theme requiring our attention is "doing the right things right does not spell client wants." The emphasis of this chapter is to provide an understanding of leadership's expectation from consultants doing the right things right as input characteristic, an understanding of the actions taken by the organization to support or strengthen the doing right things right input characteristic. Furthermore, the circumstances bringing about the realization that a doing right things right/client wants expectation-reality gap exists, and an analysis of the organization's culture, capabilities, and values identifying potential inadequacies causing the doing right things right/client wants expectation-reality gap.

Expected Result

Expectation 6

Providing industry best-practice quality readiness (upfront planning and preparation for project success), control (project execution guided by data-driven decision-making "on-time, under budget" and agreed quality), and resolution (resolve and align deliverables with next phase requirements) satisfies the client's requirements and needs. Clients are accepting the experience base of the organization's consultants and trust they will receive a level of consulting they cannot be without in executing their projects. Clients are paying for the consulting of which they offset the cost against their personal preferences.

Business Input

To deliver the expected result and project-delivery work that satisfies the client's wants, leadership introduced the concept of doing the right things right into the equation. Furthermore, to promote and prepare consultants to be advisers and strengthen the chance of achieving the expected outcome of client wants, leadership, through knowledge transfer, introduced to the organization, the team, and individual team members the following business relevant characteristics: doing the right things right and wants versus needs. As a continuous reminder to do the right things right and to produce fit-for-purpose work, leadership places the Six Sigma diagram of continuous improvement on the front page of all major work documents and presentations.

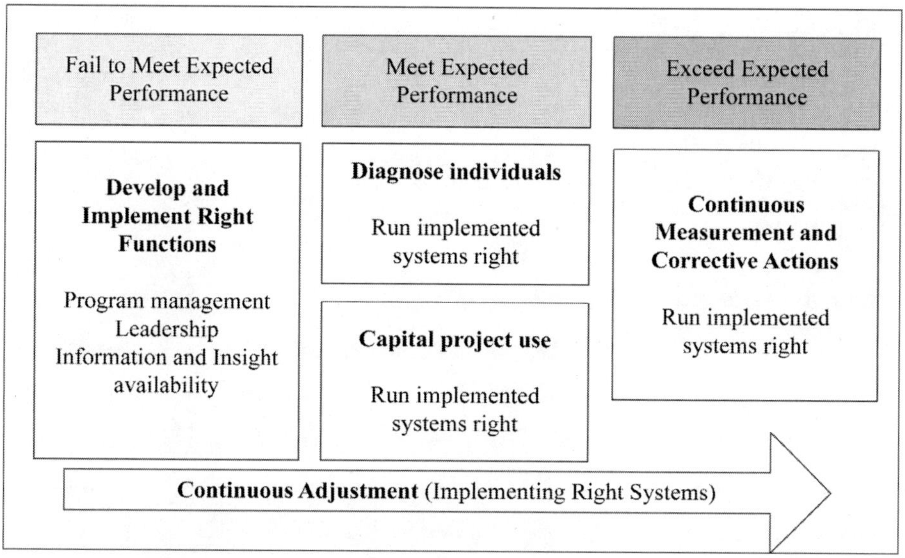

Figure 7.1: Doing the right things right (source:).

Through sharing and transfer of knowledge on the concepts of continuous measurement and corrective actions, the focus was on ensuring each consultant understands the importance of continuously collecting information and analyzing deliverables. This is to ensure development and implementation of the right systems (people, processes, and applications) and using them right to exceed performance (figure 7.1) Exceeding the client's expected performance will ensure meeting the client's wants.

Table 1: Performance Information by Consultant

	Total Packages	CP	PP	CA	SM	MED	LRG	Plan Hours	Hours Spend	Earned Hours	Rule of Credit	%-Complete	Weighted %
	30	18	12	0	28	2	0	2280	0	0	0%	0%	0%
Procurement Professional 1													
Procurement Professional 2													
Comments: added this week:													

Table 2: Performance Information by Rule of Credit

	CP	CP	CP	CP		PP	PP	PP	PP		Rule-of-Credit
	SM	MED	LRG	Total		SM	MED	LRG	Total		Total
Total Number of Packages	5	12	1	18		5	6	1	12		
% Package Distribution	28%	67%	6%	100%		42%	50%	8%	100%		100%
IFA - Package to for Review											10%
IFA Reviewed and Approved											5%
Addresses RFP Questions											10%
Compile & Issue RFP/RFQ to Vendors											15%
Technical and commercial bid evaluation											15%
Issue recommendation to Award to PM											10%
PO Approval											10%
Issue PO to Vendor											5%
Close Out											20%
Comments: added this week:											

Figure 7.2: Abstract from organization procurement performance report.

Instilling the measurement of performance, leadership developed and implemented performance-measurement reporting (figure 7.2). The emphasis is to ensure consultants analyze their work with a high level of accuracy and provide recommendations for improvement; and produce relevant and accurate information to support decision-making; produce concise reports, which means transmitting the maximum information with minimum words. Furthermore, they produce reports written for a specific audience, make unbiased recommendations—meaning, total, impartial, and objective—and present information in a format attractive to and make a clear impression with the intended reader considering structure, content, language, and presentation style. Providing relevant reporting with client buy-in will ensure identifying gaps and areas for improvement leading to meeting the client's wants.

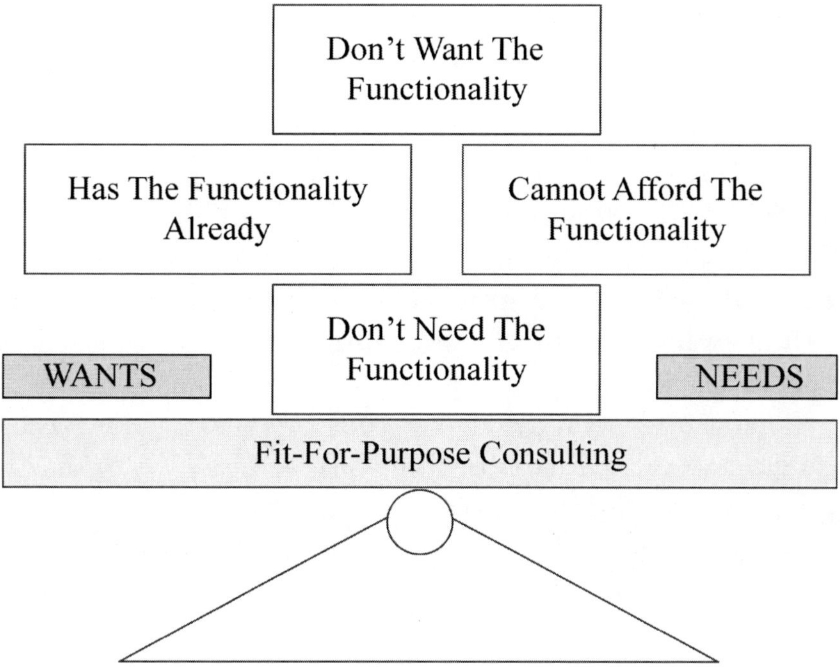

Figure 7.3: Wants versus needs (source:).

Leadership on a continuous basis iterated and reiterated the organization is built on a business model where project activities are based on the fit-for-purpose principle. Fit-for-purpose business modeled in method and approach how the consultants and teams engage with clients to develop their projects and achieve their strategic objectives (figure 7.3). From a deliverable perspective, fit-for-purpose method, final deliverables do what they intend to achieve, are good enough to do the work they were designed to do, are of a good enough standard for clients, answer the clients requirement and wants and nothing more, and are comprehensive to the extent that they answer the client's requirement and wants and nothing more. Furthermore, final deliverables are efficient enough for the stated purpose, represent the right tool to do the work consultants have to do, and fulfill the requirement specifications and stated outcome. The consultants are undertaking sufficient and efficient effort (team formation, team integration, stakeholder management, scope-of-work description, time phasing work activities, and costing work) to reach the client's intended goals.

Reality: Doing the right things right does not spell client wants.

Story 4

The cost-control consultant, a very experienced and strong technical writer, focused on delivering best-practices control and reporting. The consultant failed to ask enough qualifying questions and confirm with the client the organization's interpretation of the needs being in line with the client's want. This would have confirmed the client wanted a more simplified solution based on the project's current life cycle stage.

Table 7.1 shows when it came to consultants asking enough qualifying questions to confirm the client's needs, the organization experienced difficulties in terms of the extent, method, and condition of the "doing the right things right" input characteristic. The table further indicates when it came to doing the right things right, the organization counted on high levels of meeting client wants, while inadequacies were identified in terms of the extent, method, and condition.

Character	Difficulties Experienced or Issues Occurred	Hoped for or Counted On
	Doing Right Things Right	Client Wants
Extent	Adjusting to simpler rather than best-practice solutions	Extend the work beyond cost control to cost engineering
Time		
Method	Asking qualifying questions Method of communication to determine requirements	Asking enough questions to produce fit-for-purpose deliverables
Condition	Working with a construction manager who is old school	Building a long-term business relationship

Table 7.1: Senior team members: doing the right things right input characteristic difficulties and level of client wants.

Story 7

Though the organization was engaged with the client on a continuous basis for a two-year period, consultants were unable to get fully engaged. Consultants were unable to produce start-to-end packages of work that totally satisfied the wants of the client-procurement leadership. The organization was unable to assign consultants producing and interacting per the client's requirements, resulting in a high turnover of consultants.

Table 7.2 shows when it comes to consultants producing packages of work from start to end and totally satisfying the client's wants, the organization experienced difficulties in terms of the method and condition of the "doing the right things right" input characteristic. The table further indicates when it comes to doing the right things right, the organization counted on high levels of meeting client wants, while inadequacies were identified in terms of the extent and method.

Character	Difficulties Experienced or Issues Occurred		Hoped for or Counted On	
	Doing Right Things Right		Client Wants	
Extent			◇	Consistently use performance measurement to demonstrate to client
Time				
Method	◇	Convince client to work differently	◇	Communicate and use corporate input to convince the client
Condition	◇	Work as subordinates to client team Incorporate consultants as secondments onto the team Organization has no project management influence		

Table 7.2: Senior team members: doing the right things right input characteristic difficulties and level of client wants.

Expectation-Reality Gap

To identify the reasoning behind the doing right things right/client wants expectation-reality gap, with doing the right things right input characteristic difficulties in mind, and the level of client wants achieved, an analysis has been done on the organization's culture, capabilities, and leadership.

Table 7.3 indicates the various misalignments in organization culture (equality, ownership thinking, fit for purpose, and values) that might exist and could have led to the doing right things right/client wants expectation-reality gap.

Equality	
Limited organization structures	Consultants can enjoy themselves
Consultant participation	Equal productivity incentives
Fulfill potential	Social identity
Treated fairly	Knowing our peers
Character protected	Absence of inappropriate and disrespectful language
Work hours respected	Absence of stereotyping
Personal information protected	Taking consultants seriously
Recognition of diversity	
Ownership Thinking	
Understanding the fundamentals of the organization	Forecasting and achieving the business's key performance indicators
Understanding how the company makes money	Key performance indicators are highly visible and accountable
Understanding how each consultant adds—or takes away—value	Having self-funding incentive plans
Knowing the business's key performance indicators	Incentive plans aligning the consultants' behavior to the business's objectives
Fit for Purpose	
Deliverables do what they intend to achieve	Final deliverables are efficient enough for the stated purpose
Deliverables are good enough to do the work they are designed to do	Deliverables represent the right tool to do the work consultants have to do

Deliverables are of a good enough standard for clients		Deliverables fulfill the requirement specifications and stated outcome	◆
Deliverables answer the client's requirement and wants and nothing more		Consultants are undertaking enough and have efficient effort to reach the client's intended goals	
Deliverables are comprehensive to the extent that they answer the client's requirement and wants and nothing more	◆		

Values			
Trust	◆	Transparency	◆
Pride		Sense of urgency	
Camaraderie	◆	Commitment	

Table 7.3: Doing right things right/client wants expectation-reality gap: culture.

Table 7.4 shows the various shortcomings in the organization's core competencies that might exist and could have led to the doing right things right/client wants expectation-reality gap.

Core Competencies			
Leadership		Work quality	◆
Sense of urgency		Quantity of work	
Teamwork	◆	Accountability	
Decision-making		Adaptability	
Client focused		Initiative	◆
Business acumen	◆	Innovation	◆
Resource management	◆	Planning and organizing	
People management		Communication	

Table 7.4: Doing right things right/client wants expectation-reality gap: capability.

Table 7.5 shows the various inadequacies in organization leadership styles that might exist and could have led to doing right things right/client wants expectation-reality gap.

Styles			
Cooperative leadership	◇	Whiner	
Problem-solving leadership		Gossiper	
Leadership by example	◇	Nonstop talker	
Knowledge leadership	◇	Grumbler	
Get-up-and-go leadership		Bully	

Table 7.5: Doing the right things right/client wants expectation-reality gap: leadership.

Assessment and Checklists

With the circumstances bringing about the realization a doing the right things right/client wants expectation-reality gap exists, and an analysis of the organization's culture, capabilities, and values identifying potential inadequacies causing the doing the right things right/client wants expectation-reality gap, table 7.6 provides a list of questions and phrases to be used to assess the extent whereto the organization's culture, capabilities, values, and leadership support the referral recruitment process, contractual agreement with consultants, assignment of consultants to work, and mentoring and coaching of consultants.

Item	Description	Score
A	Culture	
	Equality	
2	Consultant participation is evident in preparedness, staying focused on the main topics, keeping control of tasks, discussing the salient issues, and contributing to ideas and information.	
15	Consultants are taken seriously as they are confident and know what they are talking about; they are engaged in multiple-level conversation, say what they need to say and get to the point, and stay serious about work most of the time.	

Item	Description	Score
	Ownership Thinking	
1	Consultants understand the fundamentals of the organization and how the organization runs the business within the following six departments: people, administration, business information management, client engagement, projects, and commercial and day-to-day operations.	
3	The organization and the individual team members understand how each consultant adds—or takes away—value.	
	Fit for Purpose	
1	Consultants produce deliverables that give what the assignment intends to deliver to achieve the project or business value.	
5	Consultants produce deliverables that are comprehensive to the extent that they answer the client's requirement and wants and nothing more.	
8	Consultants produce deliverables that fulfill the requirement specifications and stated outcome.	
B	Values	
1	Consultants have people-management competencies, including the ability to delegate, set goals, manage performance, motivate, train, develop, hire, and exit employees and contractors in a fashion that meets the company's goals.	
3	Camaraderie is demonstrated through a sense of belonging where consultants work, acceptance for who consultants are, a sense of inclusion where the organization makes everyone an insider, occasional fun events that are planned to meet diverse interests, clear messages stating that all are welcome, and understanding for those who don't choose to participate.	
4	Organization and consultants demonstrate through operating in such a way that it is easy for outsiders to see what actions are being performed based on openness, communication, and accountability.	
C	Capabilities	
3	Consultants have teamwork competencies, including the ability to establish and maintain positive working relationships and to work cooperatively to achieve results, solicit input, value team members' contributions, and place them above personal needs.	
6	Consultants demonstrate business acumen, including the ability to generate and enhance profit; recognize business opportunities; and anticipate, understand, and act on business options to lead to a positive outcome.	

Item	Description	Score
7	Consultants apply resource management in day-to-day work execution, including the ability to plan, control, and measure resources in a way that balances cost with benefits and enables the organization to meet deliverables. Resources might include money, information, inventory, supplies, people, and time.	
9	Consultants perform quality work, including speed, efficiency, and the ability to prioritize and meet deadlines and organize work. Consultants, in executing their work, demonstrate knowledge and skills, ability to meet standards, care and attention to details, follow-through to completion, and frequency of errors.	
13	Consultants have initiative and innovation utilizing knowledge and scope to constructively increase productivity and achieve goals, use resourcefulness and creativity in dealing with challenges, and anticipate and react positively to change.	
14	Intentionally blank	
D	Leadership	
1	Have consultants and team members who are seeking cooperation from all consultants, seeking cooperation from consultants whom they have no control over.	
3	Have consultants who are taking extreme measures on themselves, doing to other consultants as we would want them to do unto us: "walk the walk" and "talk the talk."	
4	Have consultants providing knowledge leadership, who know the strategies and tactics required, realizing experience and potential in the consultants, and mentoring.	
	Average Score	
Rate a score of 1, 3 or 5. Score: 1 = Seldom, 3 = Sometimes true, and 5 = Almost always true		
Interpretation of average score: 68 – 81 signs of the doing the right things right expectation-reality gap, 45 - 67 likely the doing the right things right expectation-reality gap exists, 1 - 44 certainly the doing the right things right expectation-reality gap exists.		

Table 7.6: Assessment: Doing the right things right/client wants expectation-reality gap.

Paying attention to the circumstances bringing about the realization of a doing the right things right/client wants expectation-reality gap, the outcome of the analysis of the organization's culture, capabilities, and values identifying potential shortfalls, causing the doing the right things right/client wants expectation-reality gap and the assessment, could allow the organization to:

- narrow or reduce the doing right things right/client wants expectation-reality gap,
- recruit and build a team of experienced consultants,
- adjust the doing right things right as input characteristic, and
- adjust the actions taken by the organization to support the doing right things right input characteristic.

Chapter 8 will shed light on the theme "talking and selling do not spell consulting," focusing on the talking and selling/consulting expectation-reality gap.

This page is for you, the reader, to make notes and jot down reference page numbers.

Use this table to make notes and jot down system-related reference page numbers.

Note	Page Number		
	People	Process	Application

Use this table to make notes and jot down IPO-related reference page numbers.

Note	Page Number		
	Input	Process	Output

Use this table to make notes and jot down theme-related reference page numbers.

Note	Page Number				
	Business Models	Competencies	Leadership	Values	Self-Orientation

This page is for you, the reader, to make notes and jot down ERG-related reference page numbers.

Note	Page Number
Doing the Right Things Right Does Not Spell Client Wants	

CHAPTER 8

Talking and Selling Do Not Spell Consulting

Being relevant to your customers only when you're trying to sell something means choosing to be irrelevant to them for the rest of the time.
—Stan Slap

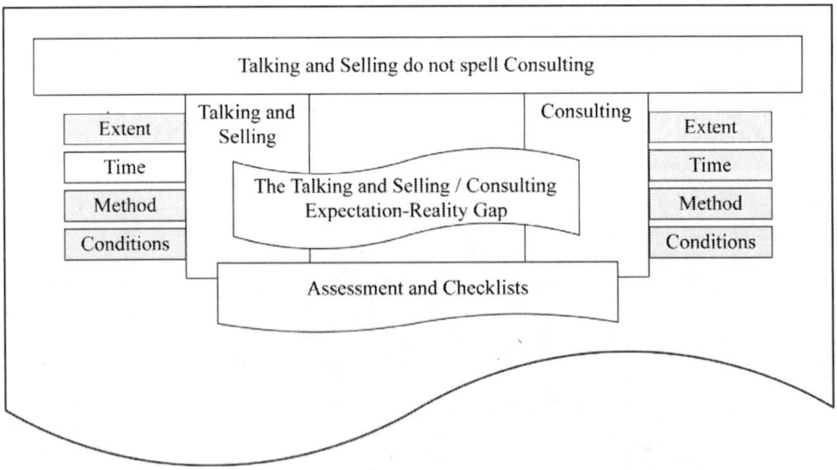

Introduction

SATURDAY, DECEMBER 14, 2020, before getting engaged in the busyness of the Christmas activities, with computer bag over my shoulder, I walk down the street visiting my favorite coffeehouse, Waves Coffee House, at 4202 Hastings Street, Burnaby, BC, Canada. The Waves slogan says it all for me: "Your place to connect." Though for the coffeehouse, the emphasis is on connecting people, my reading is to connect with my own thoughts and mind. From the earliest of days, I was intrigued by the classic movie images of a writer, cross-legged beside a round wooden table, pen in hand, a steaming cup of coffee, scribbling in a leather-covered diary.

Writers and bloggers address the "why" of working in coffeehouses in numerous articles. Sarah DeGeorge, in an article, wrote, "Leaving the house or apartment and finding a place to work, relax and also be among people and inspiration seems like an ideal escape from the compounds of your home—no matter how cozy it is and a great practice." Kylie Jane Wakefield, in an article, wrote, "Writers need to get out the house and change up their scenery or risk boredom and lack of inspiration. Coffeeshops filled with other busy people typing away on laptops provides structure, and freelancers crave structure. There's a silent social pressure to it all."

Over the years, I have found inspiration being surrounded by tasty coffee, fancy coffee cups, interior designs, and individuals or groups of students scribbling in books or typing away on computers. Today is no different; coffee in hand, overlooking people strolling along Hastings Street, I am ready to scribble.

The seventh theme requiring our attention is "talking and selling do not spell consulting." The focus of this chapter is to provide an understanding of leadership's expectation from consultants providing talking and selling as input characteristic, an understanding of the actions taken by the organization to support or strengthen the talking and selling input characteristic. Furthermore, the circumstances bringing about the realization a talking and selling/consulting expectation-reality gap exists and an analysis of the organization's culture, capabilities, and values identifying potential shortcomings causing the talking and selling/consulting expectation-reality gap.

Expected Result

Expectation 7

Like-minded seasoned consultants, together with an open communication leadership model and a thorough understanding, know it is each consultant's role, while consulting also, to identify new opportunities. With the business plan and the KPI requirements known and regularly communicated, consultants understand the importance of each consulting project to the success of the organization; furthermore, the realization that business success requires hard work and commitment, and as start-up, a bigger effort is required than from the more established competition. Consultants, as shareholders, have the emotional endurance to commit (with their inner resolve driving them) to succeed no matter the circumstances.

Business Input

To strengthen the chances of achieving the organization's objective of having a team of consultants who understand how to talk and sell to clients while working on client sites, identifying new business opportunities, and having the emotional endurance to commit to succeed no matter the circumstances, leadership adopted the concepts and methodologies of the transactional communication model, management consulting guide, and steps for dealing with difficult people.

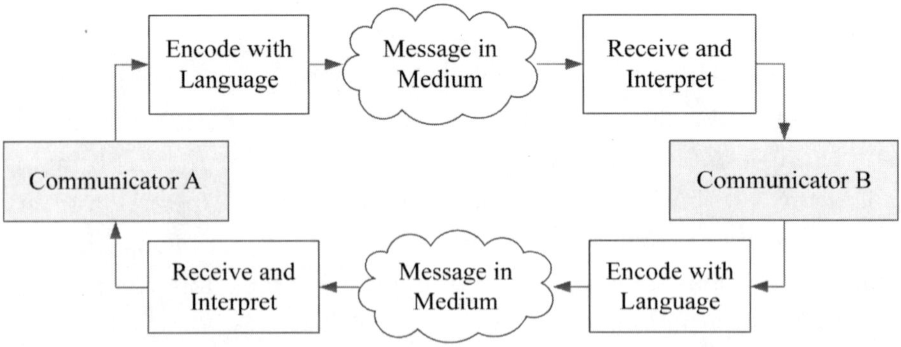

Figure 8.1: A transactional communication model (Davis Foulger 2004) (source: http://davis.foulger.info/).

Through the sharing and transfer of knowledge on the transactional communication model, the focus is on making consultants realize and understand there are always two parties involved in the creation and receiving of messages, and both parties are responsible for creating and receiving of messages (figure 8.1). Grasping the concept and emphasis on improving the consultant's face-to-face interaction with clients. The described model is used to imprint on consultants that there should always be equality between the various communicators. With a clear understanding, the client has considerably more freedom (in terms of message choice, media choice, ability to frame meaning, and ability to set the rules of interaction) and power to allocate message bandwidth than the consultant.

Phase 1: Entry	□ First contact with client □ Preliminary problem diagnosis □ Assignment planning	□ Assignment proposal □ Consulting contract
Phase 2: Diagnosis	□ Purpose analysis □ Problem analysis □ Fact finding	□ Fact analysis and synthesis □ Feedback to client
Phase 3: Action Planning	□ Developing solutions □ Evaluating alternatives □ Proposal to client	□ Planning for implementation
Phase 4: Implementation	□ Assisting with implementation □ Adjusting proposal □ Training	
Phase 5: Extension, Recycle or Termination	□ Evaluation □ Final report □ Settling commitments	□ Planning for follow-up □ Withdrawal

Figure 8.2: *Management Consulting: A Guide to the Profession* (2002) (source: http://certifications.bcs.org/upload/pdf/consultancy-cp-mgt-consulting.pdf).

The leadership team extensively shares the consulting to management process with consultants, providing a framework for what consultants do or should do, a well-established method to structure and plan their assignments and projects (figure 8.2). The guidance and knowledge transfer are intended to teach flexibility, leaving it to the imagination to introduce change with clients in a well-planned and managed approach.

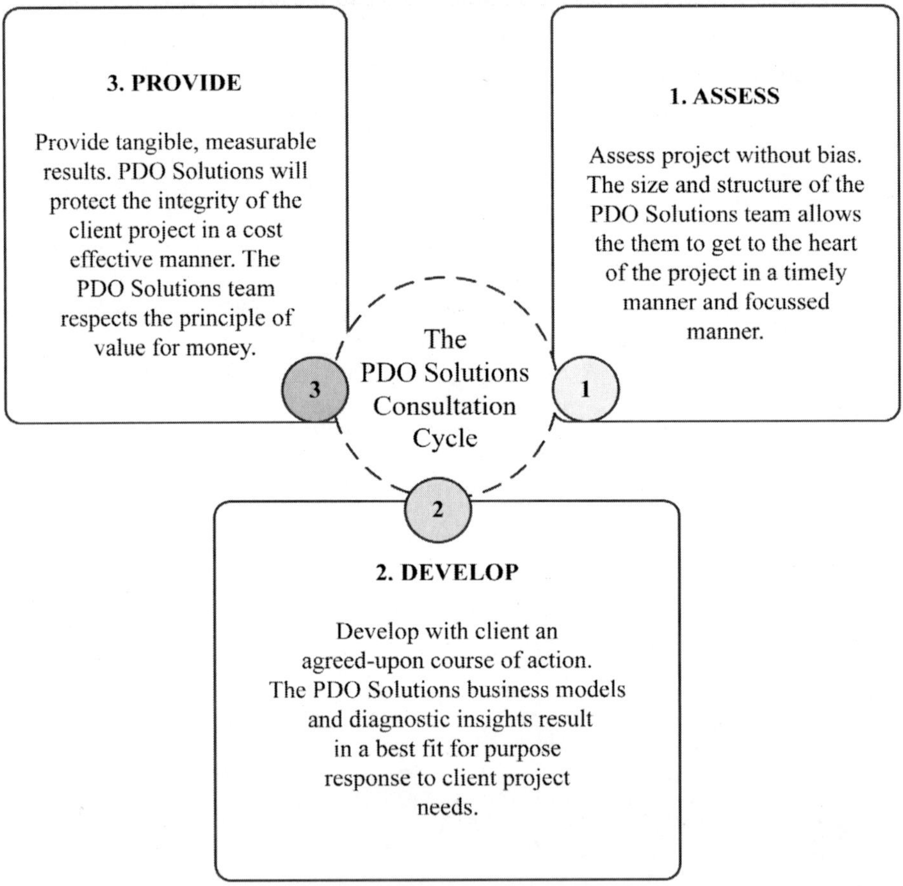

Figure 8.3: The organization consultation cycle (source: www.pdosolutions.com).

Focused on exceeding expectations, the organization developed, implemented, and trained consultants to follow a three-step work-delivery approach (figure 8.3). The three-step approach supports leadership's focus to provide fit-for-purpose consulting, allowing the consultants to clearly establish client requirements, detail the expected level of effort and desired outcomes, and then work to achieve these outcomes.

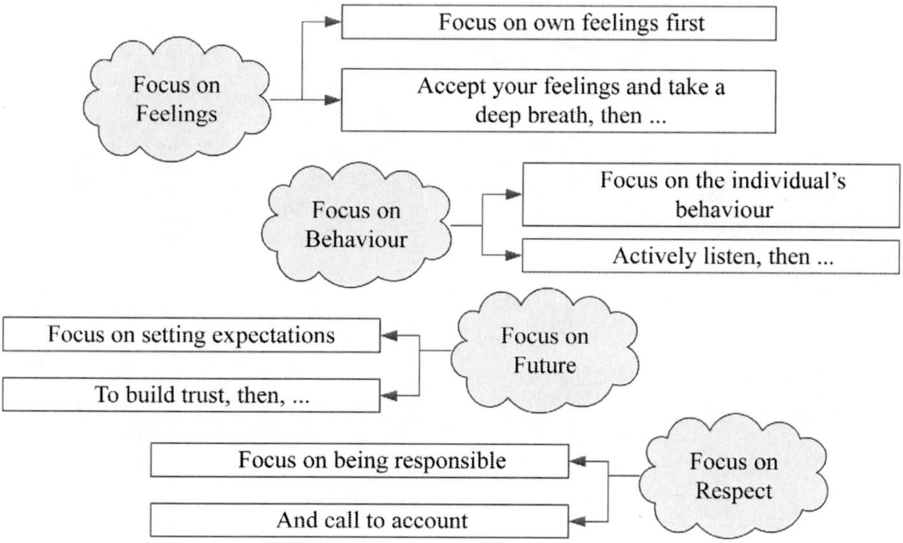

Figure 8.4: Steps in dealing with difficult people (Michael Kelly 2009) (source: http://migashco.com/cambrian/dwdp.html).

Preparing consultants to operate in the resource sector and, primarily, construction environment, leadership spends time collaborating with consultants on how to deal with difficult clients (figure 8.4), especially for dealing with personal feelings and behaviors, focusing on future and respect. Making consultants understand they must accept their feelings, understand how it might get in the way of dealing with the client, take appropriate action, and start focusing on the client's behavior. In analyzing the client's behavior, attention is given to observing body language, hearing the intonations in the voice and clues concerning their emotional state, and actively listening and communicating back your understanding. Once you've done this—and the client has acknowledged the accuracy of your words—you've created understanding. With an understanding of the topic of concern, the attention is diverted to a behavioral change by focusing on future problem-solving, allowing for building trust with the client, imprinting on consultants that we are dealing with human beings, and maintaining the minimum standard for effective communication by never leaving the client worse off than you found them, including themselves. Accepting accountability for the work the consultant is responsible for and calling the difficult client to account for the things they are responsible for.

Criteria	Current Score	Next Target Score	Actions for 12 Months	Actions for Next 6 Months	Objectives Met or Exceeded Past 6 Months	Objectives Not Met During Past 6 Months
Practitioner Value						
Current Value						
Future Value						
Emotional Expense						
Trusted Advisor						
Credibility						
Reliability						
Intimacy						
Self Orientation						
Competency						
Ownership Thinking						
Fit-For-Purpose						
Empowered People						
Project Delivery Skills						
Total Value						

Figure 8.5: Performance review criteria (Organization abstract, 2013).

Following through with the direction of Peter Drucker, Tom Peters, and Edwards Deming, who stressed "what gets measured gets managed", leadership engaged the concepts and viewpoints of Cy Wakeman demonstrated in her book *The Reality-Based Rules of the Workplace* (2013). The organization quantified the consultants' key performance indicators and incorporated them into the consultant performance review criteria (figure 8.5). The drive and motivation behind the performance review criteria is to assist consultants focusing on key elements that allow them to become the best consultants they can be.

From a participation perspective, the focus is on guiding consultants to take initiative, initiate, get going by taking first step, and introduce new fields, new knowledge, new activities, and new skills with regard to fit-for-purpose, ownership thinking, equality, team, business-related activities, client activities, business growth, innovation, business processes, and sustainability.

From a current performance perspective assisting consultants to add value, consultants take responsibility for breakthrough solutions or game-changing ideas that might have significant value to the organization. Known in the industry and company as a go-to person, one of the best the company and industry have seen. Actively teaching and monitoring people, sharing knowledge, and contributing to fellow consultants' growth and success. A model of excellence in consultant behavior of collaboration and communication as well as deliverables.

With the future in mind, support consultants to stay relevant for the future, improving how they work, regardless of whether their leaders identify a need. Fit anything for size—whether it is technology or a new position. Having a large, active social network. Consultants must surround themselves with diverse people, generations, and thoughts. Change should not impact the consultants as they are confident and believe they can figure it out. Participate in development experiences. Belong to one or more groups considered to be trendsetters in the industry. Be someone with succession or leadership potential. Have a mentor and be a mentor. Share insights freely to ensure others are not left behind.

Reality: Talking and selling do not spell consulting.

Story 2

Our intermediate consultant offended the senior project-procurement specialist by talking too much and listening too little, telling too much and asking too few clarification questions, talking in a disrespectful manner to the client, and assuming he or she knows better than the client's senior project-procurement specialist. The senior project-procurement specialist spread the word that the organization was incompetent and difficult to deal with, which made the environment more difficult for one of the other consultants to get their work done—and the client not providing follow-up work in the specific department and broader organization.

Table 8.1 shows when it comes to educating employees in the art of talking and selling to clients, the organization experienced difficulties in terms of the extent, time, and method of the talking and selling input characteristic. The table further indicates when it comes to talking and selling to clients, the organization counted on high levels of consulting to clients, while inadequacies were identified in the extent and method of consulting.

Character	Difficulties Experienced or Issues Occurred		Hoped for or Counted On	
	Talking and Selling		Consulting	
Extent	◇	Consultant performing the lower-level tasks assigned	◇	Consultant would focus on small wins and build into a larger assignment Consultant would perform lower-level tasks with the bigger picture in mind
Time	◇	Consultant performing tasks in a timely manner		
Method	◇	Consultant not building relationship with client Consultant not spending time collaborating with peers in office	◇	Consultant would collaborate with senior consultants and leaders at office Consultant would build a strong relationship with peers
Condition				

Table 8.1: Junior consultant: talking and selling input characteristic difficulties and level of consulting.

Story 3

The assigned cost-control consultant is too inexperienced to realize the client project director was a busy person who does not want to be interrupted with unimportant questions or barraged with requests for information or lengthy reports on matters that they considers to be unnecessary interruptions of their time.

Table 8.2 shows the organization, when it comes to educating employees in the art of talking and selling to clients, experienced difficulties in terms of the time and method of the talking and selling input characteristic. The table further indicates when it comes to talking and selling to clients, the organization counted on high levels of consulting to clients, while inadequacies were identified in the method and condition of consulting.

Character	Difficulties Experienced or Issues Occurred		Hoped for or Counted On	
	Talking and Selling		Consulting	
Extent				
Time	◇	Junior consultant takes the time to learn—on the client's cost—a new skill to benefit the organization		
Method	◇	Consultant collaborating with senior consultants in office Consultant focusing on working with lower-level management instead of interrupting executive management	◇	Keeping cost low and generating more work Asking questions and working with consultant in office to develop quality reporting Work with lower-level management and deliver above expectation to senior management
Condition			◇	Consultant will work closely with senior consultants in office

Table 8.2: Junior consultant: talking and selling input characteristic difficulties and level of consulting.

Story 4

Client-engagement consultants spent significant time driving five hundred kilometers to engage with the client, and two days later, presented our skills and capabilities to the client—and signed an agreement with the client a week later. Focused on providing capabilities and getting chargeability, our consultants do not manage to put themselves in the client's shoes, breaking down individual requirements into smaller pieces to determine the root cause for not being successful in delivering acceptable consulting.

Table 8.3 shows the organization when it comes to educating employees in the art of talking and selling to clients, experienced difficulties in terms of the extent and method of the talking and selling input characteristic. The table further indicates when it comes to talking and selling to clients, the organization counted on high levels of consulting to clients, while inadequacies were identified in the extent and method of consulting.

Character	Difficulties Experienced or Issues Occurred	Hoped for or Counted On
	Talking and Selling	Consulting
Extent	Focused on providing the needs and not the wants Consultant not educated enough and experienced enough in the groundbreaking work	Focused on the wants of the client Able to educate the client and client team
Time		
Method	Consultant not able to make a personal connection with the decision maker Focused on developing tools that the client does not understand	Built a relationship with the client Consultant would build a strong enough relationship with influencers to assist decision makers.
Condition		

Table 8.3: Senior team members: talking and selling input characteristic difficulties and level of consulting.

Story 6

Our project controls consultant, although a senior consultant who worked in various corporate and project environments, failed to realize our client was expecting an independent, innovative, and creative contribution with minimum interruption of the client's leadership group, without a barrage of requests for information on matters it considered to be unwarranted intrusion of its time.

Table 8.4 shows the organization, when it comes to educating employees in the art of talking and selling to clients, experienced difficulties in terms of the extent, method, and condition of the talking and selling input characteristic. The table further indicates when it comes to talking and selling to clients, the organization counted on high levels of consulting to clients, while inadequacies were identified in the extent, method, and condition of consulting.

Character	Difficulties Experienced or Issues Occurred		Hoped for or Counted On	
	Talking and Selling		Consulting	
Extent	◇	Understanding that the organization must work as a single unit	◇	Build a long-term relationship with client Deliver work with minimum interruption of executive and senior clients
Time				
Method	◇	Senior consultants collaborate with peers Scheduling time with executives, respecting their time	◇	Fit-for-purpose work delivery
Condition	◇	Senior consultants work independently Using fit-for-purpose templates	◇	Consultants would apply their individual skills and experience

Table 8.4: Senior team members: talking and selling input characteristic difficulties and level of consulting.

Expectation-Reality Gap

To identify the reasoning behind the talking and selling/consulting expectation-reality gap with the talking and selling input characteristic difficulties and level of consulting in mind, an analysis has been done on the organization's culture, consultant capabilities, and organization leadership.

Table 8.5 indicates the various inadequacies in organization culture (equality, ownership thinking, fit for purpose, and values) that might exist and could have led to the talking and selling/client wants expectation-reality gap.

Equality			
Limited organization structures		Consultants can enjoy themselves	
Consultant participation		Equal productivity incentives	
Fulfill potential		Social identity	
Treated fairly		Knowing our peers	◆
Character protected		Absence of inappropriate and disrespectful language	
Work hours respected		Absence of stereotyping	
Personal information protected		Taking consultants seriously	
Recognition of diversity			
Ownership Thinking			
Understanding the fundamentals of the organization		Forecasting and achieving the business's key performance indicators	
Understanding how the company makes money		Key performance indicators are highly visible and accountable	
Understanding how each consultant adds—or takes away—value	◆	Having self-funding incentive plans	
Knowing the business's key performance indicators	◆	Incentive plans aligning the consultants' behavior to the business's objectives	◆
Fit for Purpose			
Deliverables do what they intend to achieve	◆	Final deliverables are efficient enough for the stated purpose	
Deliverables are good enough to do the work they are designed to do		Deliverables represent the right tool to do the work consultants have to do	

Deliverables are of a good enough standard for clients	◆	Deliverables fulfill the requirement specifications and stated outcome	
Deliverables answer the client's requirement and wants and nothing more		Consultants are undertaking enough and have efficient effort to reach the client's intended goals	
Deliverables are comprehensive to the extent that they answer the client's requirement and wants and nothing more			

Values			
Trust		Transparency	◆
Pride		Sense of urgency	◆
Camaraderie		Commitment	◆

Table 8.5: Talking and selling/consulting expectation-reality gap: culture.

Table 8.6 shows the various shortcomings in organization core competencies that might exist and could have led to the talking and selling/client wants expectation-reality gap.

Core Competencies			
Leadership		Work quality	◆
Sense of urgency		Quantity of work	
Teamwork	◆	Accountability	◆
Decision-making		Adaptability	◆
Client focused		Initiative	
Business acumen		Innovation	
Resource management	◆	Planning and organizing	◆
People management		Communication	

Table 8.6: Talking and selling/consulting expectation-reality gap: capability.

Table 8.7 shows the various inadequacies in organization leadership styles that might exist and could have led to the talking and selling/client wants expectation-reality gap.

Styles			
Cooperative leadership	◇	Whiner	
Problem-solving leadership		Gossiper	
Leadership by example		Nonstop talker	
Knowledge leadership	◇	Grumbler	
Get-up-and-go leadership		Bully	

Table 8.7: Talking and selling/consulting expectation-reality gap: leadership.

Assessment and Checklists

With the circumstances bringing about the realization of a talking and selling/consulting expectation-reality gap, and an analysis of the organization's culture, capabilities, and values identifying potential inadequacies causing the talking and selling/consulting expectation-reality gap, table 8.8 provides a list of questions and phrases to be used to assess the extent whereto the organization's culture, capabilities, values, and leadership support the referral recruitment process, contractual agreement with consultants, assignment of consultants to work, and mentoring and coaching of consultants.

Item	Description	Score
A	Culture	
	Equality	
12	Consultants know who their peers are and what is expected of them, and on all levels, they foster two-way communication and trust. Although they are not reporting to each other, they embrace the fact that they are on the same team.	
	Ownership Thinking	
3	The organization and the individual team members understand how each consultant adds—or takes away—value.	

Item	Description	Score
4	Individual team members are aware of the business's key performance indicators.	
8	The organization has implemented incentive plans that align the consultants' behavior to the business's objectives.	
	Fit for Purpose	
1	Consultants produce deliverables that give what the assignment intends to deliver to achieve the project or business value.	
4	Consultants produce deliverables that answer the client's requirement and wants and nothing more.	
B	Values	
4	Organization and consultants demonstrate through operating in such a way that it is easy for outsiders to see what actions are being performed based on openness, communication, and accountability.	
5	Consultants demonstrate a sense of urgency through attitude and the process of treating key business or personal matters as if one's life depended on it. Consultants have the determination to stay focused on results and deadlines until the task or project is completed.	
6	Commitment is demonstrated through a consultant base that pledges themselves to the organization and delivers successful projects aligned with the business, culture, remuneration, and leadership model, consistently and persistently pursuing the business's purpose and conduct.	
C	Capabilities	
3	Consultants have teamwork competencies, including the ability to establish and maintain positive working relationships and to work cooperatively to achieve results, solicit input, value team members' contributions, and place them above personal needs.	
7	Consultants apply resource management in day-to-day work execution, including the ability to plan, control, and measure resources in a way that balances cost with benefits and enables the organization to meet deliverables. Resources might include money, information, inventory, supplies, people, and time.	
9	Consultants perform quality work, including speed, efficiency, and the ability to prioritize and meet deadlines and organize work. Consultants, in executing their work, demonstrate knowledge and skills, ability to meet standards, care and attention to details, follow-through to completion, and frequency of errors.	
11	Consultants have accountability competencies, including the ability to take responsibility for tasks or assignments and align words with actions.	

Item	Description	Score
12	Consultants have adaptability, showing abilities in mastering new skills and demonstrating flexibility in reacting to changing needs, procedures, and environments; work well under pressure; handle multiple assignments, and meet deadlines.	
15	Consultants have planning and organization competencies, including establishing an appropriate course of action for themselves and/or others to accomplish a specific goal, making proper assignments of people and appropriate use of resources, and ensuring which daily activities contribute to and are timely with the overall business's short- and long-term objectives.	
16	Consultants have people-management competencies, including the ability to delegate, set goals, manage performance, motivate, train, develop, hire, and exit employees and contractors in a fashion that meets the company's goals.	
D	Leadership	
1	Have consultants and team members who are seeking cooperation from all consultants, seeking cooperation from consultants whom they have no control over.	
4	Have consultants providing knowledge leadership, who know the strategies and tactics required, realizing experience and potential in the consultants, and mentoring.	
	Average Score	
Rate a score of 1, 3 or 5. Score: 1 = Seldom, 3 = Sometimes true, and 5 = Almost always true		
Interpretation of average score: 68 - 81 signs of the talking and selling/consulting expectation-reality gap, 45 - 67 likely the talking and selling/consulting expectation-reality gap exists, 1 - 44 certainly the talking and selling/consulting expectation-reality gap exists.		

Table 8.8: Assessment: talking and selling/consulting expectation-reality gap.

Paying attention to the circumstances bringing about the realization a talking and selling/consulting expectation-reality gap exists, the outcome of the analysis of the organization's culture, capabilities, and values identifying potential shortfalls causing the talking and selling/consulting expectation-reality gap and the assessment, could allow the organization to:

- narrow or reduce the talking and selling/consulting expectation-reality gap,
- recruit and build a team of business-orientated consultants,

- adjust the consulting input characteristic, and
- adjust the actions taken by the organization to support the consultant input characteristic.

Chapter 9 will shed light on the theme "a young company does not spell act quick," focusing on the young company/act quick expectation-reality gap.

This page is for you, the reader, to make notes and jot down reference page numbers.

Use this table to make notes and jot down system-related reference page numbers.

Note	Page Number		
	People	Process	Application

Use this table to make notes and jot down IPO-related reference page numbers.

Note	Page Number		
	Input	Process	Output

Use this table to make notes and jot down theme-related reference page numbers.

Note	Page Number				
	Business Models	Competencies	Leadership	Values	Self-Orientation

This page is for you, the reader, to make notes and jot down ERG-related reference page numbers.

Note	Page Number
Talking and Selling Do Not Spell Consulting	

CHAPTER 9

A Young Company Does Not Spell Act Quick

I have been impressed with the urgency of doing. Knowing is not enough. We must apply. Being willing is not enough. We must do.
—Leonardo da Vinci

Progression improvement beats delayed perfection.
—Mark Twain

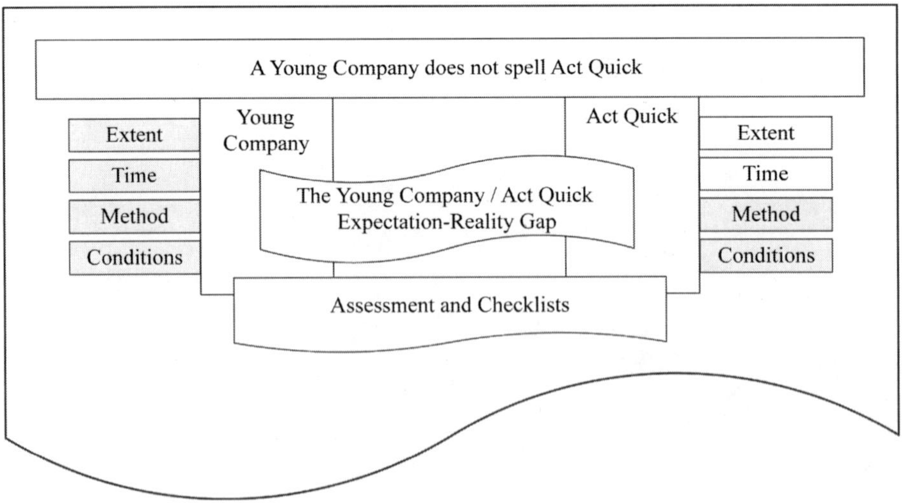

Introduction

IT IS THE last week of January 2016. A friend, peer, and colleague contacted me to provide them with a consultant to work for one of our key clients on a project in Alaska. The work was outside our core traditional consulting area and took us longer than expected to find a consultant who would add value and provide meaning to our client. Paging through the topics of my retrospective learnings, I found the topic of chapter 9, to act quick, so relevant.

The eighth theme requiring our attention is "a young company does not spell act quick." The focus of this chapter is to provide an understanding of leadership's expectation from consultants working in a young company as input characteristic, an understanding of the actions taken by the organization to support or strengthen the young company's input characteristic, the circumstances bringing about the realization a young company/act quick expectation-reality gap exists, and an analysis of the organization's culture, capabilities, and values identifying potential inadequacies causing the young company/act quick expectation-reality gap.

Expected Result

Expectation 8

Like-minded seasoned consultants engaged on referral for a young start-up organization that was still establishing itself in the project-delivery environment realize the importance to practice a sense of urgency to get work done in a short time and in a fit-for-purpose manner. The consultants understood it was the organization and individual consultants who must kick up their performance to realize valuable achievements. Furthermore, the consultants understood they must work smarter, do more research without charging the client, and deliver quality and acceptable performance.

Business Input

To strengthen the chances of achieving the organization's objective of making consultants realize working in a young start-up company requires a sense of urgency to get things done more timely and in a fit-for-purpose manner, the leadership team, on a regular basis, communicated and collaborated with consultants on the topics of why start-up organizations fail, what to expect from a start-up company, the culture required in a start-up company, why should consultants change their way of thinking, what to do, and how to succeed in start-up company.

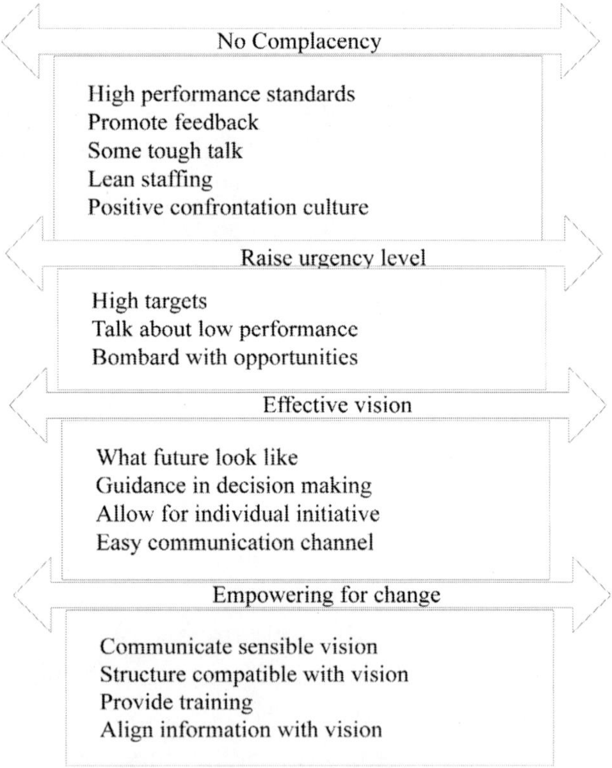

Figure 9.1: *Transforming Organizations: Why Firms Fail* (John P. Kotter, 4–14, 1996).

Knowing the move from a large corporate organization to a start-up consulting organization might have significant and traumatic impact on consultants, leadership transferred knowledge on aspects of change during such significant transformation. Assisting consultants to transition from corporate organization to start-up, the importance of a sense of urgency has been cemented as a core value in providing deliverables on an as-agreed basis. Knowing without a sense of urgency, consultants won't give the extra effort that is essential.

Besides the sense of urgency, significant focus has been placed on communicating and collaborating on the organization's vision as a mechanism to help direct, align, and inspire actions on the part of leadership and consultants. The focus on communicating and collaborating on the organization's vision was primarily to prevent the start-up actions to dissolve into a list of confusing, incompatible, and time-consuming business-management efforts and move the organization into the wrong direction. To avoid complicated and blurry direction, the leadership provided direction guided by the organization's business plan, measurable KPIs, and written and communicated elevator speech.

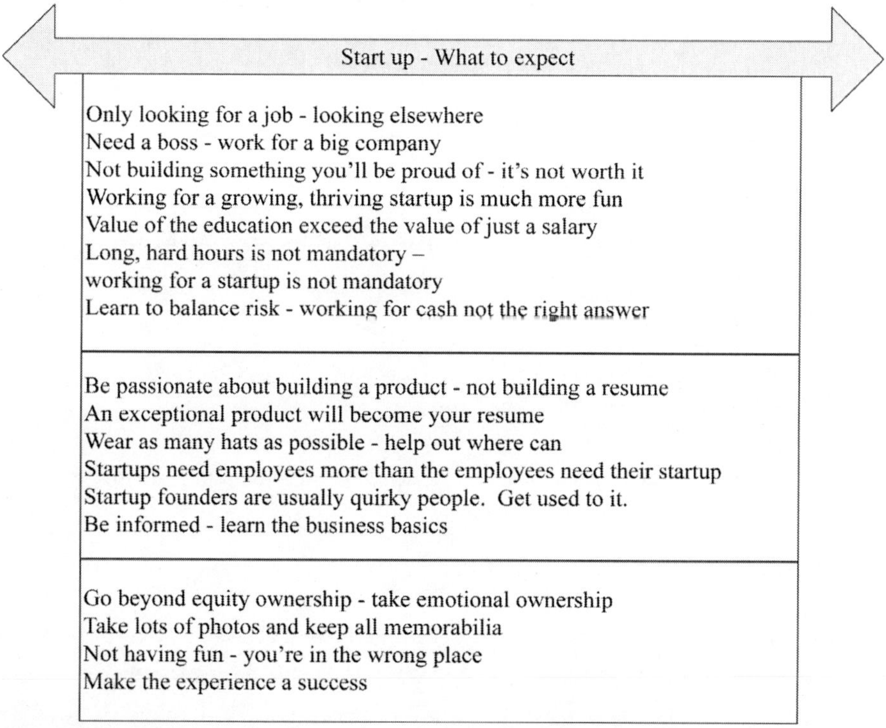

Figure 9.2: What to expect from a start-up (Shah, Dharmesh 2013) (source: https://www.linkedin.com/pulse/20130110195000-658789-17-simple-tips-on-working-at-a-startup).

Leadership, on a regular basis in weekly and monthly business meetings, around the water cooler and lunch table, addressed the importance and the honor of working in a start-up organization. Though the focus was on the learning experience, leadership paid the consultants a very competitive salary, which was very uncharacteristic for a start-up organization. Leadership at all times made it clear to the team it was not conventional, not looking for eight-to-five workers, and promoted an environment for equality, eliminating the boss and worker relationship, and strongly asked consultants to adopt a work-life balance. Leadership did its best to promote and stimulate consultants to participate and help build an organization they could be proud of. Pushing and generating opportunities for consultants to go outside their comfort zone. Adopting a total open policy introduced and involved consultants in all levels and aspects of business, allowing them to wear as many hats as they felt sometimes uncomfortable with to teach the basics and stimulate ownership and idea generation. Consultants embraced an open-door policy, open-office workspace, allowing for collaboration, communication, support, and fun and laughter.

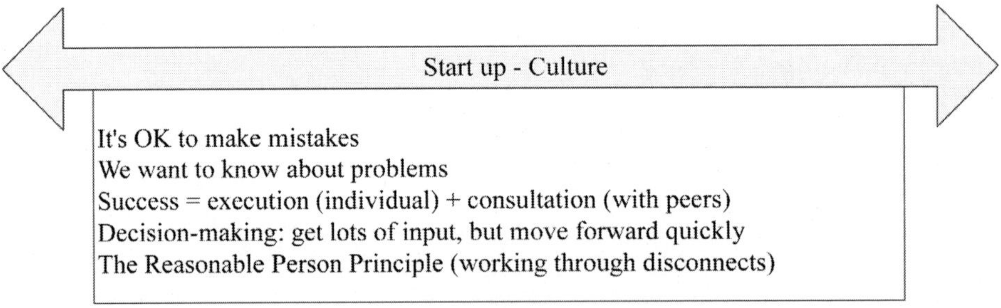

Figure 9.3: Start-up company culture (Ousterhout, John, 2011) (source: http://web.stanford.edu/~ouster/cgi-bin/startupCulture.php).

With the owner and CEO of the organization a thought and transformation leader which is typical characteristic of a start-up organization, there was no shortage in risk-taking. Leadership promoted wider decision-making with the expectation that mistakes would be made along the way, especially with the understanding the organization did not have formal IP. However, when mistakes were made, the size and implications were quickly recognized, and retrospective sessions were held to learn from the mistakes and correct them. Leadership drafted a culture plan to allow for respectful resolution to disconnect and misunderstandings and always promote and recommend working through them based on the reasonable person principle. At the same time, leadership believed if consultants truly were unreasonable and repeatedly behaved in the unreasonable manner, they must leave the organization.

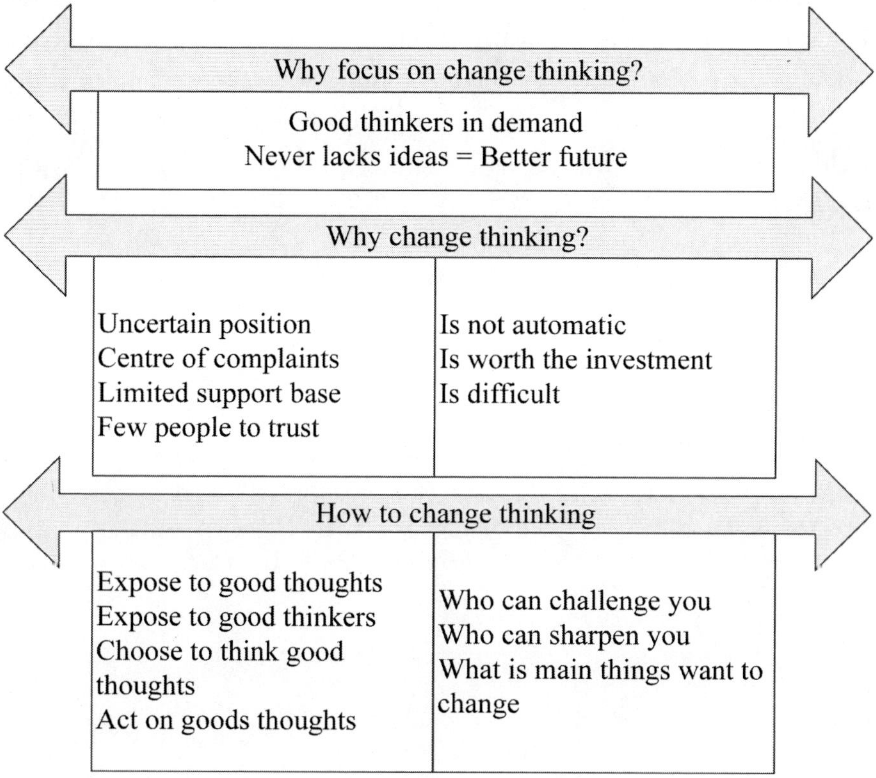

Figure 9.4: Why you should change your thinking (John C. Maxwell, x–xxi, 2009).

Realizing working in and on a start-up would be difficult and different, leadership continuously reminded consultants to change their thinking with a focus on problem-solving, idea generation, and counting on a better future. Educating and supporting consultants, leadership focused on why it was important to change the thinking and how to go about changing the thinking patterns, specifically since change does not come automatically and the start-up was new to the consultants. They had not done that type of thinking before, and it required hard work to get real great ideas. Leadership regularly introduced topics and opportunities to support and improve the process of thinking and idea generation. On the how of thinking, leadership promoted the idea and created opportunities to connect and collaborate with good thinkers who achieved success and had good task-execution ideas, created client-engagement events, and invested in attending client-engagement and consulting-enrichment events. Besides the physical connection, leadership created a culture and an environment where the consultant could practice thinking good thoughts and acting out their good thoughts.

Start up - What to do

Hire Entrepreneurs
- Smart - very enthusiastic people
- Not necessarily hire the best fit for the current, limited definition of a job
- Hire people with the potential to grow, and contribute more

Instill Company Vision
- Does things with very lean staffing and operational budgets
- Vision of the founders inspires their staff to new heights

Expand the Vision
- What we are today isn't what we're going to be – building something bigger
- Reach for the next plateau, not only in sales - also in excellence
- Refreshing the goals - keeps our team engaged
- Beyond the point of relying on profit sharing to motivate your employees

Don't Fear the #Fail
- "Experience is what you get when you don't get what you wanted" - Gary Swart -
- Come up with new ways to - serve clients, enter new markets, improve internal processes
- Opportunity to implement these ideas - don't punish if it doesn't pan out
- Congratulate willingness to take risks, encourage next idea

Adjust for Inspiration
- Don't stick with old systems
- Listening to ideas and encouraging enthusiasm.
- Don't be afraid to change
- Job descriptions, titles, department configurations, consulting lines
- Change is essential, so seize an inspired opportunity

Figure 9.5: Start-up—what to do (AngelBlog 2014) (source: http://www.angelblog.net/Startups_The_Essential_To_Do_List.html).

Leadership stressed the fact that failure in some circumstance is good since it allows time to do a retrospect and understand what is standing in the consultant's way of getting what he or she wants. The importance of being free of fear and the fact the consultant can learn to be free of fear. Recognizing fear is just a tool created by the mind allows consultants to learn how to reprogram the conditioning as it serves instead of hindering. The key to being free of fear is to get it out of heads and back into the body in the present moment. When consultants are in the present to what is happening, they are no longer controlled by the stories in their minds. This presence gives consultants the ability to act despite fear. Feedback is the fast track to success because consultant failures clearly reflect exactly what stands between the consultant and their true happiness. Failure is just a reflection of something that isn't working on the inside. It doesn't hold any hidden meaning about consultant worthiness and doesn't mean it shouldn't be tried. It is feedback on what worked and what didn't work. It contains all the information for the consultant to go back and change something on the inside so it can produce a different outcome.

If the consultants master the art of learning from failures, they will be able to literally direct their lives exactly as they want them to be. This can only be achieved through practice and more practice. Consultants must unlearn their old habits and replace them with the new, more empowering habits.

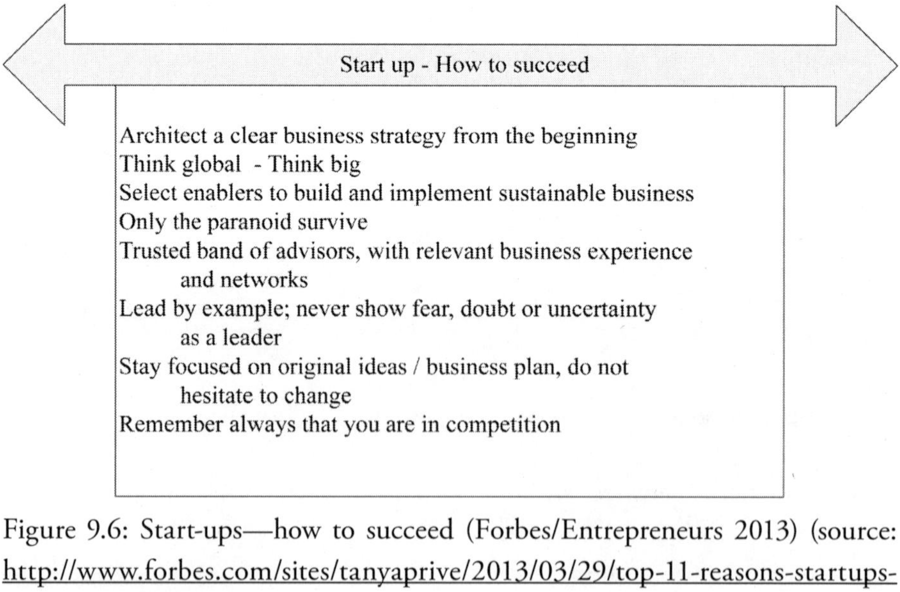

Figure 9.6: Start-ups—how to succeed (Forbes/Entrepreneurs 2013) (source: http://www.forbes.com/sites/tanyaprive/2013/03/29/top-11-reasons-startups-succeed/#641c9263b2de).

The owner from day one had a well-defined vision, communicated with the consulting team, and collaborated to ensure a common understanding would allow them to move forward and have success. Leadership developed a well-defined business plan with measurable KPIs that supported the organization's vision. It has proven to be a major force behind the organization's success, serving as a compass in tough times. Leadership created a vision incorporating various technologies and creative and innovative ideas to implement them and technologies that were specific to the contracts and controls environment on projects. Moreover, the organization showed it is not about changing and adopting to new technologies. As integral part of becoming trusted advisers, leadership introduced the concept of discipline, starting with self-control as a product of strong and self-imposed personal standard. It could not be stressed enough that without discipline, the organization would fail to succeed even in the best economy. Leadership believed self-discipline would lead to positive work ethic, and work ethic would lead to getting things done effectively and efficiently. Leadership in the day-to-day task execution and behind the scenes on an individual basis worked hard to align consultants to achieve success.

Reality: A young company does not spell act quick.

Story 1

Consultants who were used to working from templates, slow to custom-build documentation and project processes and procedures to fulfill client expectations, ultimately became the client's reason for contracting the newly started organization. Furthermore, consultants failed to proactively develop unique and nonstandard documentation, including models, templates, and procedures, and new ways of performing the project function allowing for quick response to client needs.

Table 9.1 shows when it comes to consultants embracing custom-build documentation, custom project processes and procedures, the organization experienced difficulties in terms of the extent, time, method, and condition of the "young company" input characteristic. The table further indicates when it comes to consulting in the young company, the organization counted on high levels of acting quickly, while inadequacies were identified in terms of the method and condition of acting quickly.

Character		Difficulties Experienced or Issues Occurred		Hoped for or Counted On
		Young Company		Act Quick
Extent	◇	The wish to complete the work Consultants recognize the importance of IP		
Time	◇	To work proactively on IP during downturns		
Method	◇	Consultants develop IP during time on the bench.	◇	Working as a team to develop documentation and deliverables
Condition	◇	Senior consultants visiting the office at least once per month	◇	Experienced consultants would bring high quality IP to the organization Consultants would have an urgency to develop out-standing IP

Table 9.1: Senior team members: a young company's input characteristic difficulties and level of act quick.

Story 3

On short notice, client requests—and organization assigns—a seasoned contracts-formation consultant. The very experienced consultant previously worked for major organizations, on major execution life cycle phase projects, and with large, complex template contracts. The organization failed to deliver fit-for-purpose contracts based on the specific type of contracting services and the specific life cycle stage.

Table 9.2 shows when it comes to delivering fit-for-purpose contracts, the organization experienced difficulties in terms of the extent and method of the "young company" input characteristic. The table further indicates when it comes to consulting in the young company, the organization counted on high levels of acting quickly, while inadequacies were identified in terms of the time, method, and condition of acting quickly.

Character	Difficulties Experienced or Issues Occurred		Hoped for or Counted On	
	Young Company		Act Quick	
Extent	◆	Have working and applicable documentation templates		
Time			◆	Consultants would take limited time to develop deliverables
Method	◆	Consultants taking advantage of the team's experience Consultants working independently Consultants asking for clarification during deliverable development	◆	Consultants would work with client executives
Condition			◆	Run documents by the full team for input and quality documentation development

Table 9.2: Senior team members: a young company's input characteristic difficulties and level of act quick.

Story 4

The contracts-formation consultant was very experienced, previously worked for major organizations, on major execution life cycle phase projects, and with large, complex template contracts. The organization failed to be accommodating and receptive of unusual needs from the client based on the specific type on contracting services and the specific life cycle stage.

Table 9.3 shows when it comes to accommodating and being receptive of unusual client requirements, the organization experienced difficulties in terms of the extent, and method of the "young company" input characteristic. The table further indicates when it comes to consulting in the young company, the organization counted on high levels of acting quickly, while inadequacies were identified in terms of the time, method, and condition of acting quickly.

Character	Difficulties Experienced or Issues Occurred		Hoped for or Counted On	
	Young Company		Act Quick	
Extent	◇	Have working and applicable documentation templates		
Time			◇	Consultants would take limited time to develop deliverables
Method	◇	Consultants taking advantage of the team's experience Consultants working independently Consultants asking for clarification during deliverable development	◇	Consultants would work with client executives.
Condition			◇	Run documents by the full time for input and quality documentation development

Table 9.3: Senior team members: a young company's input characteristic difficulties and level of act quick.

Expectation-Reality Gap

To identify the reasoning behind the young company/act quick expectation-reality gap with the young company's input characteristic difficulties in mind, an analysis has been done on the organization's culture, consultant capabilities, and organization leadership.

Table 9.4 shows the various misalignments in the organization's culture (equality, ownership thinking, fit for purpose, and values) that might exist and could have led to the young company/act quick expectation-reality gap.

Equality			
Limited organization structures		Consultants can enjoy themselves	
Consultant participation		Equal productivity incentives	
Fulfill potential	◆	Social identity	
Treated fairly		Knowing our peers	◆
Character protected		Absence of inappropriate and disrespectful language	
Work hours respected		Absence of stereotyping	
Personal information protected		Taking consultants seriously	◆
Recognition of diversity			
Ownership Thinking			
Understanding the fundamentals of the organization		Forecasting and achieving the business's key performance indicators	
Understanding how the company makes money		Key performance indicators are highly visible and accountable	
Understanding how each consultant adds—or takes away—value		Having self-funding incentive plans	◆
Knowing the business's key performance indicators		Incentive plans aligning the consultants' behavior to the business's objectives	◆
Fit for Purpose			
Deliverables do what they intend to achieve	◆	Final deliverables are efficient enough for the stated purpose	◆
Deliverables are good enough to do the work they are designed to do	◆	Deliverables represent the right tool to do the work consultants have to do	
Deliverables are of a good enough standard for clients	◆	Deliverables fulfill the requirement specifications and stated outcome	◆
Deliverables answer the client's requirement and wants and nothing more	◆	Consultants are undertaking enough and have efficient effort to reach the client's intended goals	◆
Deliverables are comprehensive to the extent that they answer the client's requirement and wants and nothing more	◆		

Values			
Trust		Transparency	◆
Pride	◆	Sense of urgency	◆
Camaraderie	◆	Commitment	

Table 9.4: Young company/act quick expectation-reality gap: culture.

Table 9.5 shows the various shortcomings in organization core competencies that might exist and could have led to the young company/act quick expectation-reality gap.

Core Competencies			
Leadership		Work quality	◆
Sense of urgency	◆	Quantity of work	
Teamwork		Accountability	◆
Decision-making		Adaptability	◆
Client focused		Initiative	◆
Business acumen		Innovation	◆
Resource management	◆	Planning and organizing	◆
People management		Communication	◆

Table 9.5: Young company/act quick expectation-reality gap: capability.

Table 9.6 shows the various inadequacies in organization leadership styles that might exist and could have led to the young company/act quick expectation-reality gap.

Styles			
Cooperative leadership	◇	Whiner	
Problem-solving leadership	◇	Gossiper	
Leadership by example		Nonstop talker	
Knowledge leadership		Grumbler	
Get-up-and-go leadership	◇	Bully	

Table 9.6: Young company/act quick expectation-reality gap: leadership.

Quotient and Checklists

With the circumstances bringing about the realization a young company/act quick expectation-reality gap exists, and an analysis of the organization's culture, capabilities, and values identifying potential shortfalls causing the young company/act quick expectation-reality gap, table 9.7 provides a list of questions and phrases to be used to assess the extent whereto the organization's culture, capabilities, values, and leadership support the referral recruitment process, contractual agreement with consultants, assignment of consultants to work, and mentoring and coaching of consultants.

Item	Description	Score
	Culture	
A	Equality	
3	Consultants pushing themselves to be the best they can on a personal and business level and know the real them, fulfilling their potential. Consultants accept their failures, ask for support, trust their intuition, and never stop going after their goals.	
12	Consultants know who their peers are and what is expected of them, and on all levels, they foster two-way communication and trust. Although they are not reporting to each other, they embrace the fact that they are on the same team.	
15	Consultants are taken seriously as they are confident and know what they are talking about; they are engaged in multiple-level conversation, say what they need to say and get to the point, and stay serious about work most of the time.	
	Ownership Thinking	
7	The organization has implemented self-funding incentive plans.	

Item	Description	Score
	Fit for Purpose	
1	Consultants produce deliverables that give what the assignment intends to deliver to achieve the project or business value.	
2	Consultants produce deliverables that are good enough to perform as they were designed to do, including aspects such as technical performance, maintainability, and availability.	
3	Consultants produce deliverables that are of a good enough standard for clients in terms of quality, risk, and safety.	
4	Consultants produce deliverables that answer the client's requirement and wants and nothing more.	
5	Consultants produce deliverables that are comprehensive to the extent that they answer the client's requirement and wants and nothing more.	
6	Consultants produce deliverables that are doing the right things according to the stated purpose.	
8	Consultants produce deliverables that fulfill the requirement specifications and stated outcome.	
9	Consultants are undertaking enough and have efficient effort to reach the client's intended goals.	
B	Values	
3	Camaraderie is demonstrated through a sense of belonging where consultants work, acceptance for who consultants are, a sense of inclusion where the organization makes everyone an insider, occasional fun events that are planned to meet diverse interests, clear messages stating that all are welcome, and understanding for those who don't choose to participate.	
4	Organization and consultants demonstrate through operating in such a way that it is easy for outsiders to see what actions are being performed based on openness, communication, and accountability.	
5	Consultants demonstrate a sense of urgency through attitude and the process of treating key business or personal matters as if one's life depended on it. Consultants have the determination to stay focused on results and deadlines until the task or project is completed.	
C	Competencies	
2	Have a consulting base that understands the significance of a sense of urgency. Demonstrated through the organization's and consultants' attitude and the process of treating key business or personal matters as if one's life depended on it. Consultants demonstrate the ability and determination to stay focused on results and deadlines until the task or project is completed.	

Item	Description	Score
3	Consultants have teamwork competencies, including the ability to establish and maintain positive working relationships and to work cooperatively to achieve results, solicit input, value team members' contributions, and place them above personal needs.	
7	Consultants apply resource management in day-to-day work execution, including the ability to plan, control, and measure resources in a way that balances cost with benefits and enables the organization to meet deliverables. Resources might include money, information, inventory, supplies, people, and time.	
9	Consultants perform quality work, including speed, efficiency, and the ability to prioritize and meet deadlines and organize work. Consultants, in executing their work, demonstrate knowledge and skills, ability to meet standards, care and attention to details, follow-through to completion, and frequency of errors.	
10	A common understanding exists that quantity of work is not identical with number of units, rather that each work assignment has its own measurements, rate of change, degree of development, and use of a certain standard as a unit of computation or measurement. Consultants apply the SMART principle in planning and controlling work.	
12	Consultants have adaptability, showing abilities in mastering new skills and demonstrating flexibility in reacting to changing needs, procedures, and environments; work well under pressure; handle multiple assignments, and meet deadlines.	
13	Consultants have initiative and innovation utilizing knowledge and scope to constructively increase productivity and achieve goals, use resourcefulness and creativity in dealing with challenges, and anticipate and react positively to change.	
15	Consultants have planning and organization competencies, including establishing an appropriate course of action for themselves and/or others to accomplish a specific goal, making proper assignments of people and appropriate use of resources, and ensuring which daily activities contribute to and are timely with the overall business's short- and long-term objectives.	
16	Consultants have people-management competencies, including the ability to delegate, set goals, manage performance, motivate, train, develop, hire, and exit employees and contractors in a fashion that meets the company's goals.	
D	Leadership	
1	Have consultants and team members who are seeking cooperation from all consultants, seeking cooperation from consultants whom they have no control over.	

Item	Description	Score
2	Have problem solvers who are addressing the issues that frustrate individual consultants, addressing the issues—even if they make them unpopular.	
5	Have consultants providing get-up-and-go leadership, getting up and doing what is required of them, and committing themselves to get-up-and-go business.	
	Average Score	
Rate a score of 1, 3 or 5. Score: 1 = Seldom, 3 = Sometimes true, and 5 = Almost always true		
Interpretation of average score: 101 - 121 signs a young company/act quick expectation-reality gap, 67 - 100 likely a young company/act quick expectation-reality gap exists, 1 - 66 certainly a young company/act quick expectation-reality gap exists.		

Table 9.7: Assessment: a young company/act quick expectation-reality gap.

Paying attention to the circumstances bringing about the realization of a young company/act quick expectation-reality gap, the outcome of the analysis of the organization's culture, capabilities, and values identifying potential shortfalls causing the young company/act quick expectation-reality gap, could allow the organization to:

- narrow or reduce the young company/act quick expectation-reality gap,
- recruit and build a team of business-orientated consultants,
- adjust the acting quick as input characteristic, and
- adjust the actions taken by the organization to support the acting quick input characteristic.

Chapter 10 will shed light on the theme "leadership does not spell immune system," focusing on the leadership/immune system expectation-reality gap.

This page is for you, the reader, to make notes and jot down reference page numbers.

Use this table to make notes and jot down system-related reference page numbers.

Note	Page Number		
	People	Process	Application

Use this table to make notes and jot down IPO-related reference page numbers.

Note	Page Number		
	Input	Process	Output

Use this table to make notes and jot down theme-related reference page numbers.

Note	Page Number				
	Business Models	Competencies	Leadership	Values	Self-Orientation

This page is for you, the reader, to make notes and jot down ERG-related reference page numbers.

Note	Page Number
Consulting Does Not Spell Adviser	

CHAPTER 10

Leadership Does Not Spell Immune System

The difference between successful people and really successful people is really successful people say no to almost everything.
—Warren Buffet

A genuine leader is not a searcher for consensus but a molder of consensus.
—Dr. Martin Luther King Jr.

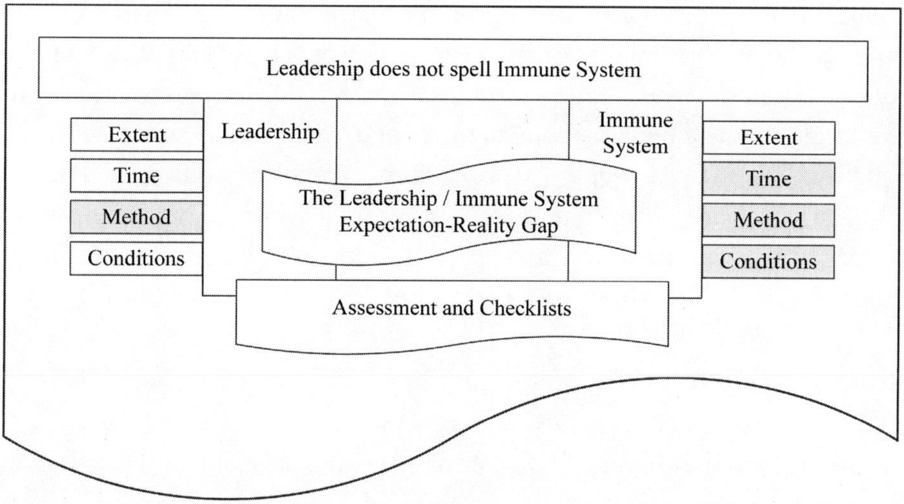

Introduction

IT IS OCTOBER 2015. I am going over company financial statements and seeing the excellent reaction to certain business decisions and directions over the past quarter and also looking back over the past four years, wondering why the organization had lost some key players and why leaders had allowed things to happen, turning my attention to the second-to-last topic of leadership does not spell immune system.

The ninth theme requiring our attention is "leadership does not spell immune system." The focus of this chapter is to provide an understanding of the organization leadership's expectation from the leadership input characteristic, an understanding of the actions taken by the organization to support or strengthen the leadership input characteristic, the circumstances bringing about realization the leadership/immune system expectation-reality gap exists, and an analysis of the organization's culture, capabilities, and values identifying potential inadequacies causing the leadership/immune system expectation-reality gap.

Expected Result

Expectation 9

Experienced consultants bring and develop leadership characteristics and experience, allowing them to keep the president and CEO of the organization on the straight and narrow when it comes to decision-making, management of consultants, focus on individual consultants' quality of work, and keeping all consultants equally accountable. Besides the formal leadership structure, consultants are developing informal leadership structures, facilitating and addressing common business concerns, and improving work conditions.

Business Input

To strengthen the changes of delivering the expected result and developing leaders who can keep the CEO accountable and on track, collaboration took place on concepts such as the difference between leadership and management, RASCQI matrix development, and the CEO's leadership style.

The term "immune system" refers to an informal process within the organization challenging leadership to carry out activities in a certain way, a form of agreement bias, an active form of leadership groupthink. The leadership groupthink processes produce an outcome, imposing itself on the decision maker, in this case, the CEO. One of the primary reasons for introducing the immune system concept is to drive out innovation and entrepreneurial activity within the organization.

The expectation is like-minded consultants would bring consistency in terms of matching attitudes, beliefs, and behaviors to leadership group norms—norms as implicit, unsaid rules shared by the leadership, guiding their interactions with the primary decision maker, peers, and consultants. This tendency to conform occurs in small groups or the leadership group as a whole and may result from subtle unconscious influences to direct and overt social pressure.

The expectation from the CEO is leadership would conform from a desire for protection of themselves in the leadership group. Understandably, leadership groupthink is a model driven by consent and conformity to group values and ethics, which might ignore a realistic appraisal of other courses of action. It is well understood that an unwillingness to conform carries the risk of social rejection. Though experience has it, peer pressure may manifest negatively. The expectation is leadership group conformity would have good consequences more often than not.

Anticipation is leadership conformity would influence formation and protection of social norms, which could be perceived as a positive power preventing distracting or risky CEO decisions. To promote and prepare consultants to be leaders and strengthen the chance of achieving the expected outcome of consultants being leaders, leadership introduced the concepts and insights of transformational leadership style, decision-making clarity state, decision map framework, and group-development process.

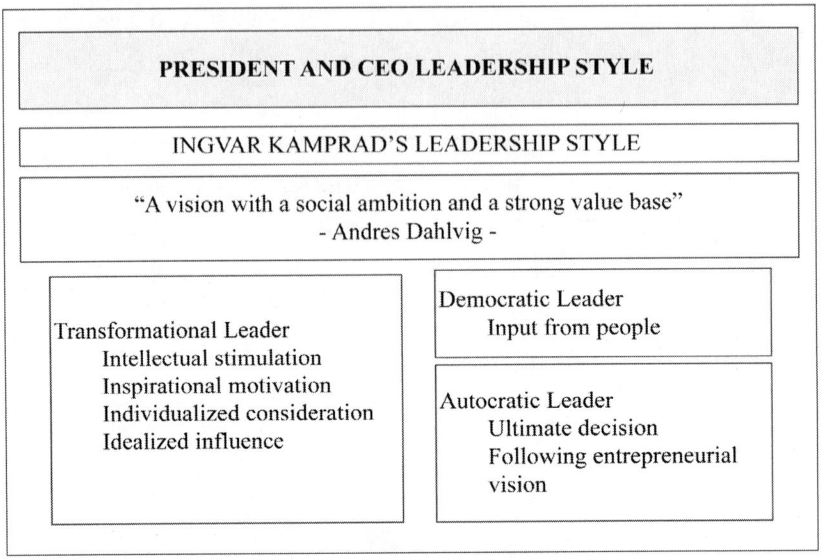

Figure 10.1: Transformational leadership style (Ingvar-Kamprads-leadership-style 2011) (source: http://hubpages.com/business/Ingvar-Kamprads-leadership-style).

With the recruitment of like-minded consultants, the owner counted on the consultants to feel they were part of the organization and feel committed with the organization, raising their dedication and performance. To ensure the organization's leaders and consultants understood the leadership style of the CEO, the CEO analyzed, studied, and regularly communicated its leadership style with the consultants. The CEO is a transformational leader. As an incomplete leader, he or she also owns some individualistic characteristics of a transactional leader. The four key elements characterizing the transformational leader are intellectual stimulation, inspirational motivation, individualized consideration, and idealized influence.

In addition, the transformational leadership style includes both a democratic and an autocratic component. The democratic component allows for frequently asking consultant input not only to get feedback but also to make consultants feel needed in the organization, certainly transforming into a higher productivity rate. However, the autocratic characteristic provides a clear indication that the ultimate decision belongs to the CEO following its vision of a small start-up consulting organization with a strong entrepreneurial character.

R = RESPONSIBLE A = ACCOUNTABLE C = CONSULTING RESOURCES I = KEPT INFORMED	President / CEO	Director People	Director Administration	Director Commercial	Director Client Engagement	Director BIM	Director Projects	Lead Project COntrols	Lead Procurement	Lead Project Accounting	Lead Systems
PEOPLE											
ADMINISTRATION											
RECRUITMENT											
Interviewing			A	A	A	A		C	C	C	C
Recruiting		A	R	R	R	R		C	C	C	C
Offer preparation and presenting	I	R	A	A	A	A					
Onboarding preparation		A									
Onboarding	I	R	A	A	A	A					
Temporary labour coordination	I	R	A	A	A	A		C	C	C	C
EMPLOYEE AND COMMUNITY RELATIONSHIPS											
DEVELOPMENT											
BUSINESS ADMINISTRATION											
FINANCIAL MANAGEMENT											
ACCOUNTS PAYABLE AND RECEIVABLE											
Safegaurd all company funds											
Purchase order issue and tracking											
Accounts payable											
Accounts receivable											
OFFICE ADMINISTRATION											
BUSINESS INFORMATION MANAGEMENT											
BUSINESS INFORMATION MANAGEMENT											
APPLICATION MANAGEMENT											
TECHNICAL INFRASTRUCTURE MANAGEMENT											
Technical infrastructure requirements											
Technical infrastructure parameters											
Remote access requirements											
PROJECTS											
PRE-PROJECT AWARD											
POST- PROJECT AWARD											
PROJECT CLOSE-OUT											
Close project											
Collect final funds											
ADMINISTRATION											
CLIENT ENGAGEMENT											
CUSTOMER RELATIONSHIPS											
Maintain current client relationships											
Engage new clients											
Develop multi-tier relationships											
MARKETS											
BUSINESS GENERATION STRATEGY											
REPORTING											
ADMINISTRATION											
COMMERCIAL											
COMMERCIAL ACTIVITIES											
Develop commercial systems											
Manage documentation and records											
Develop consulting pricing											
PARTNER OPERATIONS											
PROJECT COMMERCIAL ACTIVITIES											
NEW BUSINESS COMMERCIAL ACTIVITIES											
REPORTING											

Figure 10.2: Role and responsibility matrix (Organization abstract, 2013).

To execute the organization's formulated strategy and cultural values, business functional roles and responsibilities are identified and agreed upon, paving the way for setting goals at operational levels. As a young start-up organization, leaders fill different specialized roles at various levels in the organization.

Leadership used the RACI model or matrix to align consultants to the organization's business processes to make the business operate efficiently (figure 10.2). RACI stands for responsible, accountable, consulted, and informed. Allowing leadership to define who is accountable for the various business processes, who will provide support for the processes to be successful, who needs to be consulted if there is a problem with this process, and who must stay informed if changes are made.

After these business process roles are assigned by leadership to specific consultants for task execution, the consultants know what they are responsible for. This definition and clarity enable consultants to be more engaged; assist with consultant training; ensure consultants know who to speak with about a potential process change, alleviating frustration with leadership; save time in meetings by having the appropriate consultants and leaders present, saving the time of those who simply don't need to be there; and knowing what they need to do to contribute to the organization's success.

Leadership realizes creating a RACI matrix assigning roles and responsibilities is not enough. With the RACI matrix connected to the business strategy, action is taken to deal with conflicts and ambiguities. Resolving conflicts and ambiguities in a RACI matrix involves working across each row and up and down each column, analyzing each role and responsibility. This process allows leadership to identify and resolve situations where one consultant or leader might have too many tasks assigned, allowing the opportunity to ensure efficiencies, changing responsible to consulted and consulted to informed, and right-sizing where too many consultants are involved in a specific action.

The final step in doing the roles and responsibly matrix is for leadership to get buy-in from consultants and leaders, ensuring all consultants and leaders agree and understand the roles they are specified to play in the various business processes.

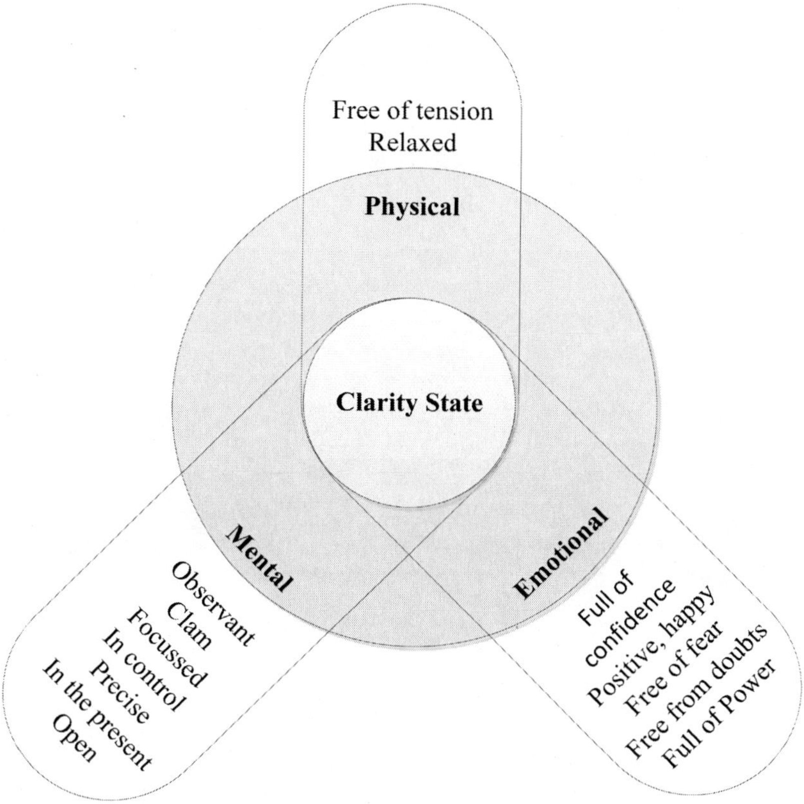

Figure 10.3: Decision-making: clarity state (Kopeikina 2005:17).

To equip leadership to be an immune system for the CEO, decision-making got a fair amount of attention. To assist in this matter, leadership introduced decision-making clarity state framework (figure 10.3). Leadership agrees with Kopeikina (2005:7) a team cannot lead without reaching clarity first, especially as clear decisions save time, eliminate unnecessary actions, release energy into acting, enable the leader to project commitment to a vision, and allow the whole team to focus on execution, which is paramount for a successful implementation. Clarity around decision-making was regularly addressed to ensure consultants were physically relaxed around tough decisions, emotionally positive, happy, released from fear, totally in the present, mentally focused on the task at hand, and charged with power, success, self-confidence, and energy.

Moreover, to eliminate the difficulties around decision-making, leadership promoted and focused on having clear objectives, clearly identifying and stating constraints, gaining and providing clear perspective, easing the difficulty in selecting options, and easing dealing with emotions.

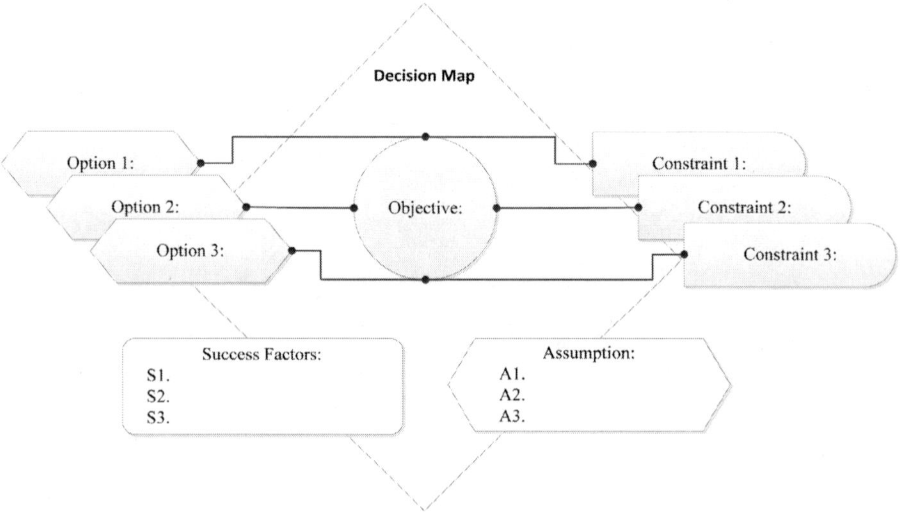

Figure 10.4: Decision map framework (Kopeikina 2005:50).

As an organization deals with complex tactical and strategic decisions integrated with a variety of strategic and unresolved issues in the organization, it is easy to become lost in the details. Leadership, to assist in addressing complex business issues, introduced an effective tool: the decision map framework (figure 10.4).

The decision map allows consultants and leaders as decision makers to clarify the difficulty or opportunity requiring resolution, arrive at the appropriate level of detail representing the most salient factors related to the decision, and keep the picture in mind while contemplating the decision. The power of a single decision map cannot be underestimated. As early as 1911, Tess Flanders said, "Use a picture. It's worth a thousand words."

Completing the decision map allows the decision maker to contemplate the decision in the clarity state, answer key and important questions about the decision, and answer the questions in the time allowed for making the decision.

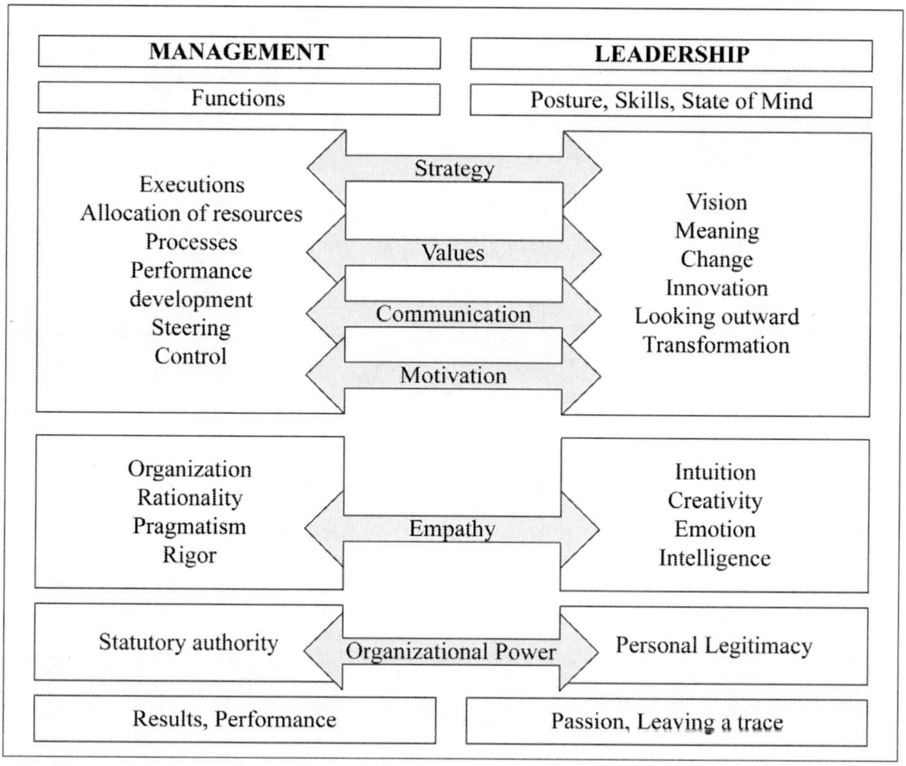

Figure 10.5: Managers and leaders: are they different? (Abraham Zaleznik 2004, 1999) (source: https://hbr.org/2004/01/managers-and-leaders-are-they-different).

Leadership, to assist with formal and informal roles and responsibilities and consultant and leader professional development, clearly addressed the old-age issue of management versus leadership (table 10.5), ensuring professional development included both traditional managerial elements of building competence, control, and the appropriate balance of power and traditional leadership elements of inspiration, vision, and human passion.

While the manager's vocabulary usually includes words such as "administering," "authority," "duties," and "objectives," the leader talks to people's minds and leverages their aspirations, needs, and abilities more than on company's procedures. The leader acts as an authoritative person, combining conceptual skills such as vision and innovation with human skills such as influencing and trust.

The focus is on making it clear to consultants and leaders, while the designation "manager" identifies—per se—an undisputed role within the organization (management of consultants, regardless to which function such resources belong), the term "leader" does not necessarily define a specific position or a role in a group.

The organization focused and communicated the managerial role on directing resources (consultants, money, material, and equipment) or systems needed to deliver something and drive them to fulfill as expected. Consultants in managerial roles perform the tasks by leveraging procedures established by the organization or the association they belong to, providing its aides with directives and instructions without necessarily providing explanations for what they are asking to do.

With the focus of this chapter in mind and leaderships vision for the organization, lots of time is spent on collaborating on leadership, which has to do with the ability—not necessarily natural potentially acquired over time—to convince and motivate people to perform certain tasks and activities, fully confident all its consultants can practice leadership and improve it over the years.

Reality: Leadership does not spell immune system.

Story 1

Senior consultants, because of a perceived lack in like-mindedness, were unable to or not feeling accountable to exercise participation and persuasive control to influence or direct the CEO of the organization to sound decision-making. In spite of a request for and the opportunity to provide a higher level of participation during the weekly Monday afternoon leadership meetings, participation in leading and mentoring of junior consultants, focusing on individual consultant quality of work, and keeping all consultants equally accountable, seasoned consultants chose to leave the organization. Furthermore, the perception was senior consultants did not fully succeed in taking ownership and creating informal leadership structures (communities), facilitating and addressing common business concerns, and improving work conditions.

Table 10.1 shows when it comes to consultants and leaders feeling accountable to exercise participation and persuasive control to influence, the organization experienced difficulties in terms of the method of the "leadership" input characteristic. The table further indicates when it comes to leadership, the organization counted on high levels of being an immune system, while inadequacies were identified in the time, method, and condition of leaders as immune system.

Character	Difficulties Experienced or Issues Occurred		Hoped for or Counted On	
	Leadership		Immune System	
Extent				
Time			◇	Senior consultants will be part of the leadership and spend hours above and beyond the corporate business hours to prepare
Method	◇	Senior consultants were not prepared Senior consultants do not have plans to show how decisions will influence Senior consultants' decisions do not fit or refer to the business plan	◇	Senior consultants will use experience to direct the CEO Senior consultants will prepare well enough to direct the CEO
Condition			◇	Senior consultants will study the leadership style of the CEO and understand how to provide support

Table 10.1: Senior team members: leadership input characteristic difficulties and level of immune system.

Expectation-Reality Gap

To identify the reasoning behind the leadership/immune system expectation-reality gap with the leadership input characteristic difficulties in mind, an analysis was done on the organization's culture, consultant capabilities, and organization leadership.

Table 10.2 indicates the various inadequacies in organization culture (equality, ownership thinking, fit for purpose, and values) that might exist and could have led to the leadership/immune system expectation-reality gap.

Equality			
Limited organization structures		Consultants can enjoy themselves	
Consultant participation	◆	Equal productivity incentives	
Fulfill potential		Social identity	
Treated fairly		Knowing our peers	◆
Character protected		Absence of inappropriate and disrespectful language	
Work hours respected		Absence of stereotyping	
Personal information protected		Taking consultants seriously	◆
Recognition of diversity			
Ownership Thinking			
Understanding the fundamentals of the organization	◆	Forecasting and achieving the business's key performance indicators	◆
Understanding how the company makes money	◆	Key performance indicators are highly visible and accountable	◆
Understanding how each consultant adds—or takes away—value	◆	Having self-funding incentive plans	◆
Knowing the business's key performance indicators	◆	Incentive plans aligning the consultants' behavior to the business's objectives	◆
Fit for Purpose			
Deliverables do what they intend to achieve		Final deliverables are efficient enough for the stated purpose	
Deliverables are good enough to do the work they are designed to do		Deliverables represent the right tool to do the work consultants have to do	

Deliverables are of a good enough standard for clients		Deliverables fulfill the requirement specifications and stated outcome	
Deliverables answer the client's requirement and wants and nothing more		Consultants are undertaking enough and have efficient effort to reach the client's intended goals	
Deliverables are comprehensive to the extent that they answer the client's requirement and wants and nothing more			

Values			
Trust	◆	Transparency	
Pride		Sense of urgency	◆
Camaraderie	◆	Commitment	◆

Table 10.2: Leadership/immune system expectation-reality gap: culture.

Table 10.3 shows the various shortcomings in organization core competencies that might exist and could have led to the leadership/immune system expectation-reality gap.

Core Competencies			
Leadership		Work quality	
Sense of urgency		Quantity of work	
Teamwork	◆	Accountability	◆
Decision-making	◆	Adaptability	◆
Client focused		Initiative	◆
Business acumen		Innovation	◆
Resource management		Planning and organizing	◆
People management		Communication	

Table 10.3: Leadership/immune system expectation-reality gap: capability.

Table 10.4 shows the various inadequacies in organization leadership styles that might exist and could have led to the leadership/immune system expectation-reality gap.

Styles			
Cooperative leadership	◇	Whiner	
Problem-solving leadership	◇	Gossiper	◇
Leadership by example	◇	Nonstop talker	
Knowledge leadership	◇	Grumbler	
Get-up-and-go leadership		Bully	◇

Table 10.4: Leadership/immune system expectation-reality gap: leadership.

Quotient and Checklists

With the circumstances bringing about the realization a leadership/immune system expectation-reality gap exists, and an analysis of the organization's culture, capabilities, and values identifying potential shortcomings causing the leadership/immune system expectation-reality gap, table 10.5 provides a list of questions and phrases to be used to assess the extent whereto the organization's culture, capabilities, values, and leadership support the referral recruitment process, contractual agreement with consultants, assignment of consultants to work, and mentoring and coaching of consultants.

Item	Description	Score
A	Culture	
	Equality	
2	Consultant participation is evident in preparedness, staying focused on the main topics, keeping control of tasks, discussing the salient issues, and contributing to ideas and information.	
12	Consultants know who their peers are and what is expected of them, and on all levels, they foster two-way communication and trust. Although they are not reporting to each other, they embrace the fact that they are on the same team.	

Item	Description	Score
15	Consultants are taken seriously as they are confident and know what they are talking about; they are engaged in multiple-level conversation, say what they need to say and get to the point, and stay serious about work most of the time.	
	Ownership Thinking	
1	Consultants understand the fundamentals of the organization and how the organization runs the business within the following six departments: people, administration, business information management, client engagement, projects, and commercial and day-to-day operations.	
2	Consultants understand how the business makes money through project work in terms of commercial agreements, delivering quality work, pricing work, reporting, and analysis.	
3	The organization and the individual team members understand how each consultant adds—or takes away—value.	
4	Individual team members are aware of the business's key performance indicators.	
5	The organization, on agreed intervals, forecasts and monitors and controls business key performance indicators.	
6	Organization leadership is clear on key performance indicators, makes it visible to all team members, and keeps responsible people accountable.	
7	The organization has implemented self-funding incentive plans.	
8	The organization has implemented incentive plans that align the consultants' behavior to the business's objectives.	
	Fit for Purpose	
B	Values	
1	Consultants have people-management competencies, including the ability to delegate, set goals, manage performance, motivate, train, develop, hire, and exit employees and contractors in a fashion that meets the company's goals.	
3	Camaraderie is demonstrated through a sense of belonging where consultants work, acceptance for who consultants are, a sense of inclusion where the organization makes everyone an insider, occasional fun events that are planned to meet diverse interests, clear messages stating that all are welcome, and understanding for those who don't choose to participate.	
5	Consultants demonstrate a sense of urgency through attitude and the process of treating key business or personal matters as if one's life depended on it. Consultants have the determination to stay focused on results and deadlines until the task or project is completed.	

Item	Description	Score
6	Commitment is demonstrated through a consultant base that pledges themselves to the organization and delivers successful projects aligned with the business, culture, remuneration, and leadership model, consistently and persistently pursuing the business's purpose and conduct.	
C	Competencies	
3	Consultants have teamwork competencies, including the ability to establish and maintain positive working relationships and to work cooperatively to achieve results, solicit input, value team members' contributions, and place them above personal needs.	
4	Decision-making including the ability to use analysis, wisdom, sound judgment, experience, and logic to solve problems and decision-making	
5	Consultants, from a business perspective, can generate and enhance profit; recognize business opportunities; and anticipate, understand, and act on business options to lead to a positive outcome.	
11	Consultants have accountability competencies, including the ability to take responsibility for tasks or assignments and align words with actions.	
12	Consultants have adaptability, showing abilities in mastering new skills and demonstrating flexibility in reacting to changing needs, procedures, and environments; work well under pressure; handle multiple assignments; and meet deadlines.	
13	Consultants have initiative and innovation, utilizing knowledge and scope to constructively increase productivity and achieve goals, use resourcefulness and creativity in dealing with challenges, and anticipate and react positively to change.	
15	Consultants have planning and organization competencies, including establishing an appropriate course of action for themselves and/or others to accomplish a specific goal, making proper assignments of people and appropriate use of resources, and ensuring which daily activities contribute to and are timely with the overall business's short- and long-term objectives.	
D	Leadership	
1	Have consultants and team members who are seeking cooperation from all consultants, seeking cooperation from consultants whom they have no control over.	
2	Have problem solvers who are addressing the issues that frustrate individual consultants, addressing the issues—even if they make them unpopular.	

Item	Description	Score
3	Have consultants who are taking extreme measures on themselves, doing to other consultants as we would want them to do unto us: "walk the walk" and "talk the talk."	
4	Have consultants providing knowledge leadership, who know the strategies and tactics required, realizing experience and potential in the consultants, and mentoring.	
6	The organization does not have consultants who are always having the worst day of their lives and are always focusing on themselves.	
7	The organization does not have consultants who are always telling stories about who did what and talking behind the backs of consultants.	
10	The organization does not have consultants who always boss other people around and tell them what to do and require reminding that it is against the company culture.	
	Average Score	
Rate a score of 1, 3 or 5. Score: 1 = Seldom, 3 = Sometimes true, and 5 = Almost always true		
Interpretation of average score: 108 - 131 signs of a leadership/immune system expectation-reality gap, 73 - 107 likely a leadership/immune system expectation-reality gap exists, 1 - 72 certainly a leadership/immune system expectation-reality gap exists.		

Table 10.5: Assessment: leadership/immune system expectation-reality gap.

Paying attention to the circumstances bringing about the realization of a leadership/immune system expectation-reality gap, the outcome of the analysis of the organization's culture, capabilities, and values identifying potential shortfalls causing the leadership/immune system expectation-reality gap and the assessment, could allow the organization to:

- narrow or reduce the leadership/immune system expectation-reality gap,
- recruit and build a team of business-orientated consultants,
- adjust leadership as input characteristic, and
- adjust the actions taken by the organization to support the leadership input characteristic.

Chapter 11 will shed light on the tenth and last theme, "inspire does not spell leadership," focusing on the inspire/leadership expectation-reality gap.

This page is for you, the reader, to make notes and jot down reference page numbers.

Use this table to make notes and jot down system-related reference page numbers.

Note	Page Number		
	People	Process	Application

Use this table to make notes and jot down IPO-related reference page numbers.

Note	Page Number		
	Input	Process	Output

Use this table to make notes and jot down theme-related reference page numbers.

Note	Page Number				
	Business Models	Competencies	Leadership	Values	Self-Orientation

This page is for you, the reader, to make notes and jot down ERG-related reference page numbers.

Note	Page Number
Leadership Does Not Spell Immune System	

CHAPTER 11

Inspire Does Not Spell Leadership

You take the front line when there is danger, then
people will appreciate your leadership.
—Nelson Mandela

A leader is best when people barely know he exists, when his work
is done, his aim fulfilled, they will say, we did it ourselves.
—Lao Tzu

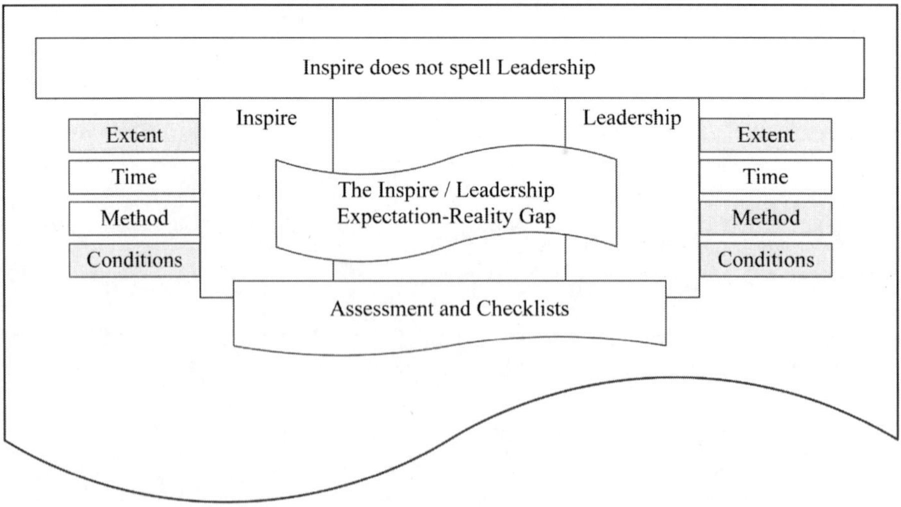

Introduction

THE YEAR 2016 started with a bang. It is January. I am attending the Cambridge House Vancouver Resource Investment Conference, and it does not matter how analysts are painting the story, it is doom and gloom for the resources sector. All indications are that resources organizations will be looking to reduce exploration costs and even offload assets, increasing the movement of assets among companies, with costs throughout the sector coming under pressure, driving labor localization projects and an increased demand for cost-effective and flexible service providers.

As a thought and transformation leader, keeping an open mind and searching for an environment to stimulate my creative thinking, a friend and I attended the Canada the Business Success Summit and Power of Success Seminar in Vancouver. With what I have seen, read, and heard at the various conferences over a span of ten days, what a better time to address the topics of inspiration and leadership. The tenth and last theme requiring our attention is "inspire does not spell leadership."

The focus of this chapter will be to provide an understanding of leadership's expectation from consultants providing inspiration as input characteristic, an understanding of the actions taken by the organization to support or strengthen the inspiration input characteristic, the circumstances bringing about the realization an inspiration/leadership expectation-reality gap exists, and an analysis of the organization's culture, capabilities, and values, identifying potential causes of the inspiration/leadership expectation-reality gap.

Expected Result

Expectation 10

After creating for a large number of consultants in the industry an environment to become the person and consultant they want to become, assisted with advice and direction in professional development, and making things happen for individuals in terms of business or project opportunities, a group of consultants comes and sticks together in the organization and does not just leave when the team dynamics get complicated, executive decisions do not work for them on an individual basis, or the business climate complicates the future of the company.

Business Input

To strengthen the changes of delivering the expected result and getting a complete understanding on why expectations are different, why expectations of the CEO are different from the leaders and followers, the organization's leaders collaborated on concepts such as leadership qualities, characteristics of the general and inspirational leader, characteristics of the transformation and transactional leader, and characteristics of coaching and mentoring.

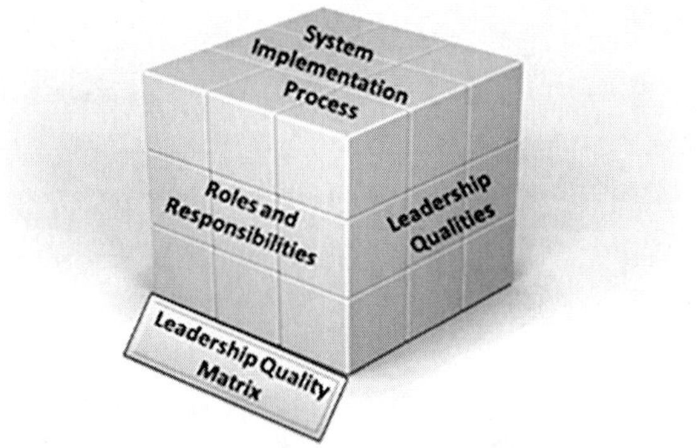

Figure 11.1: Leadership qualities (Jacobs 2012).

The leadership quality matrix is a guideline to recruitment specialists during the identification and selection of potential team members, system integrators during the placement and guidance of team members, and information system users.

Primarily, this book provides insight into a leadership quality matrix that can be applied during information system implementations. The leadership quality matrix, about information system-implementation projects, provides a three-dimensional relationship between roles and responsibilities required to support the implementation process, the various implementation process focus areas, and leadership qualities required to support the implementation process. The leadership quality matrix is built up with a thorough understanding of the various stakeholders involved, the applicable implementation process focuses areas, and leadership models to determine if potential team members have the required leadership qualities.

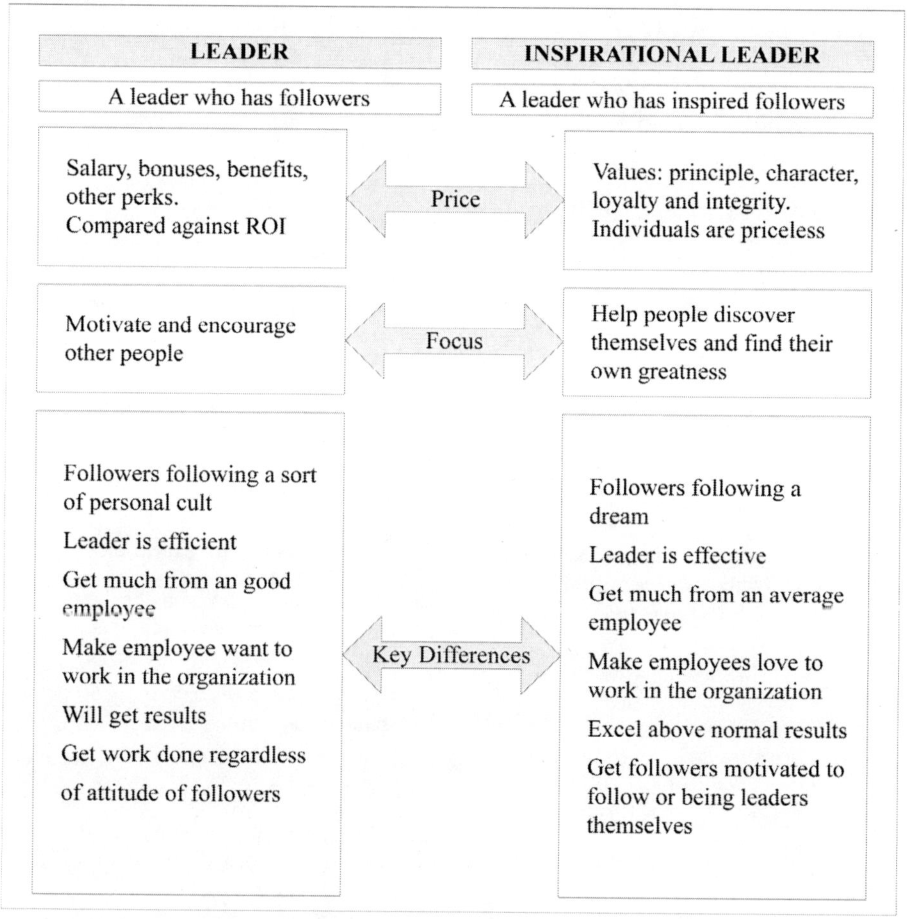

Figure 11.2: Inspirational leader versus good leader (source: http://www.slideshare.net/CommLab/inspirational-leader-vs-good-leader-whats-the-difference-4409221).

As indicated by CommLab, both inspirational leaders and good leaders come at a price. The price for good leaders is expressed in terms of dollars: salary, bonus, benefits, and perks, and the price is diligently compared to the individual's ROI. The price for "inspirational leaders" is expressed in values: principles, character, loyalty, and integrity, and these individuals are priceless.

The qualities of an inspirational leader are rather hard to define because one either has it or one doesn't. A truly inspirational leader has the passion, the commitment, the sensitivity, and the vision to see what is possible, on one hand, and to persuade people to follow which dream on the other. A good leader will motivate and encourage others to great works, but a truly inspirational leader will help others discover themselves and find their own greatness.

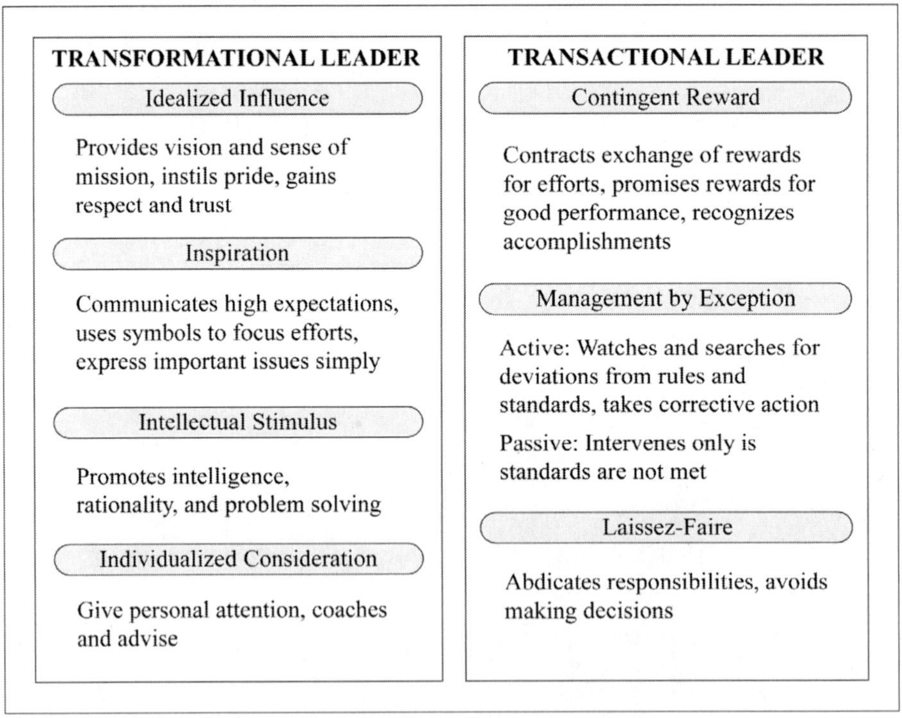

Figure 11.3: Transformational leader versus transactional leader (source: https://www.google.ca/search?q=inspiration+versus+leadership+images&biw=910&bih=451&tbm=isch&tbo=u&source=univ&sa=X&ved=0ahUKEwjstqy

Z84PLAhUQ7GMKHfDHDK4QsAQIGg&dpr=1.5#imgrc=NiYp9SMUNcsIDM%3A).

The CEO with high levels of transformational capabilities promotes the characteristics and shapes the organization's leadership to follow a more transformational leadership style. The relationship between transformational and transactional leadership should not been see as opposing approaches because they complement each other. Thus, they are not equally important since transformational leadership builds on transactional leadership. The best leaders have both transactional and transformational leadership qualities.

The core focus of the transformational leader includes effective idealized influence, inspirational motivation, intellectual stimulation, and individualized transformation; the core focus of transactional leader includes contingent reward, management by exception, and transactional laissez-faire.

Transformational leadership is more effective and more creative since it encourages those who follow them and shows greater agreement among leadership about organizational goals, improving performance by building consensus among the leadership, and increasing the follower efficiency. The transformational leadership requests response of leaders in the organization, provides greater decentralization, has the propensity to take risks, implements compensation plans geared toward long-term result, and facilitates corporate entrepreneurship.

It must be said the transformational leadership style is not perfect; on the other hand, it is suitable to chase the goals of a start-up consulting organization. Though the transformational leadership is not always superior in effectiveness to transactional leadership, it has a stronger correlation than the transactional leadership with lower turnover rates, higher productivity, lower employee stress and burnout, and higher employee satisfaction.

Transformational leadership should not be confused with charismatic leadership. The charismatic leadership wants its followers to adopt charismatic world and go no further, but the transformational leadership attempts to instill in followers the ability to question established views and eventually those established by leaders.

COACH	MENTOR
Teaching functional skills	Developing career skils
Planning	Goal setting
Company objectives	Personal development
Tactical	Strategic
Tangible	Visionary
Short term	Long term

Figure 11.4: Coaching versus mentoring (source: http://www.stuartmcfarlaneassociates.co.uk/services).

Besides introducing inspirations to the organization, the leadership has a high level of focus on coaching and mentoring of peers and intermediate and junior consultants. From a coaching perspective, the aim is to help consultants realize their potential of existing knowledge through the development of skills, attitude, and confidence, thus improving the consultant's effectiveness as a manager or leader. Implementing mentorship, the organization did promote and allowed for planning time out of a busy business schedule; creating a confidential, nonjudgmental, and safe environment; opportunity to explore new thoughts and ideas; building confidence; improved performance as a manager and leader; acquiring new skills; and equipping with development tools.

Leadership recognizes a key element of staff development is mentoring at various levels within an organization, and consultants and the organization can benefit from this very effective management tool. In an environment in which businesses must continually change to compete, mentoring provides a flexible and individual method of helping organizations realize their full potential by developing the consulting pool.

Having a mentor external to the organization helps consultants significantly in developing their leadership style and managerial skill sets.

It is beneficial in that mentoring can be used in various circumstances. It develops employees' abilities, develops employees' confidence, improves employees who are not working at an acceptable standard, and supports employees who have recently been promoted to a new role. It also supports your organization's professional development commitments and motivates and supports rising stars or underperformers.

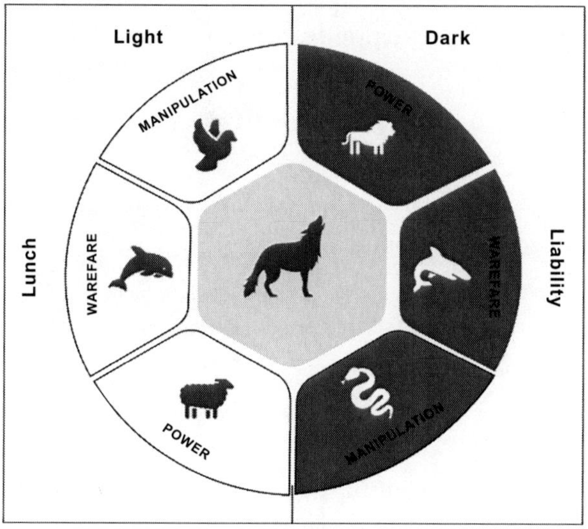

Figure 11.5: The extreme animal ecosystem (Nunno 2012).

One of the significant retrospective learnings that becoming known to the author post start-up of the organization was provided by Tina Nunno, a research vice president, Gartner group fellow, and author of *The Wolf in CIO's Clothing*. Though the book was written for CIOs, the author is certain the concepts are totally transferable to the CEO position. The CEO uses this analogy to explain to consultants and leaders what is expected of the CEO as leader of the pack. Nunno (2012:8) is indicating the ideal animal for the CEO is the wolf, which reflects an ideal balance between an intellectual, social creature inspiring loyal followership and creating group affinity and the ruthless predator leading a pack of strong fighters, winning in a competitive environment, and commanding a large territory.

Nunno (2012:30) is indicating the journey to wolf status is not a linear one from the light side to grey moderation. In the dark-side enterprise, the CEO who starts on the light side is perceived as weak. When the CEO becomes grey, its peers and the industry might perceive him or her as a weak leader who is trying to be perceived as strong by taking the middle ground. Instead, the CEO must go to the dark extremes, and when returning to the grey wolf center, he or she would be perceived as an extremely strong leader who is restraining itself by being moderate and, thus, magnanimous. The path of becoming a strong wolf leader is one of radiating out to the extremes and then returning to the grey space.

For the CEO, as wolf, to inspire loyalty, it must demonstrate the following light-side behaviors:

- use positive incentives, social skills, and collaboration to create loyalty and fellowship;
- demonstrate a strong sense of values and communicate them clearly to followers;
- listen and show empathy and caring toward other across all levels of the organization;
- take the high road by knowing when not to engage in battle and live to fight another day; and
- display selflessness and strive to give more than to receive.

For the CEO, as wolf, to inspire fear, it must demonstrate the following dark-side behaviors:

- use power and negative incentives deliberately when needed to create compliance;
- demonstrate the ability to make ethical and value trade-offs when there is no win-win solution;
- protect territory and followers, punish potential threats, and expand territory as needed;
- avoid battles when possible by being powerful, frightening, and manipulating opponents;

- take calculated rather than reckless risks and deal with large-scale and evolving attacks; and
- aspire to be viewed as a leader to be taken seriously and worthy of a strong alliance.

According to Nunno (2012:212), great leaders will wake up and ask themselves, "Am I worthy of being followed today?'

Reality: Inspire does not spell leadership.

Story 1

Consultants for whom the CEO created an environment to become the person and consultant they wanted to become, assisted with advice and direction in career development, and made things happen for them in terms of business or project opportunities were not showing resilience by sticking together. Rather, when the team dynamics got complicated, executive decisions did not work for them on an individual basis, or the business climate complicated the future of the company, they chose to leave the organization.

Table 11.1 shows when it comes to consultants and leaders showing resilience and sticking together, the organization experienced difficulties in terms of the extent and conditions of the "inspiration" input characteristic. The table further indicates when it comes to inspirational professional consultants, the organization counted on high levels of leadership, while inadequacies were identified in the extent, method, and condition of leadership.

Character	Difficulties Experienced or Issues Occurred	Hoped for or Counted On
	Inspire	Leadership
Extent	Consultants did not show willingness to stick with CEO Consultants did not show understanding and drive to make the company their own Consultants did not show any loyalty	Consultants will stand through thick and thin with CEO Consultants will give up a piece of their lives to build an organization with the CEO
Time		
Method		Teachings over the years will transform consultants to be entrepreneurial Teachings will influence consultants to break from the corporate world Influence and teachings will take on the work ethic of the CEO
Condition	Consultants did not show understanding working for an entrepreneurial organization	Consultants joining the organization understand what it takes to work in an entrepreneurial start-up company

Table 11.1: Shareholders and consultants: inspire input characteristic difficulties and level of leadership.

Expectation-Reality Gap

To identify the reasoning behind the inspire/leadership expectation-reality gap with the "inspiration" input characteristic difficulties in mind, an analysis has been done on the organization's culture, consultant capabilities, and leadership.

Table 11.2 indicates the various inadequacies in organization culture (equality, ownership thinking, fit for purpose, and values) that might exist and could have led to the inspire/leadership expectation-reality gap.

Equality			
Limited organization structures		Consultants can enjoy themselves	
Consultant participation		Equal productivity incentives	
Fulfill potential		Social identity	
Treated fairly		Knowing our peers	◆
Character protected		Absence of inappropriate and disrespectful language	
Work hours respected		Absence of stereotyping	
Personal information protected		Taking consultants seriously	◆
Recognition of diversity			
Ownership Thinking			
Understanding the fundamentals of the organization	◆	Forecasting and achieving the business's key performance indicators	
Understanding how the company makes money		Key performance indicators are highly visible and accountable	
Understanding how each consultant adds—or takes away—value	◆	Having self-funding incentive plans	
Knowing the business's key performance indicators		Incentive plans aligning the consultants' behavior to the business's objectives	◆
Fit for Purpose			
Deliverables do what they intend to achieve		Final deliverables are efficient for the stated purpose	
Deliverables are good enough to do the work they are designed to do		Deliverables represent the right tool to do the work consultants have to do	
Deliverables are of a good enough standard for clients		Deliverables fulfill the requirement specifications and stated outcome	
Deliverables answer the client's requirement and wants and nothing more		Consultants are undertaking enough and have efficient effort to reach the client's intended goals	
Deliverables are comprehensive to the extent that they answer the client's requirement and wants and nothing more			

Values			
Trust	◇	Transparency	◇
Pride	◇	Sense of urgency	◇
Camaraderie	◇	Commitment	◇

Table 11.2: Inspire/leadership expectation-reality gap: culture.

Table 11.3 shows the various shortcomings in organization core competencies that might exist and could have led to the inspire/leadership expectation-reality gap.

Core Competencies			
Leadership	◇	Work quality	
Sense of urgency		Quantity of work	
Teamwork	◇	Accountability	◇
Decision-making		Adaptability	◇
Client focused		Initiative	
Business acumen		Innovation	
Resource management		Planning and organizing	
People management		Communication	◇

Table 11.3: Inspire/leadership expectation-reality gap: capability.

Table 11.4 shows the various inadequacies in organization leadership styles that might exist and could have led to the inspire/leadership expectation-reality gap.

Styles			
Cooperative leadership	◇	Whiner	
Problem-solving leadership		Gossiper	
Leadership by example	◇	Nonstop talker	
Knowledge leadership	◇	Grumbler	
Get-up-and-go leadership	◇	Bully	

Table 11.4: Inspire/leadership expectation-reality gap: leadership.

Quotient and Checklists

With the circumstances bringing about the realization an experienced inspiration/leadership expectation-reality gap exists, and an analysis of the organization's culture, capabilities, and values identifying potential inadequacies causing the inspiration/leadership expectation-reality gap, table 11.5 provides a list of questions and phrases to be used to assess the extent whereto the organization's culture, capabilities, values, and leadership support the referral recruitment process, contractual agreement with consultants, assignment of consultants to work, and mentoring and coaching of consultants.

Item	Description	Score
A	Culture	
	Equality	
12	Consultants know who their peers are and what is expected of them, and on all levels, they foster two-way communication and trust. Although they are not reporting to each other, they embrace the fact that they are on the same team.	
15	Consultants are taken seriously as they are confident and know what they are talking about; they are engaged in multiple-level conversation, say what they need to say and get to the point, and stay serious about work most of the time.	
	Ownership Thinking	
1	Consultants understand the fundamentals of the organization and how the organization runs the business within the following six departments: people, administration, business information management, client engagement, projects, and commercial and day-to-day operations.	
3	The organization and the individual team members understand how each consultant adds—or takes away—value.	
	Fit for Purpose	
B	Values	
1	Consultants have people-management competencies, including the ability to delegate, set goals, manage performance, motivate, train, develop, hire, and exit employees and contractors in a fashion that meets the company's goals.	
2	Pride, demonstrated in defined expectations, keeps people engaged; encourages accountability, not focusing on who did what wrong rather on the solution; and reinforces expectations of outcomes, appreciation, keeping it positive, allowing each person the opportunity and strong sense of how they contribute and do the right things for the right reasons.	
3	Camaraderie is demonstrated through a sense of belonging where consultants work, acceptance for who consultants are, a sense of inclusion where the organization makes everyone an insider, occasional fun events that are planned to meet diverse interests, clear messages stating that all are welcome, and understanding for those who don't choose to participate.	
4	Organization and consultants demonstrate through operating in such a way that it is easy for outsiders to see what actions are being performed based on openness, communication, and accountability.	

Item	Description	Score
5	Consultants demonstrate a sense of urgency through attitude and the process of treating key business or personal matters as if one's life depended on it. Consultants have the determination to stay focused on results and deadlines until the task or project is completed.	
6	Commitment is demonstrated through a consultant base that pledges themselves to the organization and delivers successful projects aligned with the business, culture, remuneration, and leadership model, consistently and persistently pursuing the business's purpose and conduct.	
C	Competencies	
1	Consultants have leadership skills, including managing change; influencing outcomes; setting strategy and providing clear direction; generating commitment and enthusiasm toward business decisions; acting as a leader, role model, and ambassador for the organization; and motivating and encouraging self and other team members to work optimally.	
3	Consultants have teamwork competencies, including the ability to establish and maintain positive working relationships and to work cooperatively to achieve results, solicit input, value team members' contributions, and place them above personal needs.	
10	A common understanding exists that quantity of work is not identical with number of units; rather that each work assignment has its own measurements, rate of change, degree of development, and use of a certain standard as a unit of computation or measurement. Consultants apply the SMART principle in planning and controlling work.	
11	Consultants have accountability competencies, including the ability to take responsibility for tasks or assignments and align words with actions.	
12	Consultants have adaptability, showing abilities in mastering new skills and demonstrating flexibility in reacting to changing needs, procedures, and environments; work well under pressure; handle multiple assignments; and meet deadlines.	
16	Consultants have people-management competencies, including the ability to delegate, set goals, manage performance, motivate, train, develop, hire, and exit employees and contractors in a fashion that meets the company's goals.	

Item	Description	Score
D	Leadership	
1	Have consultants and team members who are seeking cooperation from all consultants, seeking cooperation from consultants whom they have no control over.	
3	Have consultants who are taking extreme measures on themselves, doing to other consultants as we would want them to do unto us: "walk the walk" and "talk the talk."	
4	Have consultants providing knowledge leadership, who know the strategies and tactics required, realizing experience and potential in the consultants, and mentoring.	
5	Have consultants providing get-up-and-go leadership, getting up and doing what is required of them, and committing themselves to get-up-and-go business.	
	Average Score	
Rate a score of 1, 3 or 5. Score: 1 = Seldom, 3 = Sometimes true, and 5 = Almost always true		
Interpretation of average score: 75 - 90 signs of an inspiration/leadership expectation-reality gap, 50 - 74 likely an inspiration/leadership expectation-reality gap exists, 1 - 49 certainly an inspiration/leadership expectation-reality gap exists.		

Table 11.5: Assessment: inspiration/leadership expectation-reality gap.

Paying attention to the circumstances bringing about the realization of an inspiration/leadership expectation-reality gap, the outcome of the analysis of the organization's culture, capabilities, and values identifying potential shortfalls causing the inspiration/leadership expectation-reality gap and the assessment, could allow the organization to:

- narrow or reduce the inspiration/leadership expectation-reality gap,
- recruit and build a team of business-orientated consultants,
- adjust the business plan as input characteristic, and
- adjust the actions taken by the organization to support the business plan input characteristic.

Chapter 12 will, in a nutshell, provide a summary of the ten expectation-reality gaps discussed in chapters 2–11.

This page is for you, the reader, to make notes and jot down reference page numbers.

Use this table to make notes and jot down system-related reference page numbers.

Note	Page Number		
	People	Process	Application

Use this table to make notes and jot down IPO-related reference page numbers.

Note	Page Number		
	Input	Process	Output

Use this table to make notes and jot down theme-related reference page numbers.

Note	Page Number				
	Business Models	Competencies	Leadership	Values	Self-Orientation

This page is for you, the reader, to make notes and jot down ERG-related reference page numbers.

Note	Page Number
Inspire Does Not Spell Leadership	

CHAPTER 12

In a Nutshell

Hard is trying to rebuild yourself, piece by piece,
with no instruction book, and no clue as
to where all the important bits are supposed to go.
—Nick Hornby

So, what do we do? Anything. Something. So long as we just don't
sit there. If we screw it up, start over. Try something else. If we
wait until we've satisfied all the uncertainties, it may be too late.
—Lee Iacocca

APPROXIMATELY FIVE YEARS after I started to pen down my thoughts and words in this book, I reach the final chapter, which I am labeling "In a Nutshell." It is the first week in April 2020, and the whole world is on lockdown because of the Covid-19 epidemic. I am sitting in my business office in Burnaby, British Columbia, Canada, to pen the final words of the last chapter of *My Expectations Nearly Killed My Dreams*.

As we are approaching summer 2020, resources organizations keep on reducing exploration costs and offloading assets, increasing the movement of assets among companies, with costs as predicted still coming under pressure, driving labor localization projects and an increased demand for cost-effective and flexible service providers.

I am so delighted during this time of dark and difficult social and economic conditions to spend time penning a description of my dream to start, lead, and operate a project-delivery consulting organization. A synopsis of the seven most prominent stories providing insights into the organization's business management and project-delivery consulting reach and the challenges the various project teams and I had to deal with; furthermore, my insights into the project-delivery consulting environments contributing to the insights into ten expectations that need clarity and understanding to be enablers for successful management and leadership of contracts and controls consulting organizations.

In these challenging times, I am asking myself, "How do I keep my head up?" For years, I have inspired consultants and given it my all, but I cannot help but ask myself what I could have done differently.

I truly find inspiration in the underdogs rising to the occasion, reaching their full potential, and reaching their dreams. As numerous times before, I am reaching out to the internet and listening to *Britain's Got Talent* episode 1 of 2009, with Susan Boyle singing "I Had a Dream," episode 1 of 2011 with Paul Potts singing "Time to Say Goodbye," and *America's Got Talent* episode 1 of 2019 with Kodi Lee singing "Lost without You."

Factors Causing the Expectation/Reality Gaps

Table 12.1 provides an overview of the identified reasons causing the expectation-reality gaps in the areas of equality between consultants; ownership thinking by consultants on projects and with clients and in performing administration; project activities based on the fit-for-purpose principle; a culture model based on the six pillars of trust, pride, camaraderie, transparency, urgency, and commitment; and consulting competencies and leadership.

		Like-Minded	Adviser	Action	Success	Client Engagement	Client Wants	Consulting	Acts Quick	Immune	Leadership	Occurrence
A	Culture											
	Equality											
1	Limited organization structures			X		X						20%
2	Consultant participation	X	X	X	X	X	X			X		70%
3	Fulfill potential								X			10%
4	Treated fairly											0%
5	Character protected											0%
6	Work hours respected			X	X							20%
7	Personal information protected											0%
8	Recognition of diversity											0%
9	Consultants can enjoy themselves											0%
10	Equal productivity incentives	X										10%
11	Social identity											0%
12	Knowing our peers							X	X	X	X	40%
13	Absence of inappropriate and disrespectful language											0%
14	Absence of stereotyping											0%

15	Taking consultants seriously					X	X		X	X	X	50%
	Ownership Thinking											
1	Understanding the fundamentals of the organization	X	X	X	X	X	X			X	X	80%
2	Understanding how the company makes money			X		X				X		30%
3	Understanding how each consultant adds—or takes away—value	X	X	X		X	X	X		X	X	80%
4	Knowing the business's key performance indicators		X	X	X			X		X		50%
5	Forecasting and achieving the business's key performance indicators			X	X					X		30%
6	Key performance indicators are highly visible and accountable			X	X					X		30%
7	Having self-funding incentive plans	X							X	X		30%
8	Incentive plans aligning the consultants' behavior to the business's objectives	X	X					X		X		40%

	Fit for Purpose											
1	Deliverables do what they intend to achieve					X	X	X	X			40%
2	Deliverables are good enough to do the work they are designed to do								X			10%
3	Deliverables are of a good enough standard for clients					X			X			20%
4	Deliverables answer the client's requirement and wants and nothing more	X				X		X	X			40%
5	Deliverables are comprehensive to the extent that they answer the client's requirement and wants and nothing more	X	X				X		X			40%
6	Final deliverables are efficient enough for the stated purpose					X			X			20%
7	Deliverables represent the right tool to do the work consultants have to do								X			10%
8	Deliverables fulfill the requirement specifications and stated outcome						X		X			20%

9	Consultants are undertaking enough and have efficient effort to reach the client's intended goals	X		X					X			30%
B	Values											
1	Trust		X				X			X	X	40%
2	Pride					X					X	20%
3	Camaraderie		X				X		X	X	X	50%
4	Transparency				X		X	X	X		X	50%
5	Sense of urgency	X		X	X			X	X	X	X	70%
6	Commitment	X	X	X	X			X		X	X	70%
C	Capabilities											
1	Leadership	X			X						X	30%
2	Sense of urgency			X	X				X			30%
3	Teamwork	X	X				X	X	X	X	X	70%
4	Decision-making			X						X		20%
5	Client focused		X			X				X		30%
6	Business acumen		X	X	X	X	X					50%
7	Resource management						X	X	X			30%
8	People management	X	X									20%
9	Work quality						X	X	X			30%
10	Quantity of work								X		X	20%
11	Accountability	X	X	X	X	X		X		X	X	80%
12	Adaptability	X	X		X	X		X	X	X	X	80%
13	Initiative	X		X	X	X	X		X	X		70%
14	Innovation	X			X		X		X	X		50%
15	Planning and organizing					X		X	X	X		40%
16	Communication		X					X	X		X	40%

D	Leadership											
1	Cooperative leadership		X		X	X	X	X	X	X	X	80%
2	Problem-solving leadership			X	X				X	X		40%
3	Leadership by example	X			X	X	X			X	X	60%
4	Knowledge leadership	X	X	X	X	X	X	X		X	X	90%
5	Get-up-and-go leadership	X	X	X	X	X			X		X	70%
												0%
6	Whiner											0%
7	Gossiper									X		10%
8	Nonstop talker	X	X							X		30%
9	Grumbler											0%
10	Bully	X								X		20%

Table 12.1: Factors causing the expectation-reality gap.

Difficulties Exploiting the Various Input Characteristics

Table 12.2 provides an overview of "how" consulting, management, and leadership were done exposing a specific delivery method, issues that occurred, or difficulties experienced in terms of extent, time, method, and conditions.

		Like-Minded	Adviser	Action	Success	Client Engagement	Client Wants	Consulting	Acts Quick	Immune	Leadership	Occurrence
		3	4	1	1	7	2	4	3	1	1	27
A	Extent	0	8	2	2	12	1	5	4	0	6	
	Size or scale		1		1	1		1				15%
	Degree of reach		4	1	1	7		2	3		3	78%
	Complexity level		1			4	1	2	1			33%
	Scope or magnitude		2	1							3	22%
B	Time	0	0	0	0	0	0	1	1	0	0	
	Time period							1	1			7%
	Duration											
C	Method	10	13	2	2	16	3	8	7	3	0	
	Method	3	4	1	1	3	1	1	2			59%
	Way	3	1		1	3	1	4	2			56%
	Manner	2		1		3		2				30%
	Measure											0%
	Technique		2			1	1					15%
	Instrument											0%
	Process	1	2						3			22%
	Procedure		4					1		1		22%
	Development					3						11%

	Effectiveness											0%
	Efficiency											0%
	Practicality					1				1		7%
	Reliability	1										4%
	Usefulness					2				1		11%
D	Condition	3	3	2	2	7	4	2	1	0	1	
	Prerequisite	2				4	3		1			37%
	Restrictions			2	2	1	1	1				26%
	Qualification factor											0%
	Degree of excellence		3								1	15%
	Fit for Purpose	1				2		1				15%
	Best for use											0%
	Best for ability											0%

Table 12.2: Difficulties in exploiting the various business input characteristics.

Start-Up Fulfillment

The observations and analysis in this book are based on the knowledge and experience of the author gathered over the past twenty years from a variety business and project roles:

Business Analyst

Performed objective review of client's business for the purpose of identifying the health of the company and establishing the proper prescription needed to improve its well-being.

Project Delivery Services Director

Developed and led for a leading EPCM organization a team of sixty-two consultants providing project-delivery services to mineral and mining processing, ports, and renewable power projects.

Project Controls and Risk Assessment Consultant

Managed project controls activities on various EPCM projects, including estimating, cost engineering, planning and scheduling, change management, maintenance of the risk register, and risk assessments.

Software Owner

Co-owned and developed the AliceStreet Conference Centre, a unique software solution integrating voice and video into a human intuitive conferencing environment.

Software Practice and Product Manager

Managed the development and implementation of horizontal and vertical integrated solutions to the mining and mineral processing and food and beverage sectors. Managed for an EPCM suite of project-delivery modules the development, building, and implementation, considering life-cycle considerations and a global user base.

Systems Integration Manager

Managed global centralized resource-related and production facility SAP R/3 system implementations, including the user population training and setup of relevant support infrastructure.

The real-world, quantifiable results achieved during the past twenty-five years, demonstrating the practices outlined in this book, truly do yield successful results:

- Building and leading business professional teams.
- Developing in twenty-four months a team of sixty-two consultants focused on helping clients implement successful projects, decrease project execution risk, and ultimately increase project value.

- Persistent focus on sales and profit growth.
- Co-founding a business and project consulting firm delivering approximately 15 percent profits within the first twelve months under tight financial constraints.
- Commitment to be a trusted adviser to clients.
- Focusing on delivering quality work and on the wants of clients resulted in 86 percent repeat business within the first three years of business.
- Demonstrating ownership thinking.
- Managing a production facility-related SAP implementation within twelve months, reducing onetime plant maintenance inventory by 30 percent, reducing product inventory levels on a month-by-month basis by 15 percent, reducing distribution costs by 10 percent, reducing customer complaints by 2 percent, and restructuring financial administration, resulting in 1 percent administration cost reduction.

Besides achieving these real-world, quantifiable results, the author, over the past twenty-five years, has specific nonquantifiable focus areas that contribute significantly and—further demonstrating the analysis and observations outlined in this book—truly yield successful results:

- Continuously challenged the status quo.
- Developed a business plan demonstrating a sense of industry demand for the consulting offer, the competitive landscape in the organization's space, and the dynamics of the new business environment.
- Drove for intellectual property development.
- Developed an IP strategy in eighteen months where the value from IP is measured in the context of the organization's business goals and KPIs, such as increased EBIT, increased fee rates, and increased utilization.
- Used decision-driven measurements—KPIs.
- Developed and implemented KPIs providing a high amount of strategic insight and a short-term impact.

- Embraced a strong organizational culture.
- Developed and led an organization guided by the six pillars of trust, pride, camaraderie, transparency, urgency, and commitment.

So, readers, whether you have an idea, are ready to initiate, or are in the process of building your own project-delivery consulting organization, please absorb the wisdom I have penned in this book so you will not make the mistakes the way I have—and it will help you narrowing the expectation-reality gap. I am certain once your leadership and consultants grasp these ERG themes, they will respond with urgency to become key players and gain significant momentum for your project-delivery consulting business.

REFERENCES

AngelBlog. 2014. "Startups—The Essential To Do List." Strategic Exits Corp. (http://www.angelblog.net/Startups_The_Essential_To_Do_List.html).

Baker, Mila N. 2014. *Peer-to-Peer Leadership: Why the Network Is the Leader.* San Francisco, Berrett-Koehler Publishers Inc.

Belbin, M., Belbin, N., and D. Bainbridge. 2012–2014. "Belbin Team Roles." (http://www.belbin.com/rte.asp?id=8).

Dahlvig, Anders. 2012. *The IKEA Edge: Building Global Growth and Social Good at the World's Most Iconic Home Store.* New York: McGraw-Hill.

Denning, Stephen. 2012. *The Leader's Guide to Storytelling: Mastering the Art and Discipline of Business Narrative.* San Francisco: John Wiley and Sons Inc.

Forbes/Entrepreneurs. 2013. "Top 11 Reasons Startups Succeed." (http://www.forbes.com/sites/tanyaprive/2013/03/29/top-11-reasons-startups-succeed/#50fc0e7c3b2d).

Galorath, Dan. June 7, 2008. "Better Estimation & Planning Can Help: Software Project Failure Costs Billions." (http://www.galorath.com/wp/software-project-failure-costs-billions-better-estimation-planning-can-help.php).

Harari, Oren. 2002. *The Leadership Secrets of Colin Powell.* New York: McGraw-Hill.

Hayford, J. W., S. Middlebrook, J. Horner, and M. A. Matsdorf. 1991. *Spirit-Filled Life Bible: New King James Version.* Nashville: Thomas Nelson Inc.

Kalyan City Life Blog. August 30, 2011. "Five Bases of Power by John French and Bertram H. Raven." (http://kalyan-city.blogspot.com/2011/08/five-bases-of-power-by-john-french-and.html).

Kets de Vries, Manfred. 2001. *The Leadership Mystique: A User's Manual for the Human Enterprise*. London: Pearson Education Limited.

Koestenbaum, Peter. 2002. *Leadership: The Inner Side of Greatness: A Philosophy for Leaders*. San Francisco: John Wiley & Sons Inc.

Kopeikina, Luda. 2005. *The Right Decision Every Time: How to Reach Perfect Clarity on Tough Decisions*. New Jersey: Pearson Education Inc.

Kotter, John P. 1996. *Leading Change*. Boston: Harvard Business School Press.

Krigsman, Michael. January 10, 2008. "New research: IT cost overruns, delays and contract terminations." (http://www.zdnet.com/blog/projectfailures/new-research-it-cost-overruns-delays-and-contract-terminations/565)

Krigsman, Michael. March 1, 2011. "2011 ERP survey: New IT failure research and statistic." (http://www.zdnet.com/blog/projectfailures/2011-erp-survey-new-it-failure-research-and-statistics/12486).

Lang, Amanda. 2012. *The Power of Why*. Toronto: HarperCollins Publishers Ltd.

Maister, David H. Green, Charles H., and Robert M. Galford. 2000. *The Trusted Advisor*. New York: Simon and Schuster.

Maxwell, John C. 1999. *The 21 Indispensable Qualities of a Leader: Becoming the Person Others Will Follow*. Nashville: Thomas Nelson Inc.

Maxwell, John C. 2009. *How Successful People Think*. New York: Center Street: A Division of Hachette Book Group Inc.

Merrill, David W., and Roger H. Reid. 1991. *Personal Styles and Effective Performance: Make Your Style Work for You*. Florida: CRC Press LLC.

Mollicone-Long, Gina. 2007. *The Secrets of Successful Failing*. Toronto: Pathfinders Publishing.

Nunno, Tina. 2015. *The Wolf in CIO's Clothing: A Machiavellian Strategy for Successful IT Leadership.* Brookline: Bibliomotion Inc.

Ousterhout, John. 2011. "Start-up Company Culture." http://web.stanford.edu/~ouster/cgi-bin/startupCulture.php

Pansegrouw, G. 1986. *Leadership Strategies for Organizational Transformation.* 7th Edition. NJ: Prentice Hall.

Pinto, Jeffrey K., and Ido Millet. 1999. *Successful Information System Implementation: The Human Side.* Newton Square, PA: Project Management Institute Inc.

PMI. January 12, 2012. PMP knowledge area and process groups. (http://www.pmp-certification-exam.com/pmp-processes.htm).

Shah, Dharmesh. 2013. "17 Simple Ways of Working at a Startup." (https://www.linkedin. Com/pulse/20130110195000-658789-17-simple-tips-on-working-at-a-startup).

Sibbet, D. and A. Drexler. 1993. *Team Performance: Principles, Practices Team performance guides.* San Francisco, CA. Grove Consultants International.

Spangenberg, Hermann. 1994. *Understanding and Implementing: Performance Management.* Kenwyn: Juta & Co. Ltd.

Tannenbaum, R. and Warren. H. Schmidt. May to June 1972. *How to Choose a Leadership Pattern.* Harvard Business Review (No. 73311).

Urs Bender, Peter. 1997. *Leadership from Within.* Toronto, Stoddart Publishing Co. Limited.

Wakeman, Cy. 2013. *The Reality-Based Rules of the Workplace.* San Francisco, John Wiley & Sons Inc.

RECOMMENDED READING

Covey, Stephen R. 1992. *Principle-Centered Leadership*. New York: Simon & Schuster Inc.

International Bible Society. 1998. *The Holy Bible: New International Version (Electronic Edition)*. Nashville: Parsons Technology, Inc.

Jones, Laurie Beth. 1995. *Jesus CEO: Using Ancient Wisdom for Visionary Leadership*. New York: Hyperion.

Julian, Larry. 2002. *God Is My CEO: Following God's Principles in a Bottom-Line World*. Avon, MA: Adams Media Corporation.

Krames, Jeffrey A. 2003. *What the Best CEOs Know: 7 Exceptional Leaders and Their Lessons for Transforming Any Business*. New York: McGraw-Hill.

Lencioni, Patrick. 2002. *The Five Dysfunctions of a Team: A Leadership Fable*. San Francisco: Jossey-Bass.

MacArthur, John F. 1997. *The Power of Integrity: Building a Life without Compromise*. Wheaton, Illinois: Crossway Books.

Strobel, Lee. 1998. *The Case for Christ: A Journalist's Personal Investigation of the Evidence for Jesus*. Grand Rapids, MI: Zondervan.

Swindoll, Charles. 2007. *Hand Me Another Brick: How Effective Leaders Motivate Themselves and Others*. Nashville: Word Publishing Group.

Yaverbaum, Eric. 2004. *Leadership Secrets of the World's Most Successful CEOs: 100 Top Executives Reveal the Management Strategies That Made Their Companies Great*. Chicago: Dearborn Trade Publishing.

Patterson, Dan. November 2011. "Does Better Scheduling Drive Execution Success?" *PM World Today*. Volume VIII, issue XI.

EXPECTATIONS SUMMARY

	Like-Minded	Adviser	Action	Success	Client Engagement	Client Wants	Consulting	Act Quick	Immune	Leadership
Models	X									
Business model	X									
Remuneration model										
Values										
Trust	X	X				X	X		X	
Pride	X						X			
Camaraderie	X		X				X	X	X	
Transparency	X	X	X	X	X	X	X	X	X	
Sense of urgency	X	X	X	X	X	X	X	X		
Commitment	X		X	X	X	X	X	X		
Capabilities										
Leadership	X		X	X	X	X		X	X	
Sense of urgency								X		
Teamwork	X					X	X	X		
Decision-making			X	X		X	X	X	X	
Client focused		X			X	X	X			
Business acumen					X					
Resource management			X	X		X		X	X	
People management						X	X			

Work quality						X	X	X	X	
Quantity of work										
Accountability	X	X	X	X	X	X	X	X	X	
Adaptability	X	X	X	X						
Initiative	X	X	X	X	X	X	X	X	X	
Innovation	X	X	X	X	X	X	X	X	X	
Planning and organizing	X		X	X	X	X	X	X	X	
Communication		X			X	X	X	X	X	

	Like-Minded	Adviser	Action	Success	Client Engagement	Client Wants	Consulting	Acts Quick	Immune	Leadership
Leadership										
Cooperative leadership	X	X	X	X	X	X	X	X	X	
Problem-solving leadership	X		X	X			X	X		
Leadership by example	X				X	X	X	X	X	
Knowledge leadership	X	X			X	X	X	X	X	
Get-up-and-go leadership	X	X	X	X	X	X	X	X	X	
Self-Orientation										
Whiner	X	X	X	X	X	X	X	X	X	
Gossiper	X	X	X	X	X	X	X	X	X	
Nonstop talker	X	X	X	X	X	X	X	X	X	
Grumbler	X									
Bully	X						X			

EXPECTATION-REALITY-GAP (ERG) ASSESSMENT

Item	Description	Score
A	Culture	
	Equality	
1	The organization encourages all employees to become more active and productive by giving them more roles in the decision-making process.	
2	Consultant participation is evident in preparedness, staying focused on the main topics, keeping control of tasks, discussing the salient issues, and contributing to ideas and information.	
3	Consultants push themselves to be the best they can be on a personal and business level and know the real them, fulfilling their potential. Consultants accept their failures, ask for support, trust their intuition, and never stop going after their goals.	
4	All consultants received an employee handbook to ensure they know the organization's base principles. Consultants are promoted solely based on how qualified they are to perform the work—and not because of personal relationships. All consultants are recognized and rewarded for their individual accomplishments, regardless of where they are on the hierarchical structure.	
5	Consultants work in an environment where the assignment of workplace and work is independent of age, disability, gender, race religion, sex and sexual orientation, and family partnership.	
6	Organization and consultants respect work hours and operate under the principle of getting work done in the most effective way, honoring work-life balance, and using a high level of trust to overcome the concerns of "out of sight can mean out of mind" and "when you're in the flow, time has no meaning."	

Item	Description	Score
7	A workplace exists where consultants are respected for striving toward an improved work-life balance and embracing a flexible schedule, adjusting the time and place work is completed.	
8	Consultants accept the guideline that is in place addressing the collection, use, and disclosure of personal information by organizations in a manner that recognizes both the right of consultant to protect their personal information and the need of organizations to collect, use, or disclose personal information for purposes that a reasonable consultant would consider appropriate in the circumstances.	
9	A workplace exists where, through the recognition of diversity, there is a general acceptance and understanding that everyone is unique, recognizing the individual differences of the consultants.	
10	The organization has implemented equal productivity incentives to reward consultants and ensure the organization retains top-performing consultants. The consulting incentive plan increases consultant loyalty, increases sales and profit growth, and utilizes consultants to assist with sales and strengthen client relationships.	
11	The organization promotes—and the consultants accept—the workplace, which includes consultants of a variety of genders, races, disabilities, ages, social classes, sexualities, and religions.	
12	Consultants know who their peers are and what is expected of them, and on all levels, they foster two-way communication and trust. Although they are not reporting to each other, they embrace the fact that they are on the same team.	
13	The organization leadership strongly promotes a workplace where inappropriate and disrespectful language is absent, with a strong emphasis on reinforcement of respectful statements and elimination of negative talk, sarcasm, put-downs, and disrespect.	
14	Consultants collaborate in an environment where all forms of stereotyping are absent. The organization and/or its consultants refrain from making assumptions about groups and refrain from applying these assumptions to individual consultants irrespective of their personal characteristics because of their affiliation with a certain group.	
15	Consultants are taken seriously since they are confident and know what they are talking about; they are engaged in multiple-level conversation, say what they need to say and get to the point, and stay serious about work most of the time.	
	Ownership Thinking	
1	Consultants understand the fundamentals of the organization and how the organization runs the business within the following six departments: people, administration, business information management, client engagement, projects, and commercial and day-to-day operations.	

Item	Description	Score
2	Consultants understand how the business makes money through project work in terms of commercial agreements, delivering quality work, pricing work, reporting, and analysis.	
3	The organization and the individual team members understand how each consultant adds—or takes away—value.	
4	Individual team members are aware of the business's key performance indicators.	
5	The organization, on agreed intervals, forecasts and monitors and controls business key performance indicators.	
6	Organization leadership is clear on key performance indicators, makes it visible to all team members, and keeps responsible people accountable.	
7	The organization has implemented self-funding incentive plans.	
8	The organization has implemented incentive plans that align the consultants' behavior to the business's objectives.	
	Fit for Purpose	
1	Consultants produce deliverables that give what the assignment intends to deliver to achieve the project or business value.	
2	Consultants produce deliverables that are good enough to perform as they were designed to do, including aspects such as technical performance, maintainability, and availability.	
3	Consultants produce deliverables that are of a good enough standard for clients in terms of quality, risk, and safety.	
4	Consultants produce deliverables that answer the client's requirement and wants and nothing more.	
5	Consultants produce deliverables that are comprehensive to the extent that they answer the client's requirement and wants and nothing more.	
6	Consultants produce deliverables that are doing the right things according to the stated purpose.	
7	Consultants are using the right tool(s) to produce the deliverables, and the deliverables represent the right tool to be used in the specific environment or scenario.	
8	Consultants produce deliverables that fulfill the requirement specifications and stated outcome.	
9	Consultants are undertaking enough and have efficient effort to reach the client's intended goals.	
B	Values	

Item	Description	Score
1	Consultants have people-management competencies, including the ability to delegate, set goals, manage performance, motivate, train, develop, hire, and exit employees and contractors in a fashion that meets the company's goals.	
2	Pride, demonstrated in defined expectations, keeps people engaged; encourages accountability, not focusing on who did what wrong rather on the solution; and reinforces expectations of outcomes, appreciation, keeping it positive, allowing each person the opportunity and strong sense of how they contribute and do the right things for the right reasons.	
3	Camaraderie is demonstrated through a sense of belonging where consultants work, acceptance for who consultants are, a sense of inclusion where the organization makes everyone an insider, occasional fun events that are planned to meet diverse interests, clear messages stating that all are welcome, and understanding for those who don't choose to participate.	
4	Organization and consultants demonstrate through operating in such a way that it is easy for outsiders to see what actions are being performed based on openness, communication, and accountability.	
5	Consultants demonstrate a sense of urgency through attitude and the process of treating key business or personal matters as if one's life depended on it. Consultants have the determination to stay focused on results and deadlines until the task or project is completed.	
6	Commitment is demonstrated through a consultant base that pledges themselves to the organization and delivers successful projects aligned with the business, culture, remuneration, and leadership model, consistently and persistently pursuing the business's purpose and conduct.	
C	Competencies	
1	Consultants have leadership skills, including managing change; influencing outcomes; setting strategy and providing clear direction; generating commitment and enthusiasm toward business decisions; acting as a leader, role model, and ambassador for the organization; and motivating and encouraging self and other team members to work optimally.	
2	Have a consulting base that understands the significance of a sense of urgency. Demonstrated through the organization's and consultants' attitude and the process of treating key business or personal matters as if one's life depended on it. Consultants demonstrate the ability and determination to stay focused on results and deadlines until the task or project is completed.	

Item	Description	Score
3	Consultants have teamwork competencies, including the ability to establish and maintain positive working relationships and to work cooperatively to achieve results, solicit input, value team members' contributions, and place them above personal needs.	
4	Using analysis, wisdom, sound judgment, experience, and logic to solve problems and make decisions.	
5	Consultants, from a business perspective, can generate and enhance profit; recognize business opportunities; and anticipate, understand, and act on business options to lead to a positive outcome.	
6	Consultants demonstrate business acumen, including the ability to generate and enhance profit; recognize business opportunities; and anticipate, understand, and act on business options to lead to a positive outcome.	
7	Consultants apply resource management in day-to-day work execution, including the ability to plan, control, and measure resources in a way that balances cost with benefits and enables the organization to meet deliverables. Resources might include money, information, inventory, supplies, people, and time.	
8	Consultants apply people management day-to-day work execution, including the ability to delegate, set goals, manage performance, motivate, train, develop, hire, and exit employees and contractors in a fashion that meets the company's goals.	
9	Consultants perform quality work, including speed, efficiency, and the ability to prioritize and meet deadlines and organize work. Consultants, in executing their work, demonstrate knowledge and skills, ability to meet standards, care and attention to details, follow-through to completion, and frequency of errors.	
10	A common understanding exists that quantity of work is not identical with number of units; rather that each work assignment has its own measurements, rate of change, degree of development, and use of a certain standard as a unit of computation or measurement. Consultants apply the SMART principle in planning and controlling work.	
11	Consultants have accountability competencies, including the ability to take responsibility for tasks or assignments and align words with actions.	

Item	Description	Score
12	Consultants have adaptability, showing abilities in mastering new skills and demonstrating flexibility in reacting to changing needs, procedures, and environments; work well under pressure; handle multiple assignments; and meet deadlines.	
13	Consultants have initiative and innovation utilizing knowledge and scope to constructively increase productivity and achieve goals, use resourcefulness and creativity in dealing with challenges, and anticipate and react positively to change.	
14	Consultants have planning and organization competencies, including establishing an appropriate course of action for themselves and/or others to accomplish a specific goal, making proper assignments of people and appropriate use of resources, and ensuring which daily activities contribute to and are timely with the overall business's short- and long-term objectives.	
15	Consultants have people-management competencies, including the ability to delegate, set goals, manage performance, motivate, train, develop, hire, and exit employees and contractors in a fashion that meets the company's goals.	
D	Leadership	
1	Have consultants and team members who are seeking cooperation from all consultants, seeking cooperation from consultants whom they have no control over.	
2	Have problem solvers who are addressing the issues that frustrate individual consultants, addressing the issues—even if they make them unpopular.	
3	Have consultants who are taking extreme measures on themselves, doing to other consultants as we would want them to do unto us: "walk the walk" and "talk the talk."	
4	Have consultants providing knowledge leadership, who know the strategies and tactics required, realizing experience and potential in the consultants, and mentoring.	
5	Have consultants providing get-up-and-go leadership, getting up and doing what is required of them, and committing themselves to get-up-and-go business.	
6	The organization does not have consultants who are always having the worst day of their lives and are always focusing on themselves.	
7	The organization does not have consultants who are always telling stories about who did what and talking behind the backs of consultants.	

Item	Description	Score
8	The organization does not have consultants who are always discussing every bit of detail about their personal lives and ignoring the fact that the team is working in an open-office environment and not respecting other consultants who prefer a quiet working environment.	
9	The organization does not have consultants who are continuously making silly jokes or sarcastic comments and continuously require reminders about inappropriate remarks.	
10	The organization does not have consultants who always boss other people around and tell them what to do and require reminding that it is against the company culture.	
	Average Score	
Rate a score of 1, 3 or 5. Score: 1 = Seldom, 3 = Sometimes true, and 5 = Almost always true		
Interpretation of average score: 236 - 284 signs of an expectation-reality gap, 158 - 235 likely an expectation-reality gap exists, 1 - 157 certainly an expectation-reality gap exists.		

This page is for you, the reader, to make notes and jot down reference page numbers.

Use this table to make notes and jot down system-related reference page numbers.

Note	Page Number		
	People	Process	Application

Use this table to make notes and jot down IPO-related reference page numbers.

Note	Page Number		
	Input	Process	Output

Use this table to make notes and jot down theme-related reference page numbers.

Note	Page Number				
	Business Models	Competencies	Leadership	Values	Self-Orientation

This page is for you, the reader, to make notes and jot down ERG-related reference page numbers.

Note	Page Number
Referral Does Not Spell Like-Minded	
Consulting Does Not Spell Adviser	
Business Plan Availability Does Not Spell Business Action	
Managing Right KPIs Does Not Spell Business Success	
Experienced Consultant Does Not Spell Client Engagement	
Doing the Right Things Right Does Not Spell Client Wants	
Talking and Selling Do Not Spell Consulting	
A Young Company Does Not Spell Act Quick	
Leadership Does Not Spell Immune System	
Inspire Does Not Spell Leadership	

ACKNOWLEDGMENTS

Dear Lord, it is Saturday, February 28, 2015. As I am hunched over my dining room table, scribbling away, I am witnessing daybreak over Metrotown in Burnaby, British Columbia, Canada. Realizing the beauty of nature, I feel blessed having received the knowledge, wisdom, and happiness to pen down the words for this book. Thank You for guiding me throughout this process. Once more, I have come to understand how You bless me through others.

I want to thank the people who have helped me achieve clarity in the puzzling topic of *My Expectations Nearly Killed My Dream*.

To my incredible parents, Frans and Martha, words cannot express how much I love you both. I am truly grateful for your never-ending love and encouragement. Your belief in my abilities and your constant cheering through the good as well as the challenging times allowed me to keep pushing forward. I am regretful for not visiting more regularly and providing the support and care you deserve.

My two wonderful daughters, Alicia and Mariska, thank you for hanging in there while I have been away working in Vancouver on assignment. Thank you for hanging on during some very unstable times. I am proud to see how you, as unique individuals, are busy crafting your own careers. You are beautiful and amazing, and I wish you all the best with your future professional careers.

To my brother, Michiel, congratulations on all your successes. Most importantly, thank you for being such an amazing brother and such a great friend. To my brother's family, especially his son who was paralyzed in a car accident in 2013; to Anna and her family, thank you for your support, encouragement, and inspiration over the years.

I must recognize Elaine Jang, a special friend, cofounder of PDO Solutions Ltd., colleague, and sounding board. She could just as well have developed the concepts and meaning of advocacy and allegiance. Numerous times over a cup of coffee, lunch, or dinner, I achieved significant idea breakthroughs after sound-boarding ideas and tapping into her critical thinking, experience, and knowledge base.

To the PDO Solutions team, thank you for providing me the opportunity to develop the insights printed in this book. Allowing me to lead you in performing the various project consulting assignments in Canadian mining and mineral processing and renewable power sectors is what enlightened me and forms the basis for me writing this book. A very special thank you to Elaine Jang, Paul Walychuck, Craig Rice, Brian Watters, David Bone, and Pilar Craven for standing together and supporting me during some troubled waters and tough times. Thank you. There is no way in the world I could pull this off without you all.

I want to end by expressing how grateful I am for the insights of Dr. Charles Stanley from In Touch Ministries on Sunday, March 13, 2015, on the apostolic letter written by Peter in AD 60 (1 Peter 3:1–9), confirming and stressing the fact there is wisdom in the midst of the trials we are experiencing in the business world. With the purpose of proving our faith in what we are doing, testing how devoted we are in what we are doing, assisting in purifying our ideas and thoughts, demonstrating the strength we receive to keep continuing, equipping us to deal with future trials, and understanding the proper response to what we are busy with (Hayford, Middlebrook, and Matsdorf 1991).

ABOUT THE AUTHOR

Andries J Jacobs is the founder and president of PDO Solutions Ltd, a management consulting firm, empowering leaders, making quantum leaps with their business through digital and transformation initiatives.

At the age of 33, he earned the sought-after role of Director of Business Process Support at Kynoch Fertilizer, where he transformed the vision and culture of the organization radically by using information technology and information management systems to become process-driven and tech@core.

During a 14-year career at Hatch Engineering, he acted as Project Systems Manager, Project Delivery Services Lead, SAP Practice Lead, Project Management System Product Manager, SAP Implementation Manager, and Management Consultant.

He directed and orchestrated the start-ups of three companies in the project-delivery consulting, web-based software development, and hospitality industries.

Andries has had a truly extraordinary career. His tale is of a child of farmers, reflecting ethics, discipline, high standards, hard work, and high integrity. He was born in Niekerkshoop, a small farming community in Northern Cape Province, South Africa, to parents both from the traditional South Africa farming culture.

Working as an Agricultural Economist at the South-West agricultural co-op, he benefitted from the perk of driving a company car. That allowed him to sell his much loved 1981 model Ford Cortina Truck

– a gift from my parents – and buy his first computer, an IBM Personal Desktop Computer 5150. As an early adopter, he had the immense challenge of learning how to leverage the technology to assist his bureau service clients, to do more and do better with limited resources, and adapt to changing market conditions. He thrived on the challenge of finding innovative solutions with technology as the backbone, and his curiosity in facing unfamiliar territory was sparked.

He has an amazing career and afforded three insights that continue to influence every personal and professional decision he makes: be innovative and bold with technology when experimenting and designing solutions; be aspirational and set smart goals; be confident with the skills that set you apart from your peers and make you agile. When it comes to building a set of insights that are guiding your actions, whether business or personal, he quotes the words of Hafiz "The words you speak become the house you live in".

Bridging the strategy-delivery gap and aligning business and technology are the two most significant challenges that leaders face today in becoming tech@core. Andries, as a global transformational leader with more than 25 years of experience spanning multiple industries and geographies, is uniquely poised to drive disruptive change. He leads organizations in instilling and advancing a digital vision, adapting to market changes, improving value to the customer, and maximizing ROI of technology investments.

Working in this innovative and multitasking environment allowed him to notice that a demonstrable gap exists between what is expected of team members and how they perform. What he refers to as the expectation-reality gap (ERG).

INDEX

Stories											
Story 1	27	54		87	105	123			185	206	225
Story 2	30		69			124		163			
Story 3	33	55				125		165	186		
Story 4	35		70			126	146	166	187		
Story 5	38	56				127					
Story 6	40					129		167			
Story 7	42		72			130	147				

Expectations (Themes)	16											
Like-minded expectation	17	46										
Advisor expectation	17	65										
Business action expectation	18	81										
Business success expectation	19	97										
Client engagement expectation	19	115										
Client wants expectation	20	140										
Consulting expectation	21	156										
Act-quick expectation	22	176										
Immune system expectation	23	197										
Leadership expectation	24	216										
Assessment checklist	xvii	59	77	89	106	131	146	165	185	205	225	249

Expectation-Reality Gap	xiv	xvii							
Referral / Like-minded ERG	xiv	28	34	39					46
Consulting / Advisor ERG	xiv	29	32	41	42				65
Business Plan / Business Action ERG	xiv	28							81
Right KPI's / Business Success ERG	xiv	29							97
Experienced Consultant / Client Engagement ERG	xiv	29	32	35	37	40	41	42	115
Doing Right Things Right/ Client Wants ERG	xiv	38	43						140
Talking and Selling / Consultant ERG	xiv	32	35	38	42				156
Young Company / Act Quick ERG	xiv	29	35	38					176
Leadership / Immune System ERG	xiv	30							197
Inspire / Leadership ERG	xiv	30							216

Core Competencies	14										
Leadership	14	59			108						228
Sense of urgency	14			90	108				190		
Communication	14		75						290		228
Teamwork	14	59	75				149	169		209	228
Decision making	14			90						209	
Client focus	14		75			133					
Business acumen	15		75	90	108	133	149				
Resource management	15						149	169	190		
People management	15	59	75								
Quality of work	15						149	169	190		
Accountability	15	59	75	90	108	133		169	190	209	228
Adaptability	15	59	75		108	133		169	190	209	228
Initiative	16	59		90	108	133	149		190	209	
Innovation	16	59			108		149		190	209	
Planning and organizing	16					133		169	190	209	

Expectations (Themes)		
Like-minded expectation		
	Tuckman-Jensen group-development process	50
	Belbin team roles	51
	Sibber and drexler's team performance model	52
Advisor expectation		
	Four types of client-adviser relationships	67
	Four types of relationships	68
	Breadth of business issues and depth of personal relationships	69
Business action expectation		
	Business plan	83
	Equity growth wheel	84
	European model for business excellence	85
	Balanced scorecard	86
Business success expectation		
	Six Sigma: process improvement	99
	Goal-setting theory	100
	Business plan (SMART Targets)	101
	KPI definition process	102

Made in United States
North Haven, CT
04 November 2026

21772153R00171